LAWMAKERS IN A CHANGING WORLD

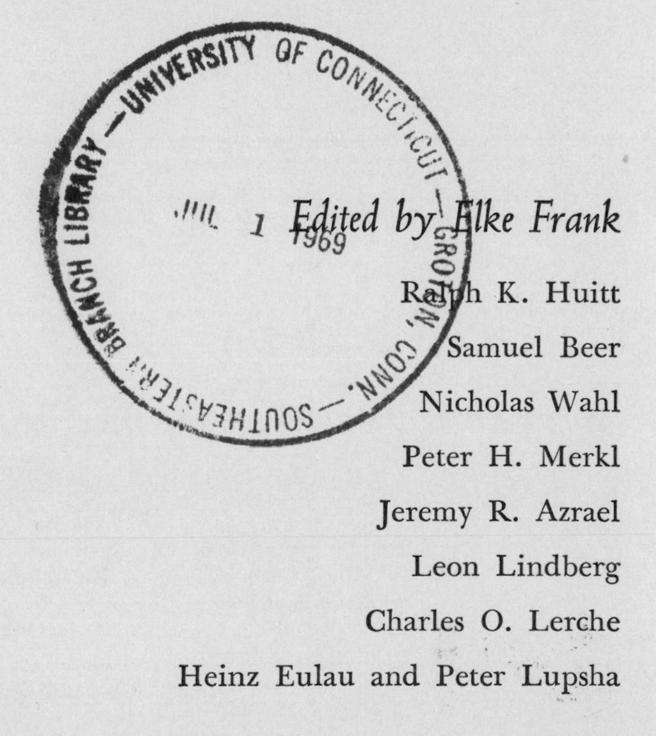

Edited by Elke Frank

Ralph K. Huitt

Samuel Beer

Nicholas Wahl

Peter H. Merkl

Jeremy R. Azrael

Leon Lindberg

Charles O. Lerche

Heinz Eulau and Peter Lupsha

PRENTICE-HALL, INC.  *Englewood Cliffs, N.J.*

Library of Congress Catalog Card Number 66-28110

Printed in the United States of America

C

Current printing (last number):

10 9 8 7 6 5 4 3 2 1

Preface

This book is a result of the fifth of an annual series of public lectures and guest seminars sponsored by the Department of Government at The Florida State University.

In the academic year 1965-66, eight professors from other universities visited the campus and brought to students and faculty at F.S.U. their views on the lawmaker in the contemporary age. Each of our lecturers approached his assignment from his own professional vantage point, brought to it his own special competency, and developed it in a method he thought best suited to his topic.

I was fortunate to act as chairman of the lecture series and as editor of these essays. The assistance of my colleagues in the Department of Government at The Florida State University made this a rewarding venture; the opportunity of meeting with the various visiting colleagues in the series made it an intellectual adventure.

The chairmanship of the 1965-66 lecture series ended my five years of teaching at The Florida State University, and I take this opportunity to express my appreciation to my colleagues and students in the Department for what was a fruitful introduction to a teaching career. Above all, my deep gratitude goes to Marian Irish who knows in how many ways she helped.

Without the encouragement and support of James Murray, Political Science Editor at Prentice-Hall, Inc., and Peter Grenquist, Director of the Spectrum series, and the editorial assistance of Bill Green, Production Editor of Spectrum Books, this book would not exist.

E.F.

The editor and other contributors were saddened to learn, shortly before the publication of this book, of the death of Charles O. Lerche of The American University.

to Marian Irish

Table of Contents

INTRODUCTION

Elke Frank

The eight essays in this volume are the product of a lecture series in comparative government. Since it is impossible to do justice to an entire political system during the course of one lecture, we decided to focus, instead, on one subsystem crucial to all government—the legislature—and on the people, relationships, and structural framework which enter into the lawmaking process. One of our essayists, Ralph Huitt, makes a good case for the focus of the collection: "the idea of studying the legislature—or any other political institution—in a comparative way is attractive. If political systems may profitably be compared, why not political institutions?"

In all eight essays the legislature as an institution is perceived in human terms. To the social scientist, institutions cannot be anything but the products of human behavior and relationships, and so this book, which is concerned with legislatures, is really about lawmakers. Each of the contributors is interested in a different group of lawmakers in a particular setting, but all essayists are concerned with lawmakers in the contemporary environment.

What are some of the distinctive aspects of our contemporary environment? What is unique about the second half of the twentieth century? Human societies have become more complex as technology has opened tremendous resources for construction and destruction, and as

---

ELKE FRANK *is Assistant Professor of Political Science at Hunter College, City University of New York. She has been a Guest Scholar at the Brookings Institution and has contributed to political science journals.*

these resources have introduced new concepts of living and dying, new patterns of relationships, new demands to be satisfied, and new problems with which to cope. Change is always with us. Our technological society is not a product of the twentieth century. Most historians would place its beginnings before the nineteenth century, but technological development and change take place at an ever increasing speed, calling for ever accelerating change in all other aspects of human life.

The changes in technology and social organizations do not take place with the same ratio of speed throughout the world. Much has been written about the discrepancies existing between various parts of the world, and when we speak of "developed," "developing," and "underdeveloped" countries, we use these labels *primarily* to distinguish between levels of technological development, though we are also aware of corresponding differences in economic, social, political, and even cultural development.

Technologically advanced societies are constantly faced with challenges to adjust politically, economically, socially, and culturally to the changes brought about by technology; social scientists are the first to admit that this is not an easy task. The developing societies which are trying to bridge the gap, to speed up their change to reach the stage of "development," face the problems of political, economic, social, and cultural adjustment in even more critical proportions.

All lawmakers then, who are responsible for ". . . establishing and maintaining the legal order, crystallizing and settling conflict, determining priorities, granting legitimacy to policies, and adapting existing rules of society to new conditions,"[1] are confronted by formidable tasks in our changing world.

To deal with all areas of our changing world between the covers of one book is impossible; some selectivity was necessary. The reader will notice immediately the exclusion of developing areas. This collection of essays includes, however, three political systems which, each in a particular way, have made classic contributions to the institution of "the legislature": Britain, the United States, and France. We also take a look at a newcomer as functioning legislative bodies go, albeit in a highly developed technological society: the Federal Republic of Germany—the so-called Bonn Republic. Further, we deal with a system which has bridged the gap from "developing" to "developed" in just two generations, which pays great lip service to the supremacy of the legislature, but whose supreme legislative body meets only a few days twice each year: the U.S.S.R.

[1] William J. Keefe and Morris S. Ogul, *The American Legislative Process* (Englewood Cliffs, N.J.: Prentice-Hall, Inc., 1964), p. 1.

Robert Dahl defines a political system as "any persistent pattern of human relationships that involves, to a significant extent, power, rule, or authority." [2] In the light of that definition, our changing world has produced political systems that go beyond the nation-state; these are to be found in some of the regional groupings of states for economic or defense purposes which have evolved into patterns of human relationship with a *persistence* much beyond that of the older alliances. We take a look, therefore, at the European Parliament to see whether here there is a potential legislature acting on behalf of a political system that exists outside the boundaries of a nation-state. In that same line of inquiry, one of the essayists discusses the activities of the United Nations General Assembly.

If a political system may go beyond the boundaries of nation-states, may it also exist on smaller scales than states? In terms of Dahl's definition it does, and there are many other political scientists who agree with him. The authors of the essay on the legislative behavior of members of city councils deal with the actions of lawmakers in a rather small political system.

Each of the contributors tackles his problem in his own way, giving the reader interested in methodology a whole range of approaches from the free-style essay of Charles Lerche to the sociograms and sociomatrices of Heinz Eulau and Peter Lupsha. Although the lecturers were part of a series in comparative government, these scholars have made contributions to political theory, foreign policy, executive-legislative relations, American government, international relations, Soviet studies, political behavior, parties, and pressure groups, and other so-called "subfields" of political science—thus pointing once again to the arbitrariness of the labels we attach to our discipline.

Despite the variety of approaches and styles, the central concern of all contributors is the lawmaker as a political actor and the legislature, or lawmaking, as a concept. Pressures on the lawmaker in the modern world, and his responses, problems, and challenges to the legislature—whether it be a city council in the San Francisco Bay region, the U.S. Congress, the German *Bundestag,* the British House of Commons, or the U.N. General Assembly—are the links between these essays.

Until the First World War, ". . . Parliaments held the center of the stage . . . for many reasons," [3] states Carl J. Friedrich, who then observes that the executive is now moving ahead and becoming the core of modern government. The first four essays reflect this observation.

In *Congress, the Durable Partner,* Ralph Huitt considers the United

[2] Robert A. Dahl, *Modern Political Analysis* (Englewood Cliffs, N.J.: Prentice-Hall, Inc., 1963), p. 6.

States Congress as a notable exception. He holds it ironical that "the representative assembly whose great historic achievement was the taming of the executive, is now almost everywhere submissive once more to him and his establishment." The former professor and long-time student of Congress who now serves as Assistant Secretary for Legislation in the Department of Health, Education, and Welfare, interprets Congress' ability to maintain its place in an executive-legislative partnership largely in institutional and pragmatic terms. To him, both the executive (composed of the President, the political appointees, and, most importantly, the bureaucrats) and the legislature have become institutionalized as lawmakers. Although congressmen make general policy and the bureaucrats fill in the details, each proceeds in different ways to perform much the same functions for the political system.

"Men who spend as much time in a social system as highly institutionalized as Congress and the bureaucracy are shaped by it in their behavior patterns." Huitt goes on to explain that in the American constitutional system, the separation of personnel produces a separation of institutions. He likens the position of the President to that of a king being forced to deal with feudal barons.

The situation differs considerably in Great Britain, as Samuel Beer sees it. In *The British Legislature and the Problem of Mobilizing Consent,* he is concerned with the inability of the British political system—one of the most powerful in the world—to deal effectively with its problems, especially in the economic sphere. Professor Beer seeks to elucidate the paradox: "Why does a government so superbly equipped to govern not have a better record of achievement?" The problem is a multidimensional one. Administrative decisions rather than parliamentary deliberations are needed to satisfy the increasing demands for quick, specific decisions which have grown out of modern technology, modern warfare, and the complexity of contemporary economic and social problems. Therefore, in Britain as in many other modern systems, administrative regulation is taking the place of general rules. The managed economy and the welfare state create two basic types of group pressures in highly concentrated form—the producers and the consumers who both converge on the lawmakers. Beer finds that the producers work primarily with the executive while the consumers are the object of party competition. Adding to this the tradition of relatively strong party discipline, Professor Beer finds crosspressures leading to what he calls "pluralistic stagnation."

He tries to find an increased role for Parliament which will enable

[3] Carl J. Friedrich, *Constitutional Government and Democracy,* rev. ed. (Boston, New York: Ginn and Company, 1950), p. 296.

Britain to break through the "policies of stalemate." Parliament should play a "lyrical function," call attention to the stalemate of crosspressures, and work at winning consent among the British public to accept restraints and ease the pressures on government. He suggests reforms in the legislative body and in the roles of the lawmakers which will equip them better for their consent-winning tasks.

To look at lawmakers in the French Fifth Republic, one would look first at President de Gaulle, secondly at the bureaucrats, and only then at members of the legislature and political parties. This is the essence of Nicholas Wahl's essay *The Fifth French Republic: Representative Government in Transition.* He comes to the conclusion that the presidency today dominates all reaches and levels of the executive branch of the French government, and the executive, in turn, is the chief lawmaking institution. All western democracies have experienced a growth of the executive, maintains Professor Wahl, joining his many colleagues in making that observation, but in France this growth goes beyond that found in most other systems.

French policy has long been initiated *tête-à-tête,* with party systems and parliament mediating between the state and the various interests. Party system and parliament have now been reduced to a *post facto* critical function, and "the result has been a direct confrontation between agents of the executive branch and agents of the groups and interests directly affected by the policy under consideration."

Wahl, like Beer, explains the shift to the executive on the part of the interests by the need for quick, efficient response to the needs of war, technology, and economics. In France, the party system broke down under the stresses, leading our essayist to speak of the "disappearance of a true party system."

The problem facing the German lawmaker in the Bonn Republic adds another dimension to our discussion. The first three essayists dealt with political systems which, taken separately and as a group, spawned the very idea of legislatures. But lawmaking in Germany has been the prerogative of the executive and his administrators throughout most of German history, as we learn in *Party Government in the Bonn Republic.* Peter Merkl traces the legacy for the legislator that came out of a strongly executive tradition, and the disastrous failure of the legislature in the new democratic-republican experiment with multiparty participation, the Weimar Republic. The result was an extreme distaste for the "party state"—a view, which Adolf Hitler turned (like so many other things) into political capital.

The bulk of Professor Merkl's essay is devoted to the transformation of the multiparty system of the first Bonn parliament into a virtual two-party system. Since German society has undergone much leveling, largely through war and technology, "the entire system of social, cultural, and economic cleavages that used to supply the particularistic division among the Weimar parties has undergone extensive change."

It seems ironic that the new Germany would try to build a stable parliamentary tradition on a two-party system at a time when the executive is gaining stature in most systems. But Merkl notes that a strong executive has never ceased to function in Germany. In the person of Chancellor Adenauer the lawmakers of the *Bundestag,* whether they belonged to the Chancellor's own CDU/CSU or to the opposition SPD or any other party group, found a strong-willed, authoritarian executive —or chief lawmaker. Chancellor Erhard's attempts at broadening the base for his office, of becoming a "people's chancellor," is largely an attempt to seek the same popular mandate in even greater concentration than is held by the lawmakers who are members of the parties and the legislature.

The "so-called crisis of parliamentarism—the multidimensional threat to parliamentary supremacy" is meaningless as an approach to *The Legislative Process in the U.S.S.R.,* according to Jeremy Azrael. His essay is devoted primarily to showing the reader the differences that exist in the U.S.S.R. between the officially espoused doctrine of parliamentary supremacy and a political reality in which "the Supreme Soviet has never played an appreciable role in the decision-making process." "Lawmaking" by the constitutionally charged bodies generally consists of "endorsement—usually *ex post facto*—of decrees in whose preparation" they have "had no meaningful voice."

Azrael notes a difference between the Supreme Soviet and regional and local soviets. He suggests that the latter do fulfill political and parapolitical functions; their most important role seems to lie in participating in the process of political socialization. To inquire into "who actually does participate in the legislative process in the U.S.S.R., given the fact that the nominal legislators and the vast majority of their constituents do not," is the main objective of Professor Azrael's essay. After an examination of the various lawmaking elites from the Stalin era to the Brezhnev-Kosygin government, he concludes that it will take "decades, not years" before the constitutionally installed legislators will also be the actual lawmakers in the U.S.S.R. Azrael shares Huitt's view, however, with regard to the "shaping" forces inherent in institutions—or as Professor Azrael puts it, "forms have a way of taking on content," and this injects a hopeful note into his conclusion.

Lawmakers who operate beyond the customary state boundaries or in a small segment within those boundaries are the subjects of study for the last three essayists.

Leon Lindberg applies David Easton's model of the political system, with some modifications of his own, to *The Role of the European Parliament in an Emerging European Community* to see whether the members of the European Parliament do, in fact, perform functions similar to those of the lawmakers within the political system of the nation-state. Lindberg takes a dim view of the European Parliament's ability to perform an allocative function, and he shows some of the complexities involved in the operation of the Parliament. In the absence of real power to allocate resources and to satisfy demands and values, Lindberg proposes that the lawmakers in the European Parliament could ultimately come to fulfill what Samuel Beer, with reference to Britain, calls the "lyrical function" of a parliament—"the exercise of indirect influence by forcing holders of actual power to pay attention" to what the European parliamentarians say.

Charles Lerche, at the beginning of his essay *The General Assembly of the United Nations: Battleground of Interests,* maintains that "The United Nations is not a world government, and the General Assembly —for all its external similarities to national deliberative bodies—is not a true legislature." What, then, justifies its inclusion in a study of lawmakers and legislatures? Lerche puts it this way: "Like any collegial body that incorporates, however imperfectly, the principle of constitutional representation, the General Assembly has been from its birth a battleground of conflicting interests."

The political system with which Lerche is here concerned is the international system—including most states of the world. If lawmakers help to establish and maintain rules of order, to allocate resources, and to determine priorities of interests, and then are charged with building consensus for that priority once it is established, then the representatives of the various states serving in the General Assembly fulfill many of the functions of legislators.

Dean Lerche examines the role of the General Assembly in the United Nations *vis-à-vis* the Security Council and the Secretariat and relates changes to the changing membership in the world assembly. In some ways, his analysis of how the "interests" of the Great Powers appeal primarily to the Security Council while the "interests" of the ever increasing smaller, developing members try to battle it out in the General Assembly, resembles the approach of Professors Beer and Wahl to "interests" in Britain and France. Dean Lerche sees "the true destiny of the General Assembly," in the representation of mass interests, "rather than in attempts to become the supreme arbiter of the entire United Nations system."

The final essay challenges the reader to jump from the largest conceivable concept of the political system—the United Nations—to one of the smallest—an American municipal council. *Decisional Structures and Coalition Formation in Small Legislative Bodies,* based on data covering ninety city councils in California, is a pilot analysis.

Heinz Eulau explains his approach to the study of legislative behavior from the micro-analytical perspective by pointing out the extreme complexity of human behavior, especially group behavior—a complexity which gets lost to the analyst who studies larger groups. Eulau and his colleague Peter Lupsha utilized only very small portions of data from what is a highly complicated and ambitious research project. In this essay, they present primarily one aspect of their study—the formation of coalitions between lawmakers in very small legislative bodies, consisting of groups generally comprising five to nine members.

A political scientist who is profoundly cautious in his interpretation of behavioral data, Professor Eulau warns the reader not to generalize from the behavior of this microcosm of lawmakers and apply the results to larger groups. Despite the fact that "small-group structures, functions, and processes may well be considered as isomorphisms of parallel properties in larger systems," knowledge gained from the study of one level cannot be transferred automatically to another.

With that admonition firmly in mind, we offer this collection of essays to the reader. The observations of our authors, each gathered by his own method and presented in his own style, are not intended to give a definitive description and analysis of the lawmaker in the modern world. Rather, these essays are meant to stimulate further inquiry into the problems, challenges, constitutional myths, and political realities facing the lawmaker in a variety of political systems, as well as into his responses to them in a changing world. The authors of an introductory book to American government introduce their discussion of American lawmakers by pointing out that it is crucial to understand that ". . . many actors—some whose names are never even mentioned in the 'list of credits'—play important roles in the drama of policy-making." [4] We hope the reader will come to that conclusion as he finishes this book.

[4] Marian D. Irish and James W. Prothro, *The Politics of American Democracy,* 3rd. ed. (Englewood Cliffs, N.J.: Prentice-Hall, Inc., 1965), p. 312.

CONGRESS, THE DURABLE PARTNER

Ralph K. Huitt

It is ironic that the representative assembly, whose great historic achievement was the taming of the executive, is now almost everywhere submissive once more to him and his establishment. The notable exception among national legislatures is the Congress of the United States. Congress cannot match the drama of the presidency but any day it sits it can remind the executive that it must be taken into account. Its leaders are men of political substance and its members can, even in their individual capacities, influence public policy. My purposes are to state briefly some reasons why Congress has maintained its place in the constitutional partnership, to consider some of the factors which affect that partnership, and to suggest some lines of inquiry which would keep a generation of legislative scholars busy and out of trouble.

I. NEVER THE TWAIN SHALL MEET

Even in a country where a fairly high percentage of a sample of the populace manages to miss almost any political question, it is a fair bet that most people know that our government is based on a separation

---

RALPH K. HUITT *is currently serving as Assistant Secretary for Legislation in the United States Department of Health, Education, and Welfare. He is on leave from the University of Wisconsin where he is Professor of Political Science. His studies on Congress and congressional committees have been published in various political science journals. He is the author of* Democratic Party Leadership in the Senate.

of powers, modified somewhat by so-called checks and balances. Perhaps some of that group also know that this formula is supposed to protect the people from tyranny, and that our forefathers were confident it would. Their confidence was shared by most of the liberal philosophers of their time. But the Founding Fathers were, above all else, practical men; they were not so much interested in a scientific separation of powers as they were in drawing on the lessons of experience to make a workable structure for the future. What they did do in deference to that shibboleth of separation which has had such an enormous influence on American political history was to provide in their Constitution that a man who holds office in one branch cannot simultaneously serve in another. At the same time, they softened the separation with checks and balances, drawing again upon experience, and by the admirable terseness of the document which they drew, they left their equally pragmatic descendents largely free to distribute and share powers as current exigencies seemed to require. The result is an untidy but, on the whole, eminently successful system. Nevertheless, there have been and are tensions in the system produced by contrary pulls of separation and commingling. Let us look first at some of the effects of separation and later at the numerous accommodations between legislature and executive which have worked to dampen those effects.

Separate Systems of Power

The process by which the English Parliament developed responsible party government is too well known to need repeating. Why should not the American system go the same way—to the extent the Constitution permits? A President elected by a majority of the people, working through a majority of his own party in Congress, should be able to enact a fair share of the program he has promised. Only some structural changes—policy committees made up of committee chairmen to adopt appropriate bills, party caucuses to pledge support to them—reinforced by a measure of public understanding of the value of responsible parties, are needed, according to earnest critics. Why have not such steps been taken? Why, in houses where most partisans vote with a majority of their party most of the time, do the blandishments of the President go unheeded, often at the most critical times?

The fragmentation of party power followed naturally from the need of Congress to establish some source of information separate from the executive and some mechanism for independent consideration of the merits of bills. In a parliamentary system the members can, at least in good logic, listen to the bureaucracy, because their own leaders are said to control the bureaucracy. But in the congressional system the bureaucrats are "they"; the men who more or less control them belong to the President. A committee was the answer: first an *ad hoc* committee, then a standing committee, then a standing committee with specialized jurisdiction. Such a committee perforce becomes a locus of power. So in time do its own subcommittees which, often over the strenuous exertions of the committee chairman, also carve out jurisdictions which they are quick to defend.

Even the dispersal of power in a committee system might not be irreparable if a party leadership could select the chairmen. But this is an exhausting procedure, often holding up appointments until most of the business is settled. The answer, as everyone knows, has been chairmanship selection by seniority, which often brings good and experienced men to power but which also, by definition, elevates those least answerable to a central party leadership. The President is not unlike a king forced to deal with feudal barons. He has certain advantages of identity with the national interest and superior visibility, as the king did, but he too must respect the rules of the game, which limit severely what he can command.

When these factors are reinforced by all the forces of localism inherent in federalism, accentuated by a long history on a vast continent with poor communication, the basic underpinnings of responsible party government are lacking.

Separate Institutional Influences on Behavior

The separation of personnel in the American system means a separation of *institutions,* and that separation has, in behavioral terms, profound influence on the day-to-day operations of American government. The Constitution, to repeat, says simply that the same man cannot hold office in both branches at the same time. A parliamentary system may actually separate powers very neatly; the minister may distinguish nicely between his executive and his legislative role. But he *can* have both roles at the same time, and so mediate between the legislature as an institution and the executive as an institution. Not so here; the institutions are clearly divided and so are the roles that go with each. What this means in behavioral terms is worth some exploration.

No dissertation on the term "institution" need be attempted. We mean simply a pattern of behavior of great stability and predictability, including the expectations people have that the pattern will be maintained.

People know what behavior to expect in a church, a court of law, a college classroom. It is convenient but not essential to have an appropriate building and symbolic trappings; men have made and accepted a church in the hold of a ship at sea. What is necessary is that the participants behave according to expectations. Confusion comes when behavior appropriate to one institution is employed in another. This was the case in the televised controversy between Senator McCarthy and the Army, in which some judicial forms were bootlegged into a legislative hearing. On the other hand, appropriate behavior validates the collective actions people take.

If men brought up in our tradition were cast upon a desert island, they would know (without a political scientist among them) that policy should be adopted by a majority, that a project should have a leader, and that an accused man should be tried by his peers, however ignorant or biased they might be. It is accepted procedure, appropriate behavior, that legitimizes social action. The social function of a court, say, is not so much the administration of justice (who can say when it deals justly?) as it is the deciding of quarrels and the imposing of sanctions, even to the taking of life, in a way society accepts as legitimate.

Needless to say, men who are inducted into any social system in which they hope to be accepted try to learn the appropriate behavior. The literature on this process of socialization is extensive and need not be reviewed here. What is worth emphasis is that men who spend much or most of their adult lives in a social system as highly institutionalized as Congress and the bureaucracy, where careers are long and status and influence depend so much on tenure, are profoundly shaped in their attitudes by the institution itself. The institution is not the only or necessarily even the most important influence, of course, but its effect can be seen in some of the ineradicable suspicions and adversions which legislators and administrators develop toward each other, which persist even when they work productively and cooperatively together. The principal purpose of this essay will be to suggest some of the differences in the institutional fabric of legislature and executive, and the influence these differences have on the people who are associated with them.[1]

[1] A good picture of the life of a member of the House of Representatives may be found in Charles Clapp, *The Congressman: His Work as He Sees It* (Washington, D.C.: The Brookings Institution, 1963) and Clem Miller (ed. John W. Baker), *Member of the House: Letters of a Congressman* (New York: Charles Scribner's Sons, 1962). The life of the Senate is depicted in William S. White, *Citadel* (New York: Harper and Row, Publishers, Inc., 1956) and Donald R. Matthews, *U.S. Senators and Their World* (Chapel Hill: University of North Carolina Press, 1960). A pioneering investigation of the role perceptions of members of four state legislatures is that of John C.

It should go without saying that the Court is a distinct institution, encrusted with the habits of centuries.[2] Like the Presidency and Congress, it is a political (as well as a legal) institution, sharing their power to make choices as to who shall get what. The Court—and especially the Supreme Court of the United States—legislates boldly and with remarkable political acumen, pushing to the testing point what Congress and the country will take. We leave it out of our discussion only because it is not part of the problem we have chosen to consider.

It is not quite accurate to say that we will contrast legislature and executive; what we really mean in the latter case is the bureaucracy. The political officers of the executive branch are a different breed than the bureaucrats. They form a kind of quasi-institution. They are not self-selected, as congressmen generally are, nor do they enjoy the tenure of either the bureaucracy or most members of Congress. They are creatures of the President, existing officially on sufferance. Their institutional life and influence on the system have largely escaped analysis and that is a pity.[3] The bureaucracy, on the other hand, is as old as human organization, and its habits, cries, and protective coloration have been subjected to intensive analysis. Moreover, it should be a safe wager that bureaucratic influence far outweighs that of the political executive officers, excepting possibly the President himself.

A good place to begin a study of any institution in which people make a living is with the conditions of employment. How are jobs got and kept? What influences salaries and promotions? These considerations probably influence the performance of professors, to take a ready example, more than the standard protestations of university presidents about the relative importance of good teaching.

The differences in the vocational aspects of the two branches of the

---

Wahlke, Heinz Eulau, William Buchanan, and LeRoy Ferguson, *The Legislative System: Explorations in Legislative Behavior* (New York: John Wiley and Sons, Inc., 1962). If my hypothesis that the legislature *as an institution* affects the behavior of its members is correct, the significance of the latter work for students of Congress is obvious.

[2] The influence of the court on its members has frustrated presidents throughout our history. For an interesting contemporary example of a dramatic conversion, see the account of the transformation of Mississippi's Supreme Court Justice Tom P. Brady from a race-baiting white supremacist to a champion of the U.S. Constitution in *Time,* October 22, 1965, pp. 94-96.

[3] Richard E. Neustadt, in David B. Truman, ed., *The Congress and America's Future* (Englewood Cliffs, N.J.: Prentice-Hall, Inc., 1965), pp. 116-20, makes an interesting case for the common stakes of elective politicians. His viewpoint is primarily that of an acute observer of the executive branch. See also Dean E. Mann (with Jameson W. Doig), *The Assistant Secretaries: Problems and Processes of Appointment* (Washington, D.C.: The Brookings Institution, 1965).

national government are striking. The congressman is a politician whose first rule of life is to take care of himself. Characteristically, he is self-selected and self-promoted. It is he who decides that the public needs him in the first place and it is he who must persuade the public this is so at each election. Generally speaking, the national party cannot help him or hurt him very much. If the local party organization is strong, this simply means that the self-selection process must employ other channels. His tenure likewise depends mostly upon his own efforts; he can be a statesman only so long as the people in his constituency are willing to let him be one.

The bureaucracy is another matter. The bureaucracy is peopled overwhelmingly by men and women who came into the service through a merit system examination, who rise in grade through largely non-competitive promotions, and who can look forward to retirement on a rather generous retirement plan. Everything in their professional lives underscores the slow but sure. They come to have faith in rules and procedures. The elements of risk and combat, of rewards and punishments that often are disproportionate and unfair—elements with which politicians live daily—are minimized.

It would seem reasonable to assume that self-selection assures generally that different kinds of men go into the separate branches. Certainly it is doubtful that either the politician or the bureaucrat could breathe easily in the environment of the other. Be that as it may, the distinct demands of each branch enforce differences.

A congressman may come from any vocation and he is required by his job to be a generalist. It is true that he specializes somewhat on his committee, and indeed may develop considerable expertise. Nevertheless, he is required to vote on a staggering variety of complicated bills, about most of which he will try to have at least a minimum understanding. The bureaucrat, on the other hand, is virtually required to be a specialist of some sort. Even if he is one of that handful of college graduates who come in as some kind of management intern, he soon finds his niche and concentrates on it if he is to move up the ladder. He is accustomed to operations in which a wide variety of experts can be brought to bear on a problem. As a matter of course he refers problems to the specialists whose skills are most appropriate to them.

The institutional fabrics into which these different kinds of men fit themselves are likewise distinctive. In Congress all members technically are peers, and at the time of the vote they are absolutely equal. The same weight of numbers which took the congressman to his house ultimately determines every issue on its floor. In the bureaucracy nothing is decided that way. The hierarchy of influence and responsibility is clearly understood; the distinctions between staff and line are appreciated; and status is reflected even in the kinds of furniture permissible to an office and the order of names on a route slip.

Furthermore, even the kinds of evidence which are acceptable in these different kinds of institutions are sharply differentiated. A congressional committee makes no attempt to get all the facts and may joyfully accept what it knows not to be facts. It is interested in hearsay, in opinion, in the shibboleths, however nonrational, around which men rally and fight. This is not to discount the careful amassing of expert testimony which many committees do; the point is simply that Congress is a representative assembly, a popularly elected body, and what may be studiously ignored in a courtroom may be exactly what a congressional committee most needs to hear. The bureaucracy, on the other hand, is a matchless machine for assembling all kinds of facts, for taking into account all kinds of expert advice. Congress itself is ultimately utterly dependent on the bureaucracy for most of the information upon which it acts.

The process by which each branch makes policy is likewise its own. Congress makes policy deliberately. The laying down of rules of general applicability for the future is its avowed business. Generality indeed is forced upon it by the complexity of modern life. Legislatures learned more than a century ago that they cannot legislate in detail for very much of the varied life they seek to regulate. The bureaucracy is capable of making policy determinations of breathtaking scope, but theoretically at least its task is to "fill in the details" of general policy, and its characteristic mode is day-by-day administration, employing standards, rules, and similar bureaucratic tools to fashion a general design.

What has been said here is familiar; any student could elaborate it from his classroom notes. The recitation nevertheless has a point: in this national government of separated institutions different kinds of men, operating in different kinds of institutional fabrics, proceed in different ways to perform much the same functions for the political system. This has operational significance: the leaders of pressure groups do not hesitate to seek from one branch what they fail to get from another but, unless they are incredibly naïve, they will adapt themselves carefully to the behavior appropriate to each. It also has significance for understanding the tensions and suspicions between branches which are endemic in the system. Perhaps most important, it suggests the crucial influence of the institution itself, with all its historic antecedents, on the behavior of the people who make their lives in it.

II. BUT OF COURSE THEY DO MEET

Despite what has been said so far, the element of collaboration between Congress and executive is far more decisive in the operation of the American system than the fact of physical separation; law and the imperatives of politics require it to be. The modifications of separation affected by the checks and balances, incorporated in the Constitution more as accommodations to experience than as an exercise in theory, is in law quite substantial. There is no need to itemize the familiar constitutional assignments of power to make the point. In practice, the separation breaks down even more. It is trite to mention the familiar designation of the President as "chief legislator." He has accepted the role happily, sending a steady stream of messages and bills to Congress in the opening months of each session. Congress, on the other hand, appears to take seriously its obligation to supervise the administration of legislation. In the Legislative Reorganization Act of 1946, Congress assigned oversight responsibility along with legislative jurisdiction to its standing committees. Congress also has invented a score of devices for "overseeing administration" (or for "meddling," depending upon the point of view). Some of the most recent—and annoying to administrators—are the use of formal legal devices to give congressional committees the last word over certain kinds of administrative actions. Probably much more important in the long run is the growing practice of the House of Representatives of passing one-year authorizations, requiring agencies to pass bills over again next year. Needless to say, if legislative advice has not been heeded in that first year unhappy accountings must be made in the second year. It may be, however, that the real significance of the one-year authorization is that the legislative committees in the House are jealous of the Appropriations Committee and do not wish to see it exercise the only check on the administration of programs during the several years of their authorized life.

The exercise of commingled powers is carried out by the two branches with a degree of pragmatism which reduces complaints of violations and overreachings to the level of political rhetoric. As Roland Young pointed out in his fine study of congressional politics in World War II, neither Congress nor the President has much to say about encroachments when the result achieved is good.[4] It is when a particular venture goes badly that the other side is open to the charge of constitutional poaching.

[4] Roland Young, *Congressional Politics in the Second World War* (New York: Harper and Row, Publishers, Inc., 1956).

Even when all this is admitted, as it would readily be by sophisticated observers, there is not much in the literature which describes the extent to which the executive and legislature share the policy process at almost every turn. It is not easy to generalize from the rich and varied studies of particular aspects of the relationship which do exist. Subject to the test of systematic analysis, I suggest that Congress plays rather a more important part in legislation than its critics usually suggest, and that it would be easy to overstate what Congress does to supervise administration.

Congress as Legislature

Some critics have assigned Congress largely a passive role in legislation. It has been suggested that the President now initiates, Congress reacts.[5] This is superficially true. Even when the impetus comes from Congress, as it did in the legislative response to Sputnik, congressional leaders like to wait for the Administration bill to have something to work on. But what is easy to miss is the origin of many bills which in time pick up enough support to become "Administration bills." One or more members of Congress may have originated the idea and done all the spade work necessary to make it viable. One thinks of the lonely voice of George Norris in the 1920s calling for a Federal river project which became, in a different political climate, the Tennessee Valley Authority.[6] Other crusades have taken less time to succeed. Area redevelopment and water pollution control are projects which began in Congress. Examples are offered in the absence of systematic analysis. It is worth mention that the individual member may engineer a public policy. I remember watching a Canadian audience, including many members of its Parliament, listen enthralled to the account of Congressman Thomas Curtis, a minority member from Missouri, of his successful effort to enact a law suggested by a woman constituent.

Needless to say, the committees of Congress maintain a large measure of control over what goes into a bill and what happens to it, regardless of its origin. A striking case occurred in the early days of the second session of the 89th Congress. The Administration had proposed the conversion of loans to college students of money directly supplied (90 per cent of it) by the government to private bank loans guaranteed by the

[5] Samuel P. Huntington, "Congressional Responses to the Twentieth Century," in David B. Truman, ed., *op. cit.*, pp. 22-25.

[6] Henry C. Hart, "Legislative Abdication in Regional Development," *The Journal of Politics*, XIII (1951), 393-417.

government. There was much opposition to the proposal, based largely on the fear that the new program could not be put in operation soon enough to meet the needs of students that year. The subcommittee of the House Education and Labor Committee which handles higher education, chaired by Congresswoman Edith Green of Oregon, met in executive session and voted unanimously to keep the National Defense Education Act loan program as it was (i.e., a direct loan program). The reason given by Mrs. Green was that the colleges needed to know what they could count on for the next school year. What is significant is the absolute confidence of the subcommittee, challenged by no one, that the change could not be made without their approval. If that confidence were not justified, the colleges obviously could not base their plans on the subcommittee action.

It may be remarked that this was a negative action. Critics of Congress, particularly those of the liberal persuasion, have emphasized that Congress is obstructive, that it cannot act affirmatively.[7] As presidents have encountered obstacles to liberal programs, these critics have urged overhaul of structure and procedure to make Congress more responsible (i.e., more responsive to the President and the constituency that nominates and elects him). But in the first session of the 89th Congress, with a topheavy Democratic majority that included some seventy generally liberal freshmen, President Johnson got approval of a massive domestic legislative program that might normally have taken twenty years. The critics were not mollified. It was the work of a transient political genius, they said; soon Congress would go back to its normal nay-saying role. But such was not the case. In the second year of that Congress the President decided, under the pressure of war and threatened inflation, to hold the line on spending. The committees in both houses, legislative and appropriations alike, would have none of it; they set about expanding the programs of the year before and inventing new ones. This bit of legislative history may require a simple explanation: that elections do count and representation does work.

Emphasizing the congressional role in legislation is not an exercise in redundancy; it is given pertinence by the volume of literature arguing that Congress is impotent. It would be misleading, nevertheless, not to put Congress in the context of a system and suggest the roles of other participants. The notion of a legislative system that includes executive, courts, interest groups, press, local constituencies, and perhaps others, is useful but not precise enough. It might be more helpful to conceive

[7] For a selection of the writings critical of Congress, see my "Democratic Party Leadership in the Senate," *American Political Science Review,* LV (June 1961), 333-44.

of a set of "policy systems," in which all parties involved in a particular category of issues share regularly in the making, alteration, and execution of policy. This would recognize the specialization necessary to effective political action. A particular policy is made by the people in the agencies, public and private, who are interested in and know about that policy area. There is an almost continuous interchange among committee members, their staffs, the executive (that is, agency personnel, White House staff, and private persons appointed to "task forces," and the like) and representatives of private associations at almost every stage of the process, from the first glimmer of an idea to compromises in conference and to administration of the act.[8] Careful research would be necessary to establish the extent to which these generalizations are true and where the breakdowns occur, but it is a fair guess that members of the appropriate committees are seldom if ever taken by surprise by executive initiative in legislation. Indeed, much initiation is simply the reasonable next step in the view of those within a given policy system and it is so recognized on all sides, even though there is opposition to it.

Congress as Overseer

The relationship of Congress to the administrative performance of the bureaucracy is equally important and invites careful study.[9] Students of representative assemblies at least since the time of John Stuart Mill have said that control of the government—the oversight function—is probably the most important task the legislature performs. It is easy to get the impression that the bureaucracy lives under the heavy frown of congressional supervision all the time. Certainly it is not pleasant to be interrogated by a congressional committee, nor to find oneself in the headlines which are congenial to the politician but not to the civil servant. But for the most part it is the politicians in the agencies, the expandable men, who face the committees in open hearings. Congressmen complain that they reach understandings with the political people which are not kept by the agency's operating personnel, who are largely beyond the reach of Congress. Without careful comparative studies designed to explore the range of patterns of relations which exist, it is

[8] For an example of this, see Stephen K. Bailey's classic case study, *Congress Makes a Law* (New York: Columbia University Press, 1950). Ernest S. Griffith refers to this coalescence of interests as a "whirlpool" in his *Congress: Its Contemporary Role,* 3rd ed. (New York: New York University Press, 1961).

[9] For a careful analysis of the process, see Joseph P. Harris, *Congressional Control of Administration* (Washington, D.C.: The Brookings Institution, 1964).

hazardous to suggest generalizations. But perhaps it is not out of order to make some tentative comments based on observation.

The first would be the prediction that appropriate studies will show that not much "oversight" of administration, in a systematic and continuous enough manner to make it mean very much, is practiced. The appropriations committees probably do more than the legislative committees (which, not surprisingly, are more interested in legislation), and the House Appropriations Committee does more than the Senate committee (because it is bigger, hears the agencies first, and permits its members no other committee assignments). Most legislative oversight occurs when hearings on new bills or authorizations occur. Closer scrutiny is likely to result from the personal interest of a chairman or ranking member, the sudden interest of the public in a program or a member's hunch that interest can be aroused, or the relationship (amounting virtually to institutional incest in a separation-of-powers system) which arises when a chairman fills the agency's top jobs with his own former staff members. The individual member's interest in administration is likely to be spurred by a constituent's protest, which subsides when the matter is taken care of.

III. WHAT SHOULD BE DONE

If the argument in the beginning of this essay—that there are similarities among particular political institutions in roughly comparable systems and that these institutional influences significantly affect behavior—has merit, then research on the legislature might profitably attempt to be comparative.

Comparative studies of legislative-administrative relations in the English parliamentary and the American presidential-congressional systems, as an example, might be worth doing. The legislature and bureaucracy in both countries stem from the same root, the feudal Great Council which advised the king. Some of its members were barons who belonged to the Curia Regis, a part of his permanent court which developed into the professional bureaucracy. The other members of the Great Council were barons invited, usually three times a year, to consult with the king and consent to taxes. They were joined in time by representatives of the communities. From these occasional meetings the bicameral legislature evolved, while the professional bureaucracy is an outgrowth of the Curia Regis itself. Thus it is that our practices and procedures (and this is true of our courts as well) bear everywhere the marks of English experience. These are worth tracing and explaining.

But our histories have diverged and there are differences. Leaving aside the tendency of some Americans to idealize the British system, what price have we paid in friction and inefficiency for an arrangement which forces the legislature and bureaucracy to negotiate without the legislator-minister as intermediary? Is that lack so decisive as some other factors that accompany it? Say, that the Member of Parliament generally is powerless to do much and the Member of Congress is not? Or that the Member of Parliament may hope for genuine power only in the executive (and so shapes his efforts that way) while a ranking Member of Congress almost surely would sacrifice power if he were to join the executive? To what extent, on the other hand, has institutional separation been bridged in the American system by the shared interest and expertise of committee and agency people, and by their mutual dependence? These questions lead not to statements of abstractly ideal systems but to an attempt to weigh the costs and gains of alternative arrangements.

What is most difficult, obviously, is to sort and assess the relative weights of influences that bear on a man in public life. The argument of this essay is that the institutional influence is a powerful one, that it shapes attitudes and values and produces a shared way of life—so much so that a seasoned member of almost any legislature in the Western world almost surely would be more at home on the floor of either house of the American Congress than most American bureaucrats would be. If this is so, it suggests that the influence of an institution in all its historic dimensions may be stronger than those which are products of a peculiar national experience. The hypothesis should be worth exploring.

The idea of studying the legislature—or any other political institution—in a comparative way is attractive. If political systems may profitably be compared, why not political institutions? It may be that legislatures appear in a system at a certain stage of development, that they perform similar political functions whatever the system, that they affect the behavior of their members in ways that are enough alike to be significant.

Needless to say, there is much of crucial importance to be done on Congress without regard to other systems or to other institutions within the American system.[10] Research on Congress with a behavioral bent

[10] Most of the remaining material is taken from a working paper prepared by the author for a conference of congressional scholars who met at Airlie House, Warrenton, Virginia, on May 20, 1964, to launch the American Political Science Association's Study of Congress. The Study of Congress is financed by the Carnegie Corporation and directed by the author and Robert L. Peabody. Most of the topics upon which scholars of the Study of Congress are working were taken generally from these suggestions.

has come a long way, it seems to me, in the last ten or twelve years. Our discipline has produced a generation of scholars sensitive to the influence on the behavior of Congressmen of the various roles they assume in the related subsystems of Congress, and to the influence on Congress of the external system with which it interacts. We have sliced into our problem enough ways to give us a notion of what is there and some confidence that we know how to proceed. What we still lack, even with the extensive descriptive and prescriptive work of several generations of predecessors, is any very clear idea, to put it simply, of how Congress works—how its principal parts do their jobs and how they are related to each other.

Empirical research can and should provide us with analytical descriptions of Congress, its subsystems, and its relations with its environment; these should (1) fill in the research gaps, suggesting models and relevant variables for future research; and (2) provide some basis for stating the functions Congress performs for the political system, evaluating the performance, and pointing out alternative structural arrangements and modes of action which seem realistically to be open to Congress. Until we have reasonably adequate models, can identify significant variables, and can know what a deceptively simple action like a recorded vote probably means, the machines stand ready to give us more help than we can use. Until we have some idea about what needs of the system are served by Congress and how it serves them, the laundry-ticket lists of congressional reforms are no more than statements of personal preferences.

Research on Congress might be categorized many ways. The categories which will be suggested here are no better than some others that might be chosen, but they should help to organize discussion. Two categories that are obvious enough are the internal system, with its norms and roles, and the relations of this system with the external system, its environment. A third category might be that of policy, or process; the budget or economic policy or foreign policy or defense, might be considered, with the approach not separating internal and external systems, but combining them as the legislative system for that kind of policy. A fourth category might deal with purely facilitative concerns. What kinds of changes would help Congress get on with its job, whatever that job is conceived to be? Improvements in personnel recruitment, pay for Congressmen, vacations, scheduling, and other items affecting the Congressman's life might readily fall into a single category, perhaps even into a single study.

The Internal System

The study of the power structure of each house—and they probably should be studied separately—might begin with the elected leaders.[11] We should not be satisfied with a description of the way the present incumbents operate; this would be little more than good journalism, at best. What is the range of behaviors open to the incumbent of a leadership position? What rewards and punishments were available to Mr. Rayburn in the time of his maximum prestige? What does an intangible like "prestige" mean and how can it be translated into power? What happened in the years of Mr. Rayburn's waning personal powers? How does the House work when the Speaker is ineffective? A close study of the division of labor among the elected leadership on both sides of the aisle, preferably with some attention to history to gain some sense of alternative possibilities, might require the collaboration of several people.

The Senate clearly is a separate study. The floor leadership seems to vary even more widely with incumbent and circumstance than the Speakership; it has fewer institutional props to support it. One crucial variable certainly is the leader's own perception of his role. Another is the occupant of the White House, whether he is of the same party as the Senate majority, and if so, what he expects of the leader and what their relations are. How can the formal party organs, such as the policy committees and the conferences, be used? Recent history suggests a cynical answer, but less recent history does not; Wilson's leader relied heavily on the conference in one of the most productive legislative periods in our history and there are senators now who argue the conference need not be useless.

In each house, the relations of the elected leaders with the committee chairmen should be explored. How does a "strong" elected leader approach his chairmen? Does he attempt to establish priorities among bills? Influence their content? Or does he just take the committee product and try to move it on the floor? These questions are doubly complicated in the House by the power of the Rules Committee. Recent history suggests at least superficially that the Speaker's principal tool is

[11] See David B. Truman, *The Congressional Party* (New York: John Wiley and Sons, Inc., 1959); Ralph K. Huitt, "Democratic Party Leadership in the Senate," *op. cit;* Charles O. Jones, *Party and Policy-making* (New Brunswick, N.J.: Rutgers University Press, 1964).

a showdown or threat of it, a weapon as likely to blow up as it is to shoot. But what about periods when Speaker and committee chairmen worked in close accord? What then was their relation with strong committee chairmen?

Perhaps no study could be more rewarding than a systematic comparative analysis of committees. Some useful and suggestive work already has been done. How do the norms of other committees differ from those found by Professor Richard Fenno to prevail in the House Appropriations Committee?[12] Are the norm systems different and more permissive in less prestigious committees? How are members recruited to committees? What does the freshman member know about this fateful decision about his career? What kind of socialization does he go through?

The chairmen should be the targets of close analysis. This means, among other things, scrutiny of the operation of seniority. It is easy to attack or defend seniority; what does not commend itself to scholarship apparently is the empirical question of its effects. How many committee majorities actually are frustrated by the tyranny of their seniority chairmen? How is this putative authoritarianism accomplished? Can committee majorities break out? What rules do they need—or are the rules already on the books? What happens when a new chairman faces 180 degrees away from his predecessor (say, Langer succeeds McCarran, Eastland follows Kilgore, on Senate Judiciary)? How does a committee deal with a senile chairman? Are there institutional devices for going around him and how well do they work? Answers to questions like these can take a lot of the fun out of the debate over seniority.

Relations among committees also are important. We think especially of the experience of legislative committees which see their floor successes at the authorization stage put in hazard by the appropriations committees. And the relations of the spending with the taxing committees. What problems come from the inescapable overlapping of committee jurisdictions? How do like committees in the two houses get along? Why do the two spending committees often fight when the taxing committees collaborate easily and well? Who wins in conference? Does it vary from committee to committee? Does the seniority system at the conference stage really deliver control of the ultimate product to the oligarchies of the houses?

The norm system in the Senate has been studied to some effect, but

[12] "The House Appropriations Committee as a Political System: The Problem of Integration," *American Political Science Review,* LVI (June 1962), 310-24.

the same cannot be said for the House.[13] Both chambers are worth more attention. What is the range of permissible behavior in each? Systematic analyses of the "outsider," who helps to define the norms by pressing at their boundaries, might be useful. What are the sanctions in these institutionalized groups which have almost no control over the selection of their members? Who is the "outsider"? Is he a personality type? Are there significant correlations with state or district, with socio-psychological origins? In what ways may he be said to be "effective"? In what ways may he be functional, in what ways dysfunctional, for the system?

The chamber floor as terrain for legislative combat might also be a focus of study. What is the relationship between the formal and the informal rules? What advantages, if any, does the skilled parliamentarian enjoy? What difference would a change in rules make? What are the strategies which might be employed by the men who lead floor fights? The literature recounts occasional coups by which advantage has been gained through knowledge and use of the rules. What is not clear is whether legislators divide labor as lawyers do, with a counterpart on the floor of the skilled advocate who takes the prepared case to the courtroom, or whether there is enough to parliamentary advocacy to justify specialization.

Another actor who occupies an ambiguous place in the power structure is the professional staff man,[14] an ambiguous figure because his influence has been both underrated and overrated. Surely he is more than a facilitator, more than extra hands to relieve the legislator of errand-running, more than a trained research mind to end legislative dependence on bureaucrat and lobbyist. Surely he is less than the real power behind the throne, as the frustrated lobbyist, and even the staff man himself, sometimes think he is. What is he like, this bright and ambitious man who submerges his own career aspirations in those of another? What does he want, what does he think he can get? How does *he* perceive his role, its satisfactions and limitations? Some remarkable men have served members of Congress; some have gone on to serve two presidents who have come out of the legislature. There is a great study to be made of the professional staff man and his relations with his principal by the legislative scholar who can enter upon it with his preconceptions firmly under control.

[13] Matthews, *op. cit.*, Ch. 5; Huitt, "The Morse Committee Assignment Controversy: A Study in Senate Norms," *American Political Science Review*, XLI (June 1957), 313-29, and "The Outsider in the Senate," *ibid.*, LV (September 1961), 566-75.

[14] See Kenneth Kofmehl, *Professional Staffs of Congress* (West Lafayette, Indiana: Purdue University Press, 1962).

Relations with the External System

The importance of the web of relationships existing between Congress and the President, bureaucracy, parties, interest groups, press, and constituencies is so patent that almost any well designed study of any of these relationships could have significance. Let me suggest only two or three.

One need which must be met before the computers really can serve us is the construction of more sophisticated models of systems of outside influence which press upon a member of Congress. The party is an example.[15] Many roll call studies have made use of "party votes," so designated because a stated majority of one party opposed a similar majority of the other. Indices of cohesion and other measures are built from them and statements are made about the influence of party on members or on this or that bloc. The curious thing is that our model of the party in the basic texts is much more sophisticated than that. A reasonably competent student in the freshman course can write that the major party "is a federation of state and local parties." Why is not this model carried over into research on Congress? Suppose that two members bearing the same party designation split their votes on a roll call. Might it not be that one is voting with the national committee party, the other casting an opposing vote *with* a state or local party which bears the same name—in a word, *both* are casting party votes?

A similarly simplistic view of *the* constituency often is employed.[16] A conception of the constituency as all the people of voting age living in the district or state is bound to lead to remarkable results. Everyone knows that the constituency so conceived will have opinions on very few issues indeed. Nevertheless, the member talks about his constituency; he says he follows its wishes sometimes or all the time, and it is not safe to assume without proof that this is double-talk or that he is a dunce. On the contrary; his perhaps tacit concept of constituency is more complicated: he responds to *different* constituencies on different issues. He may try to paint an image of himself in the broadest strokes as an

[15] An excellent bibliography on the subject has been compiled by Charles O. Jones and Randall B. Ripley, *The Role of Political Parties in Congress* (Tucson, Arizona: University of Arizona Press, 1966).

[16] For sophisticated analyses of congressional relations with constituencies employing survey research techniques and systematic interviews, see Warren E. Miller and Donald E. Stokes, "Constituency Influence in Congress," *American Political Science Review*, LVII (March 1963), 45-56; and Charles C. Cnudde and Donald J. McCrone, "The Linkage Between Constituency Attitudes and Congressional Voting Behavior: A Causal Model," *ibid.*, LX (March 1966), 66-72.

"economiser," say, for the vast number of voters who will try to remember *something* about him when they go to the polls, while at the same time he works to amend one line of a bill to please a half-dozen labor leaders who can make or break him by the kind of voter-registration effort they put on. These are "constituencies"—the people of varying degrees of influence, knowledge, and intensity of feeling who are aware of and respond to particular issues. The students of public opinion long ago learned that if they defined "public" as all the people living in a society there usually would be no public opinion. Because this was a nonsense result they defined the term in a variety of ways that would support analysis. That is what we must do with the concept "constituency."

Inasmuch as "party" and "constituency" in this sense are systems of influence, why not go for help with our models to the persons presumably influenced, the members of Congress themselves? How do *they* perceive party and constituency? The same kinds of questions might be asked about interest groups, bureaucracy, or any other putative system of influence.

One further need may be suggested. In the systematic comparative study of committees close attention should be paid to the patterns of relations between committees and the bureaucratic agencies they supervise. An unassailable truism of legislative literature makes "legislative oversight" a basic congressional task. But what goes on under the label "oversight"? Consider some of the conventional tools. Appropriations: do the subcommittees really get to the heart of the matter? Investigation: is anything really changed after the dust settles? Confirmation: what difference does it really make in agency operations *who* the top man is? Detailed legislation: but isn't it the lesson of the last century that Congress must delegate to administrators the burden of legislating in detail? Studies of the oversight exercised by particular committees make clear that some of them exercise no supervision over the agencies assigned them and have no desire to do it; others have a variety of relationships, some of which would be hard to call oversight. What determines the character of the committee's concern about administrative performance? Some of the hypothetical variables are the personality of the chairman and his perception of his role, the character of the agency and its program, the degree of constituency involvement in the program, the character and quality of the committee's professional staff. Careful and realistic additions to the literature on oversight will find an eager audience among the bureaucrats themselves.

Policy-making Process

It is not easy for a feudal system to make national policy. Whatever the advantages of dispersed centers of power (and I believe they are many), the capacity to make and carry out a plan is not among them. It is common for Congress to have inflationary and deflationary programs underway at the same time, to take away with one hand what it gives with the other. Some of our studies might profitably abandon the single house as a subsystem and look at the way one kind of policy is made across the board.[17] What is the budget process? This might be broken into spending and taxing (as Congress does it). How is foreign policy, or defense policy, fashioned? If Congress wanted to make a real effort to effect coordination in the making of some kind of national policy, what devices might be employed that have been proved by congressional experience to be useful for that purpose? If stronger party leadership generally were desired, what organizational arrangements might be strengthened, what inhibited? What would be gained and what would be the price?

These last questions, we might say finally, should be part of every study. Congress changes, as all living things must change; it changes slowly, adaptively, as institutions change. But structural arrangements are not neutral; they will be used by those who can get control of them for whatever purposes the controllers have in mind. Changes, therefore, may have unforeseen consequences. What changes seem possible of accomplishment, given Congress's history and present structure? Who seems likely to benefit, who will pay? These are questions our discipline has taught us to ask.

Suggestions for Further Reading

Bailey, Stephen K., *Congress Makes A Law: The Story Behind the Employment Act of 1946* (New York: Columbia University Press, 1950).

__________, *The New Congress* (New York: St. Martin's Press, 1966).

Clapp, Charles, *The Congressman: His Work as He Sees It* (Washington, D.C.: The Brookings Institution, 1963).

[17] For representative studies, see Holbert N. Carroll, *The House of Representatives and Foreign Affairs* (Pittsburgh: University of Pittsburgh Press, 1958); Aaron Wildavsky, *The Politics of the Budgetary Process* (Boston: Little, Brown and Co., 1964).

Griffith, Ernest S., *Congress: Its Contemporary Role,* 3rd ed. (New York: New York University Press, 1961).

Matthews, Donald R., *U.S. Senators and Their World* (Chapel Hill: University of North Carolina Press, 1960).

Truman, David B., *Congress and America's Future* (Englewood Cliffs, N.J.: Prentice-Hall, Inc., 1965).

__________, *The Congressional Party* (New York: John Wiley & Sons, Inc., 1959).

Wahlke, John C., *et al, The Legislative System: Explorations in Legislative Behavior* (New York: John Wiley & Sons, Inc., 1962).

THE BRITISH LEGISLATURE AND THE PROBLEM OF MOBILIZING CONSENT

Samuel H. Beer

The tasks of legislatures change with the times. One of the newer and more important of these tasks, and one to which not nearly enough attention has been paid, is the function of mobilizing consent. Modern governments impose vast and increasing burdens on their citizens, not only in the form of deprivations in terms of money, time, effort, and so on—as in the payment of taxes or performance of military service—but, even more important in these days of the welfare state and managed economy, in the form of requirements of certain often intricate patterns of behavior—such as conformity to wage and price "guidelines."

Yet the reasons for these impositions are usually technical, complex, and hard for the ordinary man to understand and make part of his personal motivation. If a government is to rule effectively, therefore, and since it cannot depend solely upon force, it must continuously mobilize consent and win acceptance for its policies. The legislature is one of the agencies that helps perform this task.

SAMUEL H. BEER *is Professor of Government at Harvard University, and was Chairman of the Department from 1954 to 1958. He has published articles in political theory and comparative government, parties and pressure groups in the professional journals. Among his books are* Patterns of Government: The Major Political Systems of Europe *(co-editor) and* British Politics in the Collectivist Age.

I. THE PARADOX OF POWER

This function of mobilizing consent, I wish to emphasize, is not one of the traditional functions of the legislature. It is certainly not the representative function by which in greater or lesser degree the legislature brings the grievances and wishes of the people to bear upon policy-making. It does not refer primarily to the kind of consent that is involved when the voters at an election give their approval to a certain body of men and/or to a certain program of proposals. On the contrary, it is especially the consent that must be won insofar as the voters did not originate or mandate the policies being imposed upon them.

British experience in recent years illustrates vividly this new necessity of modern government. On the one hand, we find there a governmental system that might seem to satisfy all the conditions for decisional effectiveness. "Of all governments of countries with free political institutions," Professor Bernard Crick has written, "British government exhibits the greatest concentration of power and authority. Nowhere else is a Government normally as free to act decisively, so unfettered by formal restraints of Constitutional Law, by any Federal divisions of power, by any practice of strong and active local government, or by any likelihood of defeat in the Parliament." [1]

Yet in recent years, according to many British critics, this powerful system has performed weakly. The burden of their complaint is not that it has been illiberal or undemocratic, but that it has been ineffective—in particular, ineffective in meeting the great but surely not unmanageable problems of the British economy. Here is a country that was once the workshop of the world. Yet year after year it has lagged behind the other economies of the free world. British government, it is alleged, must bear a large share of the responsibility.

It is this paradox that I wish first to develop. Why does a government so superbly equipped to govern not have a better record of achievement? Once the conditions of this paradox have been made clear, we can turn to the question of what role Parliament might have in overcoming it. This becomes precisely the question of how to enhance its role in mobilizing consent.

The Decline of Parliament

When we say that the British government is powerful we mean in the first place that it concentrates great authority in the executive. The tradi-

[1] *The Reform of Parliament* (London: Weidenfeld & Nicolson, 1964), p. 16.

tion and practice of a strong executive in Britain go back at least to Tudor times. Yet there have been ups and downs within that tradition and it will be useful to take a quick look back to the nineteenth century if we wish to understand the conditions which today support a balance of power weighted heavily in favor of the executive and against the legislature.

In this historical perspective by far the most important change in the position of Parliament has been the decline to the vanishing point of the probability that a cabinet will be defeated in the House of Commons. Consider, for instance, the period 1846 to 1860, when parliamentary independence—or unreliability, if you prefer—reached its peak. In these fourteen years the House administered eight major defeats to successive Governments. On six occasions defeat led to the resignation of the cabinet; on the other two, the cabinet dissolved Parliament and went to the country in a general election. Perhaps most interesting is the fact that in these fourteen years there were five different cabinets, with an average life of less than three years. Writing of the relations of executive and legislature, Walter Bagehot could state a cardinal truth of British government at that time when he said that the House of Commons "lives in a state of perpetual potential choice." [2]

Today cabinets must still have the confidence of the House if they wish to remain in office. As a matter of fact, however, the chance of a cabinet losing that confidence is almost nil. The last time a Government resigned because of a defeat in the House was 1923. A year later another Government suffered a defeat serious enough to cause it to call a general election. In each of these cases, however, the party supporting the Government was in a minority in the House. To find an instance when a Government originally enjoying a party majority over all other parties in the House lost on a vote that caused it to resign, we must go back to 1885 when Gladstone's Liberals split over Irish Home Rule.

The unlikelihood that a modern Parliament will exercise its power of "choice" could hardly be better illustrated than by recent events. In the autumn of 1964, Harold Wilson took office with a majority of five over the combined Conservative and Liberal opposition. In spite of dire predictions to the contrary, he remained in power and governed for a year and a half, thanks to the near perfect discipline of his supporters on the Labour benches.

All this is too familiar to need emphasis. Today if a British Government wins a party majority in the House of Commons at a general elec-

[2] *The English Constitution* (London: Oxford University Press [World's Classics series], 1928), p. 125; originally pub. 1867.

tion, it can confidently count on that majority supporting it until the next general election. In Britain this is an age not of parliamentary government, but of cabinet government.

When one asks why this great shift in the balance of power between executive and legislature has taken place and what conditions maintain this powerful executive today, the principal clue may seem to be provided by the political party. Judged by modern standards, party discipline sat lightly on the shoulders of those mid-Victorian MPs and party cohesion was at a low ebb. Today an MP may still vote against his party on a rare occasion; rather more often he will express his dissidence by abstaining. But when one makes a statistical study of party voting, the figures are so monotonously 100 per cent or nearly 100 per cent that it is hardly worth making the count. If this is an age of cabinet government, the reason in the first instance is that it is an age of party government.

Yet even a superficial glance at other legislatures will force us to take our inquiry into causes a step or two farther, for the strengthening of the executive against the legislature has been a general development in the modern world and has taken place even where party government on the British model has not been present. The United States is the obvious illustration. In this century and especially since the New Deal our presidency has radically shifted the balance of power in its favor and against the Congress. Yet party cohesion is still low in comparison with British behavior and has shown little significant increase in this century. Indeed, statistically speaking, party voting reached its peak not under Franklin Roosevelt or Lyndon Johnson, but under William McKinley.[3]

The conditions that have strengthened the executive may work through party, as in Britain, but they go beyond party. First among them, of course, has been war. As has often been remarked, military operations are peculiarly the function of the executive. They take swiftness and secrecy in decision, for neither of which qualities legislatures are well known. They also require a kind of specific and *ad hoc* action which can hardly be derived from the application of general rules and which therefore comes more readily from the executive than the legislature. Parliamentary government, and legislatures generally, flourished during that great, abnormal century of peace that stretched from the battle of Waterloo to the first battle of the Marne. These present decades of war and cold war are inevitably an age of the executive.

Yet it is not only defense activities that have expanded the powers of

[3] Julius Turner, *Party and Constituency: Pressures on Congress* (Baltimore: Johns Hopkins University Press, 1951), p. 28. *Congressional Quarterly,* XXIII: 45 (November 5, 1965), 2246.

the executive. Economic and social policy—the intervention of government in the management of the economy and the development of the welfare state—constantly make new calls upon executive action. The complexity and technicality of the issues put the administrator in a far better position than the legislator to make and adjust the rules for control of these growing sectors of government action. It is not, however, just technicality and complexity that are important, but rather what one may call *the increasing specificity of the essential governmental decision.*

The contrast I wish to draw is between government by specific decision and government by general rules. Any government, of course, involves decisions if there is to be action at all. But in the past it has been the expectation in Britain, as in the United States, that these decisions—by the policeman, the judge, the civil servant—could and would be largely controlled by laws cast in general form. Where, however, government gets as deeply engaged in the management of economic and social affairs as has British government, it must increasingly rely less upon general laws and more upon specific managerial decisions.

This trend has been a major theme of the recent inaugural lecture of the new Professor of Public Administration in the University of London. "If the Government," writes Professor Self, "is to take a greater part in the promotion of economic growth, it is hard to see how more specific interventions can be avoided. The structure of modern industry is such that general measures often cannot be realistically promulgated without awareness of their effects on particular firms." He then goes on to observe how, for example, the Board of Trade, under its procedures for controlling the location of industry, "considers every application for the location of a new factory 'on its merits.' " This is no doubt a necessary procedure if the ministry is to "take account of the special needs, and contribution to the economy, of each applicant." [4] But although the administrator in this instance is guided by a broad economic policy, his decisions are much more akin to those of the business manager adjusting to a specific situation than to those of the traditional bureaucrat administering general rules.

Largely for these reasons, the practice of delegating legislative power to the executive has grown immensely in recent times. In making these delegations of power, Parliament contents itself with a broad authorization to the executive which then determines the more specific provisions. Lawmaking by the executive under such authorizations now greatly exceeds regular parliamentary legislation, at least in quantity, the "statutory in-

[4] Peter Self, *Bureaucracy or Management?* (London: London School of Economics, 1965), pp. 13-14.

struments" embodying such acts of executive lawmaking numbering between two and three thousand a year, some of very great length and complexity.[5]

My object here is not to praise or to lament these developments, but to show their connection with the present status of the legislature in Britain. First I want to point out how this new type of decision, the managerial decision, in economic and social affairs is remarkably similar to the traditional type of decision made by men in charge of military operations. In this respect, the managed economy and war have drawn power to the executive for essentially the same reason. Secondly, I hardly need stress the important fact that as general rules become less useful to the executive in its modern efforts to manage and control the economic and social environment, so also will that great, traditional source of general rules, the legislature, probably lose its central place in the governmental system. The decline of the legislature in Britain is deeply rooted in a new pattern of policy—the managed economy and the welfare state —which in greater or lesser degree has forced itself forward in all self-governing countries.

The New Group Politics

So far, the sketch I have drawn of British government is very one-sided: a vast extension of power over society and a sharp centralization of power in the executive. But there is another side of this profile of power that makes the picture as a whole more complex and less one-dimensional. The key element is the pressure group.[6]

Pressure groups are nothing new in Britain. One can trace them back to the earliest days of representative government there. In the nineteenth century they were a major agent of political change, inspiring much of the legislation of that great age of reform. The typical pressure group of the period was a voluntary association of like-minded people who joined together to push their agitation, often for a single piece of legislation, and who might well disband once their aim had been achieved. One thinks of the Anti-Corn Law League, that model of successful middle-class reformist agitation.

The pressure groups of the present period of collectivist policy and politics are strikingly different. In Britain as in the United States, the

[5] Sir Barnett Cocks, ed., *Erskine May's Treatise on The Law, Privileges, Proceedings and Usage of Parliament,* 17th ed. (London: Butterworth, 1964), p. 610.

[6] In this discussion of group politics, I am for the most part summarizing from my book, *British Politics in the Collectivist Age* (New York: Alfred A. Knopf, Inc., 1965), especially Chap. XII.

center of the stage is occupied by organized bodies of producers representing the main sectors of a highly industrialized economy. These are the big three of business, labor, and agriculture, along with the professions—doctors, teachers, civil servants, and others.

In social base, structure, purpose, political tactics, relations with government, and the foundations of their political power these bodies greatly differ from the transient, voluntary associations of like-minded reformers which sought to win Victorian Parliaments over to their schemes of reform. The primary base of their power is the vital productive function that their members perform in the economy. If government is to control or calculably influence the performance of this economic function, it must have their cooperation. It must have access to their advice—the information and expertise which is possessed only by those actually doing the work—and especially, it must enjoy a degree of acceptance of its policy that is more than a mere grudging consent to "the law." An obvious example: you cannot operate an effective nationalized health service if the doctors refuse to work for the service, or, indeed, even if they are seriously discontented with the way it is run.

For these reasons, the officials of these organizations have over the years been drawn into a vast, complex scheme of consultation with government departments. Officially in a series of advisory committees that runs into the hundreds and less formally in constant, daily contacts, the representatives of producer groups have been joined with departments of the executive in a system of functional representation that operates outside and alongside the established system of parliamentary representation. Among the committees on which such producer groups have been represented in recent years have been such high-level bodies as the Economic Planning Board, the National Joint Advisory Council of the Ministry of Labour, the National Production Advisory Council on Industry, and, more important at the present time, the National Economic Development Council, which includes representatives of the Government, the management of private and public industry, and the Trades Union Congress, as well as independent experts, and which was designed to lead the way toward more rapid economic growth.

I call this arrangement of formal and informal contacts a system of representation because, in fact, the process of consultation is far from being a one-sided relation in which government merely listens to what the organized interests have to say and then decides its course regardless of their wishes. The very fact of government's large dependence on these bodies means that their wishes will have great weight. Looking at this new system of functional representation as a whole, one must recognize that it involves a process of bargaining as often as one of mere consultation. The *ad hoc* managerial decision is precisely the type of decision that one would expect to come from such a process of bargaining, and a large proportion of the business of economic management is performed in this network of functional representation.

I have stressed this system of functional representation, with its bargaining and its managerial decisions, because these are the most important and novel features of the new group politics in Britain. Yet the *dramatis personae* include not only producers, but also consumers. I am thinking here not of consumers in the technical economic sense, but of groups of people whose material well-being is affected in the same way by some measure of government action, actual or prospective. While the concerns of the producer groups are focused mainly on the programs of the managed economy, the concerns of these consumer groups are directed toward the array of services provided by the welfare state: social security, housing, education, and the like. These groups include old age pensioners, health service patients, tenants of state housing, and similar beneficiaries of the social services. I do not mean, of course, to try to draw a physical line of distinction between producers and consumers, for obviously every person is normally both, and producers' organizations —trade unions for instance—will be concerned with welfare programs as well as with government controls on their economic behavior.

While the producers' interests are put forward mainly in relations with the executive, consumers' interests are especially the subject of party competition. For the past twenty years or so the two big parties in Britain have been fairly evenly matched in terms of popular support. As a result they have been forced into a sharp and continuous competition for the support of groups benefiting from the services of the welfare state; competition bidding up promises of better pensions, housing, education, and the like has been a common feature of general elections. This use of terms from economics is appropriate. For if "bargaining" is characteristic of the group politics of the new system of functional representation, "bidding" is the word for the mode of competition in the parallel system of parliamentary and party representation.

In this complex manner, then, a new group politics has arisen simultaneously with, and yet as a counterbalance to, the extension and centralization of control over British society. We may breathe a sigh of relief for the liberties of the subject, for these processes of group representation are a formidable apparatus for protecting and forwarding the interests of certain minorities. Indeed, it takes no great imagination to see that the danger may be just the opposite from what a first glance at British government might suggest: that is, it is the danger not of oppressive efficiency, but rather of pluralistic stagnation. One British observer has recently written:

> *The interests have grown too strong. Try to introduce change into any British institution and the log jam piles up at once. It is natural for an American faced by the overlapping committees and agencies in Washington and the separation of powers to sigh for the efficiency of the British governmental machine where issues flow smoothly along from the committees for decision at Ministerial or Cabinet Committee level, all interests having been consulted. Yet the very efficiency and tidiness of the machine is its undoing. The interests are so faithfully represented and bring such pressure to bear indicating how far each is prepared to move—which is usually little distance at all—that the degree of movement is negligible.*[7]

There is perhaps a shade of masochism in this indictment—the British are in an excessively self-critical mood these days. Yet in crucial fields of policy one can convincingly establish a connection between the new group politics and tendencies to inaction and stagnation. Two critical failures of British economic policy will illustrate the point. Since the war the rate of economic growth of the British economy has consistently lagged behind that of the other principal countries of Western Europe. One major reason for this lag has been the relatively low proportion of national product used each year for net new investment in manufacturing. There is no simple explanation for this lag. Yet the situation has certainly not been helped by policies favoring expenditure on consumption. Insofar as resources are diverted to satisfy immediate consumption needs—whether through individual purchase or provision by the welfare state—there will be that much less available for enlarging Britain's productive capital. I do not suggest that the choice is an easy one for a government to make—especially when its margin of favor with the electorate is constantly threatened by a competitor bidding for the votes of the same consumer groups in which the government itself has found crucial support.

A second and related problem has been inflation. With almost cyclical regularity the British economy has fallen into a crisis in its balance of payments with the rest of the world. Typically a cause of the trouble has been an inflationary rise of prices. While there has been no single cause

[7] Noel Annan in a review of my book, cited above; *New York Review of Books,* V: 7 (November 11, 1965).

of these price rises, very often the pushing up of wage costs by trade union pressure and by competition among employers for scarce labor, has been an important contributing factor. In order to meet this problem, governments—both Labour and Conservative—have attempted to establish what has come to be known as an "incomes policy." This means in simplest terms some form of restraint on wages and other income so that they rise no more than productivity.

One might well think that since inflation and payments crises are so obviously against the interests of all groups, it should not be too difficult for government to arrange a bargain with unions and managers that would result in the necessary restraint. And governments have devoted great efforts and much time to the bargaining process. Yet even when the official representatives of the groups have been able to agree, it has been difficult, if not impossible, to win acceptance of the policy of restraint among the rank and file and among leaders at lower levels. The failure of government policy in this crucial area of economic concern has been one of the most striking examples of how the new group politics has flourished undaunted by the imposing powers of modern British government.

The economic problems of which I have spoken are essentially political problems. I do not deny that there is a good deal more that economists would like to know about the causes of inflation and the conditions of economic growth. At the same time, modern economic analysis does give governments far greater understanding of these matters than was possessed by governments and their advisers in the 1920s and 1930s. The problem is therefore not so much to devise economic programs which, if they were carried out, would meet the problems. It is rather to win such understanding and acceptance of government programs among the public, as individuals and as members of producer and consumer groups, that they will adjust their own behavior to the requirements of these programs. The central problem in short is to win consent—and winning consent is a political problem and a political process.

II. WHAT CAN PARLIAMENT DO?

My paradox is complete: a system which by the very extension and centralizing of power undertaken to deal with modern problems has set in train political consequences that make it exceedingly difficult to deal with those problems. The question now is: Has Parliament a role in helping Britain overcome these essentially political difficulties?

The Functions of Parliament Traditionally and Today

It may help us see the possibilities if we briefly consider some of the conventional views of the functions of legislatures in general and of Parliament in particular. I will take these in the chronological order in which they have flourished, but I want to emphasize that in greater or lesser degree they still give us insight into what actually goes on today.

One of the oldest conceptions of the role of Parliament is that of controlling and restraining the executive. An acute Tory thinker of the last generation claimed that throughout British history, from the origins of the constitution in the Middle Ages, this had been the essential function of Parliament. In the view of L. S. Amery, there are and always have been two main elements in British government: one is the central, initiating, energizing element—formerly the monarchy, today the cabinet—while the other is the checking, criticizing, controlling element—the Parliament, and nowadays especially the Opposition.[8] The task of the Government is to govern; the task of Parliament is to criticize and control—that is, to present grievances and to let the ministers and bureaucrats know what the people will not stand.

This bipolar model still tells us a great deal about British government. It provides, for instance, an illuminating rationale for much of the procedure of the House of Commons. As stated in Standing Orders and in long-honored conventions, the rules of the House presuppose on one side a Government—that is, not merely a number of ministers, but a unified ministerial body which has a program of business that it will put before the House—and on the other side, an Opposition similarly organized and ready to act. Within this framework, the activity of the House is organized under various formal headings. One authoritative classification, for instance, relates the forms of procedure to the following functions of the House: (1) control of finance; (2) formulation and control of policy; and (3) legislation.[9] This is a helpful scheme, but when we examine how the procedural forms under these headings are actually used, they usually turn out to constitute criticism and control. The nominal function of a procedural form is usually not its real function. In a debate on an adjournment motion, for example, one does not discuss whether or not to adjourn. In the debates on the estimates, the House rarely discusses the

[8] *Thoughts on the Constitution*, 2nd ed. (London: Oxford University Press, 1953), Chap. I.

[9] "Suggestions for Reform in Procedure" Clerk of the House, Sir Gilbert Champion, in *3rd Report from the Select Committee on Procedure*, H.C. 189-1, 1946, xxiii.

amount to be appropriated, but rather some aspect of departmental policy which the Opposition has chosen to attack. Whatever their nominal content, the forms of procedure of the House are used very much in accord with the bipolar model. The Government governs, but subject to a continuous flow of criticism varying in scope, timing, specificity, and so on.

The opportunities for criticism are clear enough, but may one also speak of them as a means of control? To be sure, in these days of monolithic majorities, such criticism is not expected to result in defeats for the Government—not, at any rate, in defeats serious enough to cause a resignation or dissolution. Yet such criticism is not without influence. By building up points in these debates, the Opposition may hope to sway voters when they next go to the polls. Moreover, one cannot neglect the real though immeasurable influence that criticism may have without reference to electoral consequences. The House itself is a community with its own standards of excellence in the light of which, quite apart from party considerations, reputations are made and lost. Furthermore, this community blends with a special public linked by communication centers such as the clubs of Pall Mall, university common rooms, and the editorial offices of the better daily newspapers and weekly political journals. No self-respecting minister or civil servant can enjoy having acts of injustice or stupidity for which he is responsible exposed to the scrutiny and comment of such circles in the House and adjacent to it. In trying to understand what influences British Governments and politicians, it is certainly a mistake to neglect the sanctions of these critics and to consider only those of the electorate. To be sure, only the voters can ultimately withdraw or confer power. But not the least of the sweets of power is to use it in such a way as to earn the praise of a discriminating public. Otherwise, one may have power without glory.

This criticizing and controlling function of Parliament, although perhaps its most ancient task, is still important today. Another function, that first became prominent in a later historical period, however, gives the legislature a more positive role. In the light of this function, the essential task of the legislature is to legislate, to make laws—in a fundamental sense, to lay down the lines along which the country will be governed. Two major historical views that attribute this function to Parliament are the Liberal and the Radical.[10] The Liberal conceived of Parliament as performing this lawmaking function under the guidance of its own sense of what was right and prudent without regard to pres-

[10] I have discussed these attitudes and theories in *British Politics in the Collectivist Age,* Chap. II, "Liberal and Radical Politics."

sure from the outside. In short, he took Parliament to be a deliberative body, making its determinations in response to reasons and forces arising within it. According to the Radical democrat, Parliament was also to be the chief lawmaker, but with the important proviso that it express the will of the people. In some versions, this relationship was to be secured by means of a party program approved by the voters at a general election and conceived as giving the Government a "mandate" to carry out what was promised.

Today, of course, Parliament is not the chief lawmaker, if by that we mean that it lays down a set of general rules which so far control the actions of administrators that they need merely apply them by deduction to particular cases. As we have previously observed, a continually larger proportion of government action consists of managerial decisions governed only broadly by statutory authority and formulated in many cases by the *ad hoc* bargaining of public and private bureaucrats. Moreover, even those broad statutory grants of power to the executive have not originated with the rank and file of the legislature. The initiative in legislation, as in other policy-making, is exercised almost exclusively by the executive. If we want to know what laws will be debated in a coming session of Parliament, we do not take a poll of MPs. We look rather at the Speech from the Throne in which ministers state the objects for which they will seek legislation. Indeed, not only does the Government largely monopolize the initative in drafting and proposing bills to Parliament, it also gets substantially all legislation for which it asks. Under modern conditions of cabinet and party government, it would be misleading to picture Parliament as the law-making power.

Yet, again speaking in terms of realities, we cannot neglect the influence of the legislature, in particular the parliamentary party upon which the Government depends for its "mechanical majorities." When the governing party went to the country, it took a position on many public questions. It may have presented a detailed program; at the least, it gave an impression of its broad approach to problems. This public stance in part reflects and in part creates a body of ideas and sentiments among the party's MPs which the Government cannot easily disregard. "Collectively and individually," D. N. Chester has recently written, "Ministers cannot get far out of line with the views of their supporters in the House. The electoral campaign and Party manifestoes, the basic attitudes of active Party members, are as much part of the heritage of the Government as of their supporters and almost as compulsive on their actions." [11]

[11] D. N. Chester, "The British Parliament," a paper presented at the Conference on the Future of the Legislative Power, Princeton University, April 14-17, 1966, p. 19.

An ancient task of the party whips is to keep leaders informed of feeling among the rank and file and of whether the limits of their loyalty are being approached. A more modern instrument for taking such soundings and for enabling leaders to anticipate disaffection is provided by the elaborate organization of back-benchers that has grown up in both parties in the past fifty years and especially since World War II. In both parties there are regular weekly meetings of what we would call the party caucus; in addition there are many specialized committees roughly corresponding in their subjects of concern with the main departments of state. In both parties leaders keep in touch with these meetings, and discussion at them can be fierce when the party is divided over some question of policy or leadership. Indeed, it is sometimes said that the most interesting debates in the Palace of Westminster take place not on the floor of the House, but in the rooms where the party meetings are held. If the ancient function of criticism is nowadays performed especially by the Opposition, the more modern function of keeping the actions of government in line with its electoral commitments depends in no small degree upon such pressures from the back-benchers of the governing party.

As a model of what actually goes on, the notion of Parliament as chief lawmaker, whether in its Liberal or Radical versions, is a gross distortion—a common fate of models. Yet it does give us a systematic insight into a function of the legislature that is a necessary supplement to the view that Parliament's role is to criticize and control. At times Parliament does behave as a deliberative body—for instance, when amending bills in the less partisan atmosphere of standing committee where the special knowledge of members has a chance of being attended to by civil servants, ministers, and other MPs.

Moreover, although pure mandate theory is an exaggeration, Parliament performs its criticizing and controlling function in the context of a lively system of democratic and party politics. It is the principal forum from which the parties appeal to voters for their support in the next general election. "Governing," writes Professor Crick, "has now become a prolonged election campaign." "Parliament," he goes on to observe, "is still the agreed arena in which most of the continuous election campaign is fought," and the principal device by which "the Parties obtain something like equal access to the ear of the electorate in the long formative period between the official campaigns." [12] One must not exaggerate the attention given to Parliament. Those newspapers that carry reasonably full reports of parliamentary debates are read by only 11 per cent of

[12] *Op. cit.*, pp. 25-26.

the population—that is, rather more than 5 million persons. About the same number (though not necessarily the same people) have been identified as the "serious public" who declare themselves to be "very interested" in political affairs and who follow them between elections.[13] These people are only a fraction of the total electorate, but as opinion leaders they play an important role in the formation of the opinion that is expressed at elections.

To Mobilize Consent

There are two aspects of this opinion that are of interest to us. On the one hand, it includes those "electoral commitments" which were made by the leadership of the winning party and will be in some degree pressed on that leadership by their parliamentary followers. This aspect of the electoral process is a primary concern of traditional democratic theory which emphasizes the flow of public will into governmental action by means of such commitments. In this view, voters use elections to oblige government to follow their wishes.

For the purposes of this paper, however, another aspect of the electoral process is more important. This is the fact that these "electoral commitments," so to speak, commit not only the Government, but also the voters. They constitute a set of expectations—some specific, most rather vague—about the future course of government policy which the voters in substantial numbers have shown themselves to share. These expectations originated with the public itself probably in only a few instances and in a very distant sense. As our previous discussion suggested, they may well have been initially communicated to the electorate by means of the party battle in Parliament. The important point is that the expectations, however they originated, have laid a foundation of consent and acceptance for relevant government programs in the future. A first step in mobilizing consent has been taken.

With some stretching of democratic theory, we may say that this process is one way in which the legislature fulfills its representative function. The voters did not originate the commitments and there was perhaps some "dependence effect" [14] in the way they were brought to accept them.

[13] Richard Rose, *Politics in England* (Boston: Little, Brown and Co., 1965), p. 89, and *Influencing Voters: A Study of Political Campaigning in 1964* (to be published) Chap. XI, note 19.

[14] "As society becomes increasingly affluent," writes John Kenneth Galbraith, "wants are increasingly created by the process by which they are satisfied." For example, "producers may proceed actively to create wants through advertising and salesmanship." Galbraith calls this the "dependence effect." *The Affluent Society* (Boston: Houghton Mifflin Co., 1958), p. 158.

Still, the electorate made the choice and the legislature, more or less faithfully, carries out its will. It is immediately clear, however, that such an expression of popular will—such a set of commitments and expectations—can realistically control the course of government in only the most limited sense. Many—and quite possibly the most painful—decisions will have to be taken after the election.

How to legitimize these decisions may be a problem for democratic theory. Our concern here is to point out that winning consent for them among the people they affect will certainly be a problem for the government. For modern government cannot and does not rely solely upon the legitimizing effects of periodic elections. It must make continuous efforts to create consent for new programs and to sustain consent for old ones. *It must mobilize consent between as well as at elections.*

In so mobilizing consent, various elements of British government make a contribution. The "exhortations" to which ministers resort from time to time in an effort to win voluntary cooperation with some painful policy have not been uniformly successful. Still, the kind of leadership ministers provide, and especially the confidence the prime minister is able to arouse, are vitally important. Likewise, the spirit and the incentives that government imparts to the bargaining process can make a difference. My concern here, however, is briefly to suggest the possibilities of an enlarged role for Parliament.

I do not know of a theoretical exploration of this function by a political scientist. It has, however, been recognized as an important function of the American Congress by one of the most effective and scholarly of the new generation in the United States House of Representatives. Writing of "the emerging role of Congress," John Brademas has isolated and described an important aspect of the modern legislator's relationship with his constituents. Referring specifically to the recently enacted education, anti-poverty, and medicare programs, he reports that as he traveled around his district, he was constantly questioned by "state and local authorities, officials of private organizations and individuals on how the programs work."

It is more than a question of red tape and filling out applications, [*he writes.*] *Many local leaders may not understand the purposes of the legislation or see its relevance to their communities. The Congressman or Senator, by organizing community conferences, mailing materials and in other ways, can supply important information, interpretation, justification and leadership to his constituency. . . . These activities of explaining, justifying, interpreting, interceding, all help, normally,* to build acceptance for government policy, *an essential process in democratic government. . . .*[15]

When Congressman Brademas writes of how the legislator can "build acceptance for government policy" he means exactly what in this paper has been called mobilizing consent. In his illustration he refers to programs which have already been enacted into law, but which are not understood or fully accepted even among those whom they benefit. That he sees the necessity to "build acceptance" for these particular programs is especially interesting, as they are concerned with direct "welfare" benefits rather than more remote objectives, such as economic growth. Yet even in the case of such "popular" programs and among people who stand to benefit from them, he finds a need to "build acceptance."

The welfare state and the managed economy bring many benefits, but inevitably they also impose many new and complex coercions—often in the very process of conferring benefits. A great deal is expected of the citizen in the form of new necessities that oblige him to conform his behavior to the complex requirements of economic and social policy. On the one hand, the burdens that government imposes on citizens are very demanding and, on the other hand, the reasons for these impositions are often highly complex and technical. To win both the mind and the heart of the citizen to an acceptance of these coercions is a major necessity, but a severe problem. And if, as Congressman Brademas shows, this problem is substantial in our own country, it is far more acute in Britain where welfarism and economic management have become more comprehensive and elaborate.

The democratic process, focused by the legislature upon periodic elections, can do a great deal to meet this problem. Yet much more is required—a more continuous, intimate interchange between authority and those subject to authority. The process of policy-making itself, insofar as it is carried out in public, can be shaped as a means of winning consent to the very coercions then being explained, defended, and attacked. If I may again quote Professor Crick: "The truth is that if anything useful and significant is to be done in a free society, it must be done publicly and in such a way as to consult, involve and carry with it those affected." [16] *Consent in this instance does not spring from some previous interaction of government and voter at a general election, but is the*

[15] "The Emerging Role of the American Congress," a paper presented at the Conference on the Future of the Legislative Power, Princeton University, April 14-17, 1966, pp. 11 and 12. My emphasis in the quotation.

[16] *Op. cit.*, p. 177.

constantly renewed product of a continual exchange of communications.

In performing the function of winning consent in either of these modes, Parliament displays glaring inadequacies and as one goes through the current literature advocating reform of Parliament, one can catch many glimpses of how these inadequacies might be remedied. I refer those interested in the detail of these proposals to Professor Crick's excellent little book, *The Reform of Parliament.* Here I shall simply bring out a few main points.

In the first place, the level of secrecy should be reduced. It is not plausible to expect people to identify with the output of the governmental process when only the product and not the process itself is revealed to the public gaze. Defense matters no doubt require much secrecy. So also in Britain does the system of party government and cabinet responsibility by which sharp conflicts within a party, a Cabinet, or the civil service are removed from public knowledge and scrutiny. Too much public scrutiny could—as the example of Washington, D.C., warns us—exacerbate personal relations and abrade the channels of communication and decision within the Whitehall machine.

Yet it is nevertheless clear to the growing body of British critics that the level of secrecy in British government is excessively high. The reporting of parliamentary news is faulty. Party leaders in office and in opposition hold too few press conferences. The restraints on reporters at Westminster are too strict. Another area in which the veil of secrecy could be lifted is the parliamentary party. Already the debates in meetings of the parliamentary parties seep out, often in distorted form. It would add greatly to the vitality of British government if the press were admitted on a regular basis to these debates.

If the public is to be given a greater sense of participation, not only must secrecy be reduced, but MPs must be given better instruments for understanding, explaining, and—inevitably—criticizing what the government is doing. A major reform toward this end would be to substitute for the present non-specialized committees of the House, a system of committees, each with a sphere of competence parallel to one or more ministries. Such committees would take the committee stage of bills, but more important they would have some of the functions of reviewing administration—"legislative oversight"—that the specialized committees of Congress perform. The essential point is that such a committee system would not only enable MPs themselves to gain some competence in a substantive field of government, but would also provide a focus for public attention upon government action in these fields. For the same general purpose, MPs need much more expert staff assistance. The specialist committees should have such staff and the House Library should be expanded.

A government today is strong for any purpose—economic, social, or military—only so far as it can mobilize consent among its citizens. As events of recent decades have shown, democratic governments are more likely to have this power than non-democratic governments. A leading instance is the comparative war effort of democratic Britain and Nazi Germany. Although it started far behind Germany in mobilizing its resources for war, Britain was much more successful in total mobilization. After the war, the German Minister for War Economy, Albert Speer, said: "You won because you made total war and we did not."

Today Britain confronts the political problem of breaking through the politics of stalemate and at once releasing and concerting untapped energies among her people. There is no simple solution to this problem and no single agency of government or politics can be expected to cope with it. It is, however, essentially a task of mobilizing consent in which the legislature could be given a much more important role.

Suggestions for Further Reading

Beer, Samuel H., *British Politics in the Collectivist Age* (New York: Alfred A. Knopf, Inc., 1965).

Birch, A. H., *Representative and Responsible Government: An Essay on the British Constitution* (London: George Allen and Unwin, Ltd., 1964).

Butler, D. E., and Anthony King, *The British General Election of 1964* (London: Macmillan & Co., Ltd., 1965).

Crick, Bernard, *The Reform of Parliament* (London: Weidenfeld & Nicolson, 1964).

Eckstein, Harry, "The British Political System," in Beer and Ulam (eds.) *Patterns of Government: The Major Political Systems of Europe* (New York: Random House, 2nd edn., 1962).

Finer, Samuel E., *Anonymous Empire: A Study of the Lobby in Great Britain* (London: Pall Mall Press, Ltd., 1966, 2nd edn.).

McKenzie, R. T., *British Political Parties* (2nd edn. London: William Heinemann, Ltd., 1963).

Rose, Richard, *Politics in England* (Boston: Little, Brown and Co., 1965).

Self, Peter, *Bureaucracy or Management?* (London: London School of Economics, 1965).

THE FRENCH PARLIAMENT
From Last Word to Afterthought

Nicholas Wahl

I

Traditionally, policy-making in French parliamentary government was practically synonymous with the legislative process. The long struggle for political democracy in France had sought to enshrine the governance of laws, not men, and especially laws that were legitimized by popular consent. Since the Revolution popular consent has usually been interpreted as the consent of parliament, hence the governance of parliament. Under the Third and Fourth Republics, parliament fulfilled its dominant role in policy-making by performing two functions: first, it served as the principal agency of mediation between French society and the state, integrating rival interests and producing ultimate compromises over public policy; second, it cast these compromises into the form of laws or grants of legislative power to the executive. In the process of debate and voting on the laws, parliament bestowed upon them legitimacy.[1]

[1] This interpretation of the functions of parliament is adapted from the discussion of parliaments in Carl J. Friedrich, *Constitutional Government and Democracy* (Boston, 1950). The analysis and argument of the present article constituted one section of a paper entitled "The Fifth Republic: 1965," presented to the meeting of the American Political Science Association, Washington, D.C., September 8-11, 1965.

NICHOLAS WAHL *is Associate Professor of Politics and Chairman of the Program in Modern European Studies at Princeton University. He is the author of* The Fifth Republic: France's New Political System *and co-author of* Patterns of Government: The Major Political Systems of Europe.

Today these two functions are essentially carried out by the executive branch of the French Government, beginning with the Prefect in the departments and ending with the President of the Republic in the Elysée Palace. And although the French parliament continues to exercise the formal constitutional power to legislate, policy-making—and, therefore, the norms that are cast into law—is primarily the work of the executive. This was, of course, the intention of the new constitutional order created in 1958. At that time, General de Gaulle and his Minister of Justice, Michel Debré, the constitution's main drafters, were both convinced that the existing multiparty system was immutable and that stable governing majorities were unlikely under any conditions. Therefore, to give governmental policy the coherence and continuity they felt was vital to their policy goals, they sought by constitutional means to protect the policy-making process from the unsettling effects of shifting majorities in the lower house, the National Assembly. The "rationalized" legislative process provided by Title V of the 1958 constitution reflects this desire to limit the impact of a permanently divided parliament upon policy-making.

To begin with, Article 34 substantively names, and therefore limits, the subjects upon which parliament can legislate. Article 42 requires that parliamentary debate on Government bills must start with the official Government text. Article 43 limits parliamentary committees to six for each house, thus reducing the "exposure" of a bill to detailed parliamentary criticism. Article 44 allows the Government to limit amendments from the floor and enables it to protect its original version of a bill by calling for a "single vote" on all or part of the bill being debated. Article 47 empowers the government to enact the budget by decree if parliament has not approved it within seventy days of tabling. Article 48 gives priority on the parliamentary docket to Government bills. Finally, Article 49 provides that a bill on which the Government has called for a confidence vote automatically becomes law, no matter what the vote in its favor, unless a motion of censure is carried by an absolute majority of the deputies. These constitutional provisions, as well as those providing for a strengthened upper house, the President's discretionary right of dissolution, and the Constitutional Council, were all meant to arm the executive against the legislature. In this way the drafters hoped to escape the kind of deadlock over policy that had been the prime target of Gaullist criticism under the Fourth Republic.[2]

[2] For the rationale of the drafters and the expected working of the 1958 constitution, see the present author's *The Fifth Republic: France's New Political System* (New York, 1959), Chaps. I and II. The intellectual origins and the drafting process of the

But while all of these new powers have been used by the Government to dominate the legislative process, the main source of executive power over policy-making has really been the plebiscitary authority of the chief of state, Charles de Gaulle. Until the presidential elections of December 1965 this authority came from a combination of de Gaulle's historical relationship with French opinion and his repeated direct appeals to the voters for support of his policies. Throughout the first four crisis years of the Fifth Republic de Gaulle settled most of the difficult policy problems by direct negotiation with the leaders of the outstanding interests—the French army in Algeria, the Moslem Algerian nationalists, and the civilian opposition to both his overseas and domestic programs. To strengthen his hand in these negotiations and to finally legitimize the decisions he made, de Gaulle regularly took to the air waves. In January and July there were usually televised speeches to the people, in April and October there were similarly broadcast press conferences, and in between, when crisis or the preparation of future decisions required it, there were special appeals. By 1963 the Algerian war, the most important policy problem facing de Gaulle when he assumed the presidency, had been settled by a direct confrontation between the state, in the person of de Gaulle, and the organized and, indeed, armed interests involved.[3]

It was natural, therefore, that all matters of public policy should gradually become subject to a similar decision-making process. De Gaulle and his ministers, moreover, discovered that Government policy was indivisible and that the methods used to effectively resolve one range of problems quickly became the methods used for solving all important problems. The Algerian model of direct confrontation became the pattern for policy-making in the domain of domestic economic and social problems, and the legitimization of the Algerian settlement by the President's direct, plebiscitary appeal to opinion became the norm for legitimizing most governmental decisions.[4]

Thus in recent years one can say that the policy-making process in France has resolved itself into a direct confrontation between the state and organized interests in society. It has become a series of direct nego-

---

constitution are described in the author's "The French Constitution of 1958: The Initial Draft and its Origins," *The American Political Science Review,* LIII: 2 (June 1959).

[3] The negotiations between de Gaulle and the "interests" involved in the Algerian war are most dramatically described, at least in part, by one of the ministers in the Debré government: Robert Buron, *Carnets Politiques de la Guerre d'Algérie* (Paris, 1965).

[4] Cf. Georges Lavau, "Forces politiques, forces nouvelles et institutions," *Revue Française de Science Politique,* XIII: 3 (September 1963), 689ff.

tiations that lead to a settlement which is mainly legitimized by the President's authority. Parliament's traditional functions of mediating between state and society and then legitimizing the norms by sovereign lawmaking have both been largely absorbed, in fact if not fully in theory, by this process of direct confrontation. To be sure, parliament must still pass the laws, but its contribution to the actual settlement on which these laws repose is in effect simply a *post facto* critique followed by a ratification of decisions that have been made outside its sphere. Both the integration of interests and the legitimization of policy decisions now take place outside parliament.

Ironically—in view of the expectations of the constitution's drafters—this reduced role for parliament is not primarily the result of such constitutional innovation as the "rationalized" legislative process. Neither the alarms of the Algerian war, nor the President's natural drift toward plebiscitary rule, nor the near-majority strength of the Gaullist party in the lower house, nor, of course, the turning of organized interests to the executive was produced by constitutional engineering. The fact is that under the Fourth Republic and, indeed, under the prewar Third Republic, French parliaments had frequently delegated legislative authority to the executive and French Governments had directly engaged organized interests in policy-making dialogues outside of parliament.[5] But while neither of these phenomena has been considered extraordinary in other Western democracies, in France until 1958 they were always viewed as temporary expedients, normally to be avoided. Their repeated use was quite rightly felt to undermine the functions of mediation and legitimization by which parliament dominated policy-making.

Like most apparent institutional changes, the rise of a new policy-making process which eliminated parliament's dominance had been underway for many years. General de Gaulle was but one of many observers of French politics who were unaware of this development—hence his obsession with the need for binding parliament into a web of constitutional limitations. Once he returned to power under the Fifth Republic, de Gaulle quickly discovered that both opinion and organized interests already had withdrawn their confidence in the mediating and legitimizing functions of parliament. As someone who has long prided himself in

[5] This view has best been argued by François Goguel, Secretary General of the Senate, especially in his "L'Avenir des Institutions Politiques Françaises" (unpublished paper for the FUTURIBLES conference, Paris, April 5-7, 1965) and in his "The Evolution of the Legislative Power in France" (unpublished paper for the conference on the Future of the Legislative Power, Woodrow Wilson School of Public and International Affairs, Princeton University, April 14-17, 1966).

adapting to the "nature of things," de Gaulle was not one to resist carrying this trend to its logical conclusion.

II

It is true, of course, that policy has long been initiated in France by a direct confrontation of the state and organized interests—in city streets, on rural highways, or in private and public offices. Today, laws, ordinances, decrees, and regulations originate, as always, primarily in the ministries. But the initiative for the process comes more than ever before from a continuing range of direct contacts: from quiet talks between a minister and the head of a professional association or between a Prefect and a local notable, in a hostile exchange between the Prime Minister and a national leader of opinion, by "events" such as strikes, peasant road blocks, or milk poured into a country ditch. Even prior to the present regime much important domestic legislation rarely began in a plenary debate of parliament, in a committee report, or by a private member's bill.[6]

At present most Government legislative proposals are extensions of traditional forms of delegated legislation. "Program laws," including the Plan, and "laws of orientation" are the vehicles of major legislation. They are vast norm-setting *ensembles,* prepared over months if not years, and they are meant to commit the state to action over a long time span. Ministerial stability has allowed the Government to undertake protracted and fastidious soundings and negotiations before submitting a proposal of this sort to parliament. This process naturally involves direct dealings between the state and the interests concerned and, obviously, these dealings are meant to gradually eliminate the conflicts that in the past nourished parliamentary debate and offered material for the lengthy process of parliamentary amendment of Government bills. Furthermore, once these highly general laws have been passed, the process of direct negotiation continues over the administrative and executory contents of the skeletal law, again outside and beyond the view of parliament. As French observers have pointed out, the time factor in the form of ministerial longevity, long commitment of state action, and the related long-range planning and expectations of the "consumers" of this kind of legislation,

[6] An "insider's" view of the initiation of policy under the Fifth Republic can be gained from another book by the former minister Robert Buron: *Le Plus Beau des Métiers* (Paris, 1963), Part III. The best analysis of the legislative process under the Fourth Republic is, of course, in Philip Williams' *Crisis and Compromise: Politics in the Fouth Republic* (London, 1964).

has become an important element in reinforcing the trend toward policy-making by direct confrontation.[7]

Similiarly, with the weight of pressure group activity shifting from parliament and the parties, these traditional mediating agencies have declined in direct relevance to policy-making; they have lost authority as a consequence, and thus, in circular fashion, their decline has also reinforced the process of direct confrontation. Just as the decay of the French party system, the absence of a true governing party, and—even more vital—the lack of a credible and stable opposition have all encouraged the new policy process, so the growing habit of organized interests to seek redress directly from the executive has made it well nigh impossible for the traditional party system to restore itself. The effects of this situation, as well as one of its contributing causes, are reflected in such parliamentary customs as the rebirth of absenteeism among the deputies, the rarity of roll call votes requiring presence, the still-birth of the new provision for question day, and the headlong and feverish participation of the more ambitious young deputies in communal and regional affairs.[8]

To illustrate the changing nature of policy-making in the new French political system, brief analysis of a legislative case study might be useful.[9] In the early spring of 1960 agricultiural organizations, spearheaded by new interest groups such as the CNJA (*Centre National des Jeunes Agriculteurs*), staged widespread demonstrations in favor of governmental action to alleviate their grievances.[10] The more traditional farmers' organizations, such as the FNSEA (*Fédération Nationale des Exploitants Agricoles*), turned by ancient habit to parliament and activated their deputies on all benches to sign a petition requesting the President to call parliament into special session. Considering this request to have been made under a

[7] Two excellent retrospective assessments of the new institutions' impact on policy-making are: Georges Lavau, "Réflexions sur la régime politique de la France," *Revue Française de Science Politique,* XII: 4 (December 1962) and Georges Vedel, et al., "Les Institutions Politiques de la France," *Entretiens du Samedi, Association Française de Science Politique* (Paris, February 1964).

[8] The habits and mores of parliament, as well as the analysis of the substance and methods of the legislative process are regularly chronicled in the bimonthly *Revue du Droit Public et de la Science Politique* (Paris) and occasionally in the *Revue Française de Science Politique* (Paris).

[9] The case summarized here is one of the few subjected to detailed study: cf. Gaston Rimareix and Yves Tavernier, "L'Elaboration et le vote de la loi complémentaire à la loi d'orientation agricole," *Revue Française de Science Politique,* XIII: 2 (June 1963). The author has supplemented this analysis by reference to newspaper accounts and interviews with deputies, officials, and French specialists in the legislative process.

[10] Cf. Yves Tavernier, "Le syndicalisme paysan et la politique agricole du gouvernement," *Revue Française de Science Politique,* XII: 3 (September 1962).

"binding instruction" from the agricultural organizations, de Gaulle rejected the petition as contrary to Article 27 of the constitution, thereby checking parliamentary initiative on the matter. The farmers' groups then shifted their fire to the cabinet. Prime Minister Debré consulted with the various organizations and decided to propose a long term structural reform of French agriculture in the form of a law of orientation, largely inspired by the proposals of the young leaders of the new and progressive farmers' unions. The law passed in 1961 provided for basic though necessarily slow reforms such as the gradual regrouping of the family-sized farms into economically more viable units, the development of agricultural training, and the reorganization of distribution circuits.

Frustrated in their appeals for the usual state subsidies, the older organizations continued to pressure parliament and to incite their members to direct action. The Minister of Agriculture, Edgard Pisani, then began an effort to resolve the crisis, scrupulously avoiding parliament where the traditional subsidy-minded interests held sway. He tabled a supplementary legislative proposal in the fall of 1961 but held it back from parliamentary consideration. Early in 1962 he opened an informal dialogue with the leaders of all agricultural organizations over the proposed legislation, regularly seeing them in his office or having his staff consult with them on their suggestions for changes. In May Pisani held a formal negotiating session with all the leaders and in June, prior to the announced meeting of the Council of Ministers at which the Government bill was to be given final approval, he "leaked" the terms of his revised bill to the press. Soon thereafter, now well educated by public reaction to his text, Pisani initiated another round of negotiations with the agricultural groups, but this time in small working parties at which only civil servants and technical advisers were present. Finally, armed with what he considered a document that embodied both the consensus of agricultural opinion as well as the objectively required solution suggested by his experts, he brought his bill to the Council of Ministers.

At this stage parliament made the penultimate effort at asserting its right to modify the bill. The "political" ministers—that is, former deputies, including the Gaullists—urged crippling modifications as suggested by their party organizations on the prompting of the traditional agricultural interests. Joining the old parties in this effort was the Gaullist UNR, for the Government party no less than the opposition was sensitive to the threats of electoral retaliation by the powerful old-line farmers' unions. But de Gaulle, impressed by both the support Pisani had generated among the younger progressive farmers, as well as by the effectiveness with which he had used the process of direct confrontation, arbitrated against the crippling amendments in the Council of Ministers. The bill was then submitted to parliamentary debate, where it easily withstood further change from the committees and the floor, and was enacted within three weeks—an unusually short period for this kind of legislation.

The significant points of this case study are worth explaining in greater detail. First, it should be remarked that initiative for agricultural reform came from direct action by organized interests and a direct response from the administration. Parliament, whether on opposition or Government benches, was excluded from negotiations over the text of the bill. The Government's proposals were drafted in meetings between the staff of the Minister of Agriculture and the leaders of progressive French agriculture, weak in numbers but willing to break with traditional palliatives and older methods of promoting their cause. Successive drafts of the proposals were submitted directly to all agricultural organizations for further negotiation, although Pisani made it clear that the principle of structural reform rather than subsidy would be retained. At the same time that part of his large personal staff was negotiating with and gathering intelligence from the farmers' groups, Pisani passed over the cabinet level and the Prime Minister in order to win personally de Gaulle's approval for the reforms. Parallel to the Minister's direct discussions with the farmers, however, de Gaulle's staff organized a similar if abbreviated dialogue with the same organizations in order to offer the President an independent basis for judgment. Then, just before final Government action on the proposal, Pisani revealed the essentials of the reform to public opinion and to interested pressure groups such as labor. To general surprise, many trade union leaders warmly approved the agricultural reform bill—a position rare for working-class organizations in the past.

When the bill came before the Assembly, therefore, an impressive array of group support had already been marshaled behind the Pisani reforms. Employing its full armory of tools for expediting the legislative process, the Government quickly passed the bill into law. The only concession to parliament was the usual short dialogue between the Government and the members of its majority, in particular the agriculture "study group" of the Gaullist UNR. There, and later in committee and on the floor, UNR deputies not only gave voice to many opposition objections, but they also echoed opposition critiques of the manner in which Pisani had drafted the bill and delayed parliamentary consideration until there remained little for the deputies to add to the policy. They were especially bitter about what they called Pisani's "personal" technique of direct negotiations with agriculture, his refusal to consult even Gaullist deputies. For, notwithstanding their formal pledge of loyalty to the Government, the UNR deputies realized how grave was the threat to their dwindling authority with such a legislative process becoming the rule.

The Pisani reforms did indeed become law for all intents and purposes the day de Gaulle had arbitrated in their favor in the Council of Ministers. In the fall of 1962, the legislative elections returned a larger and more homogenous group of Gaullist deputies than those of 1958. Constituting almost a majority and no longer threatened by internal schisms over Algeria, the new group had few illusions as to the reasons for their success. Their size and automatic loyalty guaranteed an untroubled future for the new policy process of direct confrontation. Today, in return for keeping parliament within its new role as a relatively docile critical forum operating after policy has been set, the various study groups of the UNR have been allowed to comment on policy negotiations at an early stage through regular meetings with ministers. More important, they have been allowed a modest and prearranged amending power in the hope of winning some electoral favor from the interests which they occasionally serve as defenders.[11] But this crumb from the table of direct confrontation does not really represent much of a concession to a French parliament that has finally produced a workable governing majority. If anything, the appearance of a stable and disciplined parliamentary majority since 1962 has further established the process of direct confrontation by finally eliminating any last slim hopes on the part of recalcitrant interests for avoiding direct negotiations with the Gaullist state. Given the disunity of the opposition, there would be small point to the alternative were it to exist.

III

It is worth recalling briefly, at this point, how different the expectations of 1958 were concerning the legislative process. The "rationalized" procedure prescribed by Title V of the constitution was vital for both de Gaulle and Debré because they firmly expected only a modest Gaullist victory at the polls. To them this meant a continuing series of inherently shaky coalition Governments and the traditional risk of concomitant ministerial instability. Domestic policy-making, of which parliament had always been especially jealous, was to remain, in the Gaullist view, a process of bargaining between a vulnerable Government and an Assembly forever subject to the shifting majorities that could offer power to a new set of leaders through ministerial crisis. So convinced were the new

[11] Cf. Claude Emeri, "Les forces politiques au parlement," *Revue Française de Science Politique,* XIII: 3 (September 1963).

regime's founders of parliament's indestructible reserve power that for the first two years they barred even the most petty accretions to parliamentary prestige. Debré, for example, rejected out of hand the long standing proposal to improve the Assembly's ridiculously inadequate research and office facilities, while de Gaulle regularly refused to allow the appointment of a junior minister to the job of parliamentary liaison and often vetoed the appearance of a senior minister before parliamentary committees. Debré was proud of his personal creation of a question day and he expected that it would become a much valued escape valve for the Assembly's frustrated though ever vigorous hunger for interpellation of the Government. Similarly, the principal architect of the new constitution foresaw, erroneously of course, that debate in plenary session would still be a vital stage of policy-making—the scene for the forming and reforming of concurrent majorities in accordance with the subjects discussed.

Not content with the buttressed confidence vote procedure and the then strangely underestimated procedure for a "single vote" (*vote bloqué*) under Article 44, Debré tried hard to make of the new Senate an effective check upon the potentially unruly lower house by increasing its legislative role. He finally settled for a constitutional text which he thought would make the Senate an occasional alternate recourse for the Government, especially on the budget. Debré also supported the introduction of a novel joint conference committee stage in the legislative process (*commission mixte paritaire*) because it seemed to offer the executive still another chance to undo what he expected to be regular damage at the hands of the deputies. But these forecasts were no more accurate than was de Gaulle's expectation to maintain presidential power within a "reserved sector" (*domaine réservé*) in which his personal prestige could be invested only in decisions concerning foreign, defense, and colonial policies.[12]

As time passed the President discovered that conflict over agricultural and social policies could become just as difficult to resolve as conflict over his "favorite" issues. Indeed, he was obliged to intervene on the domestic front because he came to realize that ineffective decision-making in economic and social affairs might easily lead to a reduction of his freedom to act on foreign and defense problems. Other discoveries of this kind were soon to follow. The unexpectedly large Gaullist group

[12] De Gaulle's views on the subject are more fully explained in the author's "The French Political System," in Samuel H. Beer and Adam B. Ulam, eds., *Patterns of Government: The Major Political Systems of Europe*, 2nd ed., (New York, 1962), Chap. 13.

in the Assembly made dependence on Title V of the constitution less vital for both the Government program and ministerial stability. The emergence of an opposition majority in the upper house made the expected employ of the Senate as an ally of the Government impossible. And while Debré continued to pursue his dream of true cabinet Government by urging a greater effort at "implanting" the UNR in the provinces and giving its parliamentary group added luster by regular consultation with ministers, de Gaulle discouraged these efforts. Once again the fear of losing his freedom to act on international matters was the motive: a Gaullist party that was strong in the country in the years after 1958 could be prey to the French Algeria lobby. Were it to be fully involved in policy-making, the option of a negotiated peace in Algeria might well be foreclosed.

The *coup de grâce* to the 1958 system was delivered by the appointment of Georges Pompidou as Prime Minister, by the constitutional revision, and by the near majority victory of the UNR—all in 1962. The new Prime Minister had never held elective office and had no interest in changing an established policy process that both met the approval of his chief and accorded with personal habits gained in an administrative career. The size, docility, and homogenous nature of the 1962 UNR group—purged of its French Algeria wing—had made Debré's dream of cabinet Government for France now almost realizable, but it was too late.[13] The habits of the new policy process were now set and they included little real power for either a Government party or the parliament as a whole. Even more important, the elections had completed the decimation of the opposition that had begun in 1958. Now divided into four roughly equal and thoroughly incompatible groups, their total number came only within eighty or so votes of the Gaullist majority. Rather than the problem of managing concurrent majorities that Debré had foreseen as dominating the Assembly, the problem that emerged was a problem strictly for the opposition leaders: how could they fashion concurrent opposition minorities into an over-all posture of constructive opposition that might maintain, if not nurture, their slight authority in the eyes of opinion?

The deputies elected for the first time in 1962, having no veteran parliamentary status to preserve, adapted quickly to the diminished prestige of parliament. Whether opposition members or Gaullists, they abandoned the Assembly at every opportunity and flung themselves into

[13] The Gaullist UNR won 234 seats in November 1962, just eight short of an absolute majority. For the party's behavior in parliament see Georges Lavau, "L'UNR-UDT au lendemain de sa victoire," *Revue Française de Science Politique,* XIII: 2 (June 1963).

a fury of local activity. These mainly youngish men, often from business or the civil service, were quick to grasp the essential "truth" about the regime that was emerging from the Algerian war. In the policy process of direct confrontation the place of parliament as an intermediary was untenable. For the deputy once again to reenter the decision-making circuit he would have to become individually a negotiator in the process, either as a minister or, more easily, as the representative of an organized interest—not in parliament, but rather in the process of direct confrontation. However, since economic and social groups now delegated their own men to deal directly with the Government, many of the new deputies sought personal power as the negotiators for local collectivities, often as mayors but increasingly in more novel ways. Recent reforms in French provincial administration—such as the committees for regional economic development and the appointment of regional prefects—when added to existing regional planning groups founded by private initiative, have encouraged the growth of a series of subnational arenas in which the state and organized interests can negotiate.

Locally minded deputies have found that expending their efforts in these committees rather than in parliament has proven more profitable. Where formerly it was in Assembly debate and legislative maneuvering that future ministers were trained and tested, it is now increasingly in these many intermediary bodies that young leaders can deploy the prowess that is often rewarded by ministerial office. An ambitious young opposition deputy in these regional committees may well become the negotiator for local interests fearful of proposed Government policy, ultimately threatening the state with the direct action of his troops. An ambitious young majority deputy may attract attention by taking the lead in mobilizing local support for a Government proposal or serving as spokesman for central policy-making. In both cases the new French deputy has reintroduced himself into the circuit of policy-making by becoming the agent of one of the parties to the direct confrontation of state and interests that has been taking place independently of parliament and the party system. Naturally, however active and popular many of these new deputies may be, the very nature of their activity is not likely to help their political party, much less reconstruct the party system.

IV

In the last analysis, the decline of parliament's role in policy-making must be attributed to the failure of the French party system. After all, the rise of a modern party system had been essential to the development of democratic parliamentary Government. It was universal suffrage, the subsequent creation of mass parties, and the principle of ministerial responsibility that led to the growth of party Government—whether singly or in coalition, but in any case the only means for parliament to become effectively involved in the policy-making process.[14] The necessary condition of democratic parliamentarism was the existence of a governing majority in parliament, produced by the party system. In the historic circumstances of the Third and Fourth Republics, the French party system produced governing majorities by various types of a party coalition technique known as the "concentration of centers" or "republican concentration." With the exception of the Popular Front and the immediately post-liberation majorities, all governing majorities since 1919 have been coalitions of this sort. But during the last years of the Fourth Republic the Algerian war accelerated trends in French politics that made coalition building by "concentration" increasingly difficult. Because the war was being defined as an "ultimate" issue, the Algerian problem split every party. Only the most thorough party realignment could have allowed "concentration" to produce once again stable governing majorities.[15]

In retrospect the referendum and elections of 1962 probably offered the party system its last chance to effect the kind of reform that could restore to parliament its role in policy-making.[16] Had the long awaited party realignment taken place before the referendum, conditions for limiting the plebiscitary nature of the Fifth Republic would have emerged, for a credible party system would have attracted organized interests and thus reestablished the mediating role of parliament. Instead, the opposition chose what hindsight now suggests was the worst possible strategy. They vigorously opposed the popular change to direct election of the President and they formed a totally non-credible electoral coalition of incompatible and purely negative resistance to the regime. This *Cartel des Nons* was inspired by simple error, rather than by a doctrinaire blindness. The old parties continued to believe that de Gaulle would shortly leave power, his Algerian task now completed and a relative decline of Gaullist strength at the polls virtually certain.

[14] This interpretation is developed by Otto Kirchheimer in his "European Parliaments" (An address to the Ninth National Conference of the United States National Commission for UNESCO, Chicago, October 23-26, 1963).

[15] The importance of center "concentrations" for the working of French parliamentary government is stressed by Maurice Duverger, "L'Eternel Marais: Essai sur le Centrisme Français," *Revue Française de Science Politique,* XIV, 1 (February 1964).

[16] Party strategies as well as detailed analyses of the campaign and the results of the 1962 legislative elections and referendum are best found in François Goguel, ed., *Le Référendum d'Octobre et les Elections de Novembre 1962* (Paris, 1965).

The result of the referendum of 1962 approving de Gaulle's constitutional revision prepared the final blow to the party system. It was this that neither opposition nor, indeed, Gaullists had fully understood—hence their error. Conservative voters who had overwhelmingly supported the constitutional change decided to confirm this support by deserting the traditional conservative parties. At the subsequent legislative elections they thereby transformed the Gaullist party into what is, for practical purposes, the first majority party France has ever known. Whether fully conscious of the trap he was setting or not, de Gaulle had maneuvered the old parties into a position where available alternatives were limited to the unknown and threatening adventure of thorough party realignment, or the easy and familiar course of an incompatible electoral coalition—that is, defeat and discredit.

A result of this discredit in the years since that election has been the assumption by other organs of the body politic of some of the more important functions of political parties. It is now a commonplace in France that pressure groups are turning from parties and parliament in order to concentrate on direct dealings with the administration. But it is less often remarked that in these continuing negotiations professional organizations such as those of agriculture and business are becoming *pari passu* the spokesmen for a broad range of their members' concerns, including some that are purely political. Thus business associations have protested directly to the Government over its foreign policy in the Atlantic area while agricultural unions have both supported and attacked the Government's regional administrative reforms. Even more striking is the evidence that in the absence of effective party mediation, groups with special grievances such as the marginal farmers of Brittany have actually set about creating *ad hoc* protest organizations in order to equip themselves to initiate a direct confrontation with the executive.[17]

Moreover, as noted previously, the Fifth Republic's passion for planning and regional development has produced another range of Government-inspired organs that are also serving as surrogates for party mediation between the Government and the governed. As one observer has put it:

Little by little an imposing array of intermediaries is being constituted by committees of regional and departmental economic development, regional planning commissions, commissions of the National Planning Commissariat, mixed corporations for communal economic development

[17] This phenomenon is noted by Georges Lavau, "Forces politiques, forces nouvelles, et institutions," *op. cit.*, p. 697 n.9.

and re-equipment, specialized organizations of varied scope and power, and inter-communal districts and associations. Henceforth it will be at least as necessary to influence and pressure this structure as it was useful in the past to control a few deputies in parliament.[18]

Whether or not this development will ultimately bring de Gaulle to transform the Senate into a corporatist upper house with actual legislative power remains to be seen. For the moment, however, one must admit that the job of party rejuvenation is not facilitated by these new institutions and that the party system of the future will somehow have to offer something as good or better if it is to replace or even accommodate this growing system of corporate representation and mediation.

Party activity before, during, and since the presidential elections of December 1965 provides little evidence that a new party system will soon emerge. Yet not only the return of parliament to policy-making, but also the future of the Fifth Republic, depend on party realignment. A discredited party system and the absence of party government are but one element in a circular relationship of factors that have given the Gaullist regime its present character. Because the parties had failed to produce governing majorities and coherent solutions to policy problems, the legislative process and parliament declined as the centers of policy-making. The executive, which for years had been increasing its independent role in the actual determination of policy, naturally filled the vacuum thus created. In the crisis circumstances of the Algerian war de Gaulle was obliged to assert and then to intensify his personal plebiscitary authority in order both to resolve policy problems and to legitimize the solutions to which parliament was able to contribute so little.

The circular process continued, for with the growing dominance of de Gaulle's presidency over all aspects of Government policy, the irrelevance of the traditional legislative process became ever more clear. This in turn further discouraged the new political class from considering parliament or the parties as the principal vehicles for their ambitions. Simultaneously, other groups in society replaced the parties in the mediating process, just as the executive had replaced the legislative branch as the integrating and legitimizing institution of politics. As for the future, it might well be that this circular process has altered the behavior and expectations of French political leaders and interest groups to the point where there is no possible return to a more traditional form of

[18] Pierre Viansson-Ponté, "Vacances et Veillée d'Armes: Les Nouvelles Habitudes," *Le Monde* (Paris, July 3, 1965). The government's program for regional development is described by Olivier Guichard, *Aménager la France* (Paris, 1965).

parliamentary Government. And with respect to popular habits and expectations, it is well to remember that over a third of the electorate of the 1970s will be comprised of those who will have known no other regime than the Fifth Republic.

What seems evident, at any rate, is that if the legislature has ceased to have an important role in French policy-making, the reasons for its decline are not primarily constitutional. It was party Government that gave parliaments their role in policy-making and it was the decline of the French party system *as a system* that promoted the executive to its present eminence. In politics, as in life, responsibility for losing something of value lies more often than not with the one who had it last.

Suggestions for Further Reading

Other than the books and articles mentioned in the footnotes, the following works may be found useful:

Avril, Pierre, "Un Président Pour Quoi Faire?" (Paris, 1965).
__________, "Le Régime Politique de la Ve République" (Paris, 1964).
Christoph, James B., ed., "Cases in Comparative Politics" (Boston, 1965).
Defferre, Gaston, "Un Nouvel Horizon" (Paris, 1965).
Delvolvé, Pierre, and Henry Lesguillons, "Le Contrôle Parlementaire sur la Politique Economique et Budgetaire" (Paris, 1964).
Duverger, Maurice, "Institutions Politiques et Droit Constitutionnel," 8th ed. (Paris, 1965).
Goguel, François, and Alfred Grosser, "La Politique en France," 2nd ed. (Paris, 1964).
Mendès-France, Pierre, "A Modern French Republic" (New York, 1963).
Pickles, Dorothy, "The Fifth French Republic," (London, 1962).
Priouret, Roger, "La République des Députés" (Paris, 1959).

PARTY GOVERNMENT IN THE BONN REPUBLIC

Peter H. Merkl

A comparison of parliamentary government in Great Britain and France directs attention to the pivotal role of political parties and of the party system in the various types of executive-legislative relations. German parliamentary government is no exception to this rule. No other verbal formula, perhaps, can express the different attitudes toward the penetration of representative institutions by political parties as succinctly as the contrast between the English term "party government" and the German "party state" (*Parteienstaat*). Both concepts denote a modern democratic state with political parties in the Government and the Opposition. To English and American ears, "party government" is an ideal political system in which parliamentary government merges with a system of stable, moderate parties which take turns at governing and criticizing governmental policies so that the voter can make an effective choice between alternative sets of leaders and policies. Responsible party government has been the model for most of the older nations of the British Commonwealth and has preoccupied American political scientists since the days of Woodrow Wilson.[1]

[1] For a survey of the earlier theories of responsible party government, see Austin Ranney, *The Doctrine of Responsible Party Government* (Urbana: University of

PETER H. MERKL *is Associate Professor of Political Science at the University of California in Santa Barbara. He has contributed articles to various political science journals and is the author of* The Origin of the West German Republic, Germany: Yesterday and Tomorrow, *and* Rassenfrage und Rechtsradikalismus in den U.S.A.

On the other hand, the term "party state" of German constitutional jurisprudence, from its earliest use in the days of the Weimar Republic, mirrored the misgivings of many Germans about the unfamiliar ways of parliamentary democracy. To begin with, the term lacked the well defined character of the English "party government." It set no limits to the number or character of the parties included. Parties hostile to democracy and to the parliamentary system were just as much considered a part of the "party state" as the parties loyal to the system. Neither did it set forth any rules of the political game or establish such roles as Government and Opposition with any precision. But there was no mistaking the note of suspicion in the term "party state"—the distrust in the parliamentary figures and party politicians who were inheriting power from the *Kaiser*, the aristocrats, and the trusted bureaucracy of the old regime. In the phrase "party state" one can also discern the distaste of many Weimar Germans for the bargaining and what they considered the disorderly haggling among the parties. Even the terms party or partisan interest were contrasted unfavorably with the public interest or the common good by most of the literature of that period. Being partisan meant being selfish, or placing the interest of a partial group above those of the whole community.[2]

The party state of Weimar parliamentary democracy finally succumbed to the impact of the Great Depression and to the rising Hitler movement. Today, more than forty years after the birth of the Weimar Republic, Western Germany in many ways approaches British style "party government." Looking back at the decades of crisis and transition, it may be well to reflect on the difference between executive-legislative relations in the "party state" and in "responsible party government." Why was it so difficult for the Weimar Republic to achieve this latter system? Just what makes the Bonn system a closer approximation of party government than the Weimar Republic could ever have hoped to have been?

I. THE FAILURE OF THE WEIMAR PARTY STATE

Regarding the setting for British-style party government in the Weimar Republic of Germany, there are many unfavorable circumstances to ac-

---

Illinois Press, 1962 [paperback]). Also Elmer Schattschneider, *Party Government* (New York: Holt, Rinehart and Winston, Inc., 1942).

[2] The literature on the *Parteienstaat* is quite extensive. The following are a representative sample: Otto Koellreutter, *Die politischen Parteien im modernen Staate* (Breslau: Ferdinand Hirt Verlag, 1926); Heinrich Triepel, *Die Staatsverfassung und die politischen Parteien* (Berlin: O. Liebermann Verlag, 1930); and Hansfritz Roeder, *Parteien und Parteienstaat in Deutschland* (Munich: M. Huber Verlag, 1930).

count for. First of all, there had not even been a national German parliament until 1871. By the end of World War I, this Parliament, the *Reichstag*, had as yet acquired very little control of the executive branch. In particular, the *Reich* chancellor and his cabinet were not responsible to the *Reichstag* but only to the monarch until a few weeks before military defeat and the revolution pulled down the whole monarchic edifice of Imperial Germany. The political parties of the Imperial *Reichstag*, consequently, viewed themselves primarily as instruments of the representation of the people against a government they could not control. Each *Reichstag* party and every deputy considered himself the spokesman of a particular electoral district or a clearly defined group of German society. It was his function to stand up for the interests of those he represented: to protest, to oppose, even to propose, but not to govern. This notion was not at variance with nineteenth-century liberal views of representation, or of state and society. Governmental responsibility was thus left to the *Kaiser* and his chancellors and ministers, who were generally men without a parliamentary or partisan profile of their own.[3]

With the downfall of autocracy and the advent of the Weimar Republic, the political leaders were well aware of the fact that under the new parliamentary constitution they were supposed to take on governmental responsibility. Yet old habits die a slow death, and there were many circumstances that conspired to perpetuate the oppositional attitudes of the past.

The framers of the Weimar Constitution were evidently plagued by considerable doubts about the wisdom of turning over a monopoly of decision-making power to the parliamentary executive, chancellor and cabinet, and by implication to the parties supporting them in the *Reichstag*. Instead of centering the chief policy-making power in a British-style cabinet, therefore, they divided it between the parliamentary executive and a strong *Reich* president. Popularly elected to a term of seven years, the *Reich* president represented the new sovereign—the people—as the *Kaiser* had represented the old sovereign—the monarchy. The *Reich* president thus could actually point to a more popular mandate than the *Reich* chancellor and his cabinet. The framers of the Constitution naïvely assumed that the identity of the electorate of both

[3] See also Wilhelm Treue and Wolfgang Treue, *Parlamentarismus in Deutschland* (Bonn: Bundeszentrale für politische Bildung, 1963) and the sources cited there. The March issue, 1964, of the *Politische Vierteljahresschrift* and Ernst Fraenkel, *Deutschland und die westlichen Demokratien* (Stuttgart: Kohlhammer Verlag, 1964) discuss parties and parliamentary government in a broadly comparative framework. See especially the descriptions of the German views of parliamentarianism before and after 1918, in Fraenkel, *op. cit.*, pp. 95ff.

Reichstag and president would make dualism or conflict between the two executives unlikely. They also expected the spheres of executive power to remain separated neatly, since the *Reich* president was to appoint chancellor and cabinet for the making of governmental policy, and then to keep in the background until a state of emergency would require his intervention. Little did the framers of the Constitution expect that the use of the ill-defined presidential emergency powers would be so frequent and indiscriminate as to determine the character and fate of the Republic. What had been designed as an executive "emergency brake" on the wagon of the party state turned out to be more important than the steering wheel.

The lesson of distrust in the ability of the *Reichstag* parties to exercise governmental responsibility was not lost on the party leaders who frequently preferred to remain outside the Government, even though their parties might support it. Their own diffidence often manifested itself also in selecting nonpartisan experts for ministerial posts. The Weimar Constitution showed its suspicion of parties also with its recurring use of the popular referendum and the initiative which enable the voter to take direct action over the heads of their elected *Reichstag* deputies. Thus, the temptation was great for the parties to leave weighty and unpopular decisions to the *Reich* president or to the electorate itself.

A Fragmented Party System

If, on the one hand, the executive-legislative relations evolved by the Weimar Republic discouraged the parties from taking on governmental responsibility, on the other hand, they spared no effort to facilitate the task of opposition and obstruction from many sides. By questions and interpellations which called cabinet ministers on the carpet, and by unprecedented parliamentary investigations of the once sacrosanct executive branch, the *Reichstag* could make the most of its power to harass the Government. Several significant groups in the *Reichstag* used all means to oppose and obstruct not only the Government of the day, but parliamentary democracy itself. The economic and political crises of the Weimar Republic likewise made it far more attractive for a party to remain in opposition, or at least to avoid being blamed for circumstances beyond its political control, by avoiding governmental responsibility.[4]

[4] See especially Friedrich Glum, *Das parlamentarische Regierungssystem in Deutschland, Grossbritannien und Frankreich*, 2nd ed. (Munich, Berlin: Beck Verlag, 1965) and Werner Conze in Erich Matthias and Rudolf Morsey, eds., *Das Ende der Parteien* (Düsseldorf: Droste Verlag, 1960).

The rampant proliferation and particularistic character of German parties comprised another major factor in propagating older attitudes. Right at the end of the war, to be sure, many party leaders thought of merging several smaller parties into one in an effort to build a broader political base. A number of traditional party names were changed so as to end with "people's party" (*Volkspartei*) to denote the quest for a mass following from many layers of society.[5] Throughout the Weimar years, the different parties in the *Reichstag* strove to develop their own trade unions, farm organizations, and veterans' organizations in order to strike broader roots in many parts of German society.

Despite these efforts, the number of parties condemned each one to a permanent minority status. Too many parties were competing with each other, as the following brief glance at the political spectrum will illustrate. Starting from the left wing, there were the Communists (KPD), the Social Democrats (SPD), and, for a while, two further Socialist groups. Next came the Catholic Center Party (Z) whose Bavarian branch (BVP) insisted on maintaining a separate party. The two Liberal parties (DDP and DVP), and at times several smaller middle-class groups, represented a variety of economic interests. Finally, the German Nationalists (DNVP) and smaller conservative groups shared the spotlight on the right with numerous tiny right-wing extremist parties from among whom the National Socialist Movement (NSDAP) of Hitler rose in a great landslide in the last years of the Weimar Republic.

At one time, close to forty distinct parties competed in the national elections. Even the largest of them generally received no more than 15 to 20 per cent of the popular vote, and only on rare occasions as much as 30 per cent. Such a permanent minority status at times of crisis, when successive governing coalitions invariably got blamed for economic breakdowns and political emergencies beyond their control, was very unlikely to encourage the taking on of a stance of governmental responsibility. Only a party with a popular majority or within reach of winning a majority can fully know what governmental responsibility means, through years of crisis or of triumph, for better or for worse. A permanent minority is naturally inclined to regard the larger questions of statesmanship with the myopic eyes of particularistic selfishness. Even for stalwart friends of the embattled Republic it seemed much safer to ride out the

[5] The Catholic Center Party, for example, tried to change its name to Christian People's Party (CVP). The Conservatives (DNVP), National Liberals (DVP), and the Bavarian offshoot of the Center Party (BVP) all insisted on the label of a "people's party" which had earlier been used only by left-wing Liberals, such as the Saxonian People's Party or the more recent Progressive People's Party.

years of crisis in the opposition, or by merely tolerating rather than participating in the Government in office.

The Problem of Missing Consensus

Responsible party government was frustrated also by the obvious lack of consensus on the fundamentals and procedures of government. The Communists on the extreme left and the so-called "folkish" groups on the extreme right were plotting for the violent overthrow of the Republic. At times, the sizable groups of the Independent Socialists on the left and the conservative German Nationalists on the right definitely favored forms of government other than the parliamentary democracy of Weimar. The original three-party coalition of Weimar—the Social Democrats, the Center Party, and the Democrats—which wrote the Weimar Constitution and constituted the first provisional government after the war, lost their popularity in the first *Reichstag* elections, and regained it only sporadically.

In the declining years of Weimar, a new tide of popular disaffection with parliamentary democracy rose at the same time that emergency decrees and cabinets without parliamentary support signified the abandonment of the basic executive-legislative ground rules of the political system. The assertion of presidential emergency powers was taken even by the moderate parties of the Republic as a sign that they did not really have to take on governmental responsibility while the *Reich* president was taking charge. In 1932 a clear majority of German voters actually turned out to vote for the totalitarian parties of Communism and National Socialism in a pointed protest against the failure of the "party state" to steer the country through the mounting economic crisis of the Great Depression.

While the masses thus cried out for an authoritarian replacement of the bankrupt "party state," ironically enough, Weimar constitutional lawyers were still debating whether parties really fitted into a system of true representative government. They seriously discussed the relative merits of such alternatives to party government as corporatism, or the authoritarian, or administrative state. The parliamentary parties indeed had never quite become the depositories of governmental responsibility in the First German Republic. The Constitution attempted to deny them the right to impose party discipline on the individual deputy. The extra-parliamentary parties and even the organized interests constantly interfered with the parties' autonomy. Even in such fields as labor legislation or foreign policy, where notable decisions and legislative enactments were made in the 1920s, it was generally not a particular party or coalition of parties that was responsible for the achievements, but more often *ad hoc* blocs made up of interested segments of several major parties. Considering the fact that well organized interests and lobbies had frequently broken up the existing major parties along functional lines behind the scenes, toying with schemes of corporate representation as an alternative to the party state was not as absurd as it may seem today.

All of these facts and considerations played a significant role in the thinking of party leaders after 1945, and especially in the deliberations of the framers of the Bonn Constitution. There was a widespread conviction that the system of executive-legislative relations under the Weimar Republic had been a failure, although it was not entirely clear what particular aspect of it had been at fault. Of the seventeen coalition governments with legislative majority support or its equivalent in the years from 1919 to 1932, three had fallen on a question of confidence, one upon the dissolution of the *Reichstag,* three after an election, another four because of foreign policy crises or internal revolt, and no less than six cabinets fell because of internal convulsions or instability in one of their coalition parties. Were the parties to blame or was it the institutional design? To supply a background for an understanding of the present development, the dilemmas raised by the crises of the Weimar Republic have to be compared with the details of the design decided upon at Bonn. By the same token, only a thorough analysis of what caused the "party state" of Weimar to fail can open up insights into what is stable and enduring about party government in the Bonn Republic.

II. THE WEST GERMAN PARTY SYSTEM

Following World War II, no other factor was as important to the eventual development in the direction of responsible party government in the Bonn Republic as the actual changes in the party system. The difference is particularly obvious in the number, the size, and the character of the parties represented in the West German *Bundestag,* the Parliament of the Federal Republic of Germany. In fact, the entire system of social, cultural, and economic cleavages that used to supply the particularistic divisions among the Weimar parties has undergone extensive changes.

From Multiparty System to Two-Party Government

The returns of the state and local elections of the early postwar period gave every indication that the Weimar multiparty system would be revived. The first *Bundestag* of 1949-53 still consisted of representatives of nine parties, including the Communists (KPD), the regional Bavaria Party (BP), the conservative German Party (DP), the Economic Reconstruction Party (WAV), the revived Center Party (Z), and refugee representatives who later joined the Refugee Bloc (BHE), as well as the three largest parties, the Christian Democrats (CDU/CSU), the Social Democrats (SPD) and the Free Democrats (FDP). Decimated from election to election by restrictive electoral laws and by the successful drive of Adenauer's Christian Democrats for an electoral majority, the number of parties shrank to the last named three by 1961.

Of these three parties, the Christian Democrats (CDU/CSU), Social Democrats (SPD) and Free Democrats (FDP), the first two have each demonstrated a definite capacity to win a majority of the popular vote. Their combined total of the vote has grown from about 60 per cent to over 90 per cent. It therefore seems appropriate to speak of a two-party system in West Germany at the present time, even though there is still a third party, the FDP. Not unlike the British Liberal Party, which has survived in spite of the two-party system, the German FDP is clearly a minor party with little growth potential. In fact, it may well fall victim someday to the clause in the West German electoral law which denies representation to parties polling less than 5 per cent of the vote. It is also conceivable that the two major parties may change the prevailing electoral law in order to deprive the FDP of what they consider its undeserved key position.

Contemporary Party Orientation

The West German parties of today also differ from their Weimar predecessors in their basic character. The futile attempts of 1919 to transform many of the particularistic, hidebound parties of old into broadly based "people's parties" have wrought fundamental changes in the two major parties after 1945.

The CDU/CSU was built on the basis of the old Weimar and pre-Weimar Center Party which already had succeeded in recruiting its members and voters from all different social classes in the midst of the prevailing system of class parties. There had been one severe limitation, however, which had kept the Center Party imprisoned in a tower of exclusiveness in spite of all its efforts at becoming a Christian People's Party in 1919: the Party was limited to the Catholic minority, for one of the chief reasons for its rise had been the discrimination against Catholics under Bismarck. This limitation kept the Party from ever polling more than about 20 per cent of the nationwide popular vote throughout the Weimar Republic. The Christian Democrats of 1945, on the other hand, made a determined and by and large successful effort to attract Protestants as well as Catholics which soon resulted in a share of the popular vote of 30 per cent and more.[6]

When Adenauer's determined drive for a majority of *Bundestag* seats was successful in 1953 and 1957, it not only made the CDU/CSU the first German party to get a majority of the popular vote, but also rallied a body of voters so evenly distributed over the main social groupings of German society, including the blue-collar workers, as to approximate a cross section of the electorate.[7] Only a few groups, such as farmers, women, and Catholics, are still rather disproportionately represented among the CDU/CSU voters.

The Social Democrats took longer to shake off the rigidity of their old Marxist orientation and restriction to labor votes. But in recent years they also have come around to a determined attack on their sources of electoral weakness. Their Bad Godesberg Program of 1959, in particular, was a landmark in the effort to change the public image of the party to that of a broad "people's party." [8] Since 1959 the new emphasis on selecting attractive candidates and on wooing rural voters and even members of the Catholic church have confirmed the significance of the Bad Godesberg Program as a reformation. The electoral success of the party, long confined within the "magical 30 per cent barrier," has demonstrated with nearly 40 per cent in the 1965 elections that this second major party of the Bonn Republic is well on its way to contesting the headstart of the CDU/CSU.[9]

The third party, the FDP, is the only one that has not followed the

[6] On the rise of the CDU, see especially Arnold J. Heidenheimer, *Adenauer and the CDU* (The Hague: Martinus Nijhoff, 1960) and the German sources cited there. Also, Max Gustav Lange, ed., *Parteien in der Bundesrepublik* (Stuttgart, Düsseldorf: Ring Verlag, 1955), and Ossip K. Flechtheim, *Dokumente zur parteipolitischen Entwicklung in Deutschland seit 1945* (Berlin-Grunewald: Dokumentenverlag, Dr. Wendler, 1962-63).

[7] In the 1961 elections, for example, approximately 20 per cent of the CDU/CSU voters were drawn from unskilled labor, about 33 per cent from skilled labor and lower white-collar groups, about 33 per cent from the middle layer, and another 14 per cent from upper-middle and upper classes of West German society. SPD voters were composed of 20 per cent unskilled workingmen, 55 per cent skilled and white-collar workers, 22 per cent middle layer and 3 per cent upper-middle and upper class.

[8] Douglas A. Chalmers traces this development in some detail in his *The Social Democratic Party of Germany* (New Haven: Yale University Press, 1964).

[9] The new style of campaigning by the SPD also mirrors this change in emphasis from doctrinaire rigidity to flexible engineering. See this writer's "Comparative Study and Campaign Management: The Brandt Campaign in Western Germany," *Western Political Quarterly,* XV (December 1962), 681-704. Also, by this writer, *Germany: Yesterday and Tomorrow* (London: Oxford University Press, 1965), pp. 313ff.

trend toward becoming a broadly based "people's party." It is still in many respects a liberal "party of representation" of the old style, a party made up of individualistic notables who are as reluctant to become involved in matters of party bureaucracy and organization as they are to accept party discipline in the *Bundestag* or the state diets. The FDP was in virtual eclipse during the years 1953-1961 when the governing CDU/CSU majority made the cooperation of the FDP superfluous.[10] Since 1961, however, the party has enjoyed the accidental advantage of being the balance between the two almost evenly matched major parties. In the government coalition since 1961, the FDP was repeatedly able to get its way on various issues in spite of the embittered resistance of its coalition partner, the CDU/CSU, which has four times as many deputies in the *Bundestag*.[11]

Along with the number and character of the more important parties, it should be emphasized that the basic nature of the social and political cleavages typical of the Imperial and Weimar years has changed. The most important cleavage before the rise of Hitler was the class antagonism between bourgeoisie and proletariat. This cleavage defined the confrontation of labor and management. It also defined the embattled position of bourgeois parliamentary democracy, bourgeois civilization, bourgeois morality, and bourgeois family life. There were legions of militants who regarded themselves proudly as the "vanguard of the proletariat" and further millions of veterans, including the extreme right wing, who were clamoring for the day when the bourgeois civilization would disappear along with white shirt collars, neckties, and the institution of bourgeois marriage. Today even the symbols of this belligerent confrontation of three decades ago seem to have lost their significance in the public mind. In public opinion polls, it has turned out, nobody wants to call himself a "proletarian" any more. The word that once defined class antagonism is now considered quite negatively, or as a synonym of vulgarity. Its opposite term of reference, "bourgeois," is similarly hazy, though vaguely positive, in meaning. A majority of respondents in public polls who identified themselves as regular SPD voters, for example, call their party bourgeois.[12]

The voting habits of the different socio-economic groups today show the extent to which the old lines of social cleavage have been obliterated.

[10] See *Germany: Yesterday and Tomorrow*, pp. 282ff. and Gerard Braunthal, "The Free Democratic Party in West German Politics," *Western Political Quarterly*, XIII (June 1960), 332-48.

[11] For details, see *Germany: Yesterday and Tomorrow*, pp. 257-62.

[12] See *Jahrbuch der öffentlichen Meinung, 1957*, p. 266 and the essays of Ralf Dahrendorf collected in his *Gesellschaft und Freiheit* (Munich: Piper Verlag, 1961).

German blue-collar workers turn out to vote for the CDU almost as heavily as for the SPD. White-collar voters and public employees also split their allegiance between the two major parties. If it were not for the needs of a part of the remaining fraction of the German electorate, one might say that a two-party system would be quite sufficient for West German society. The remaining part of society—farmers, businessmen, and professional people—divide their votes between the CDU/CSU, the FDP, and a number of small, regional, and generally right-wing groups which are no longer represented in the *Bundestag*.[13]

As German sociologists have pointed out, the new basic political alignment in West German society owes much to fundamental structural changes that have occurred since the 1920s. The destruction of the landed nobility east of the Elbe River and the old aristocratic ruling class in general has left ample room for the rise of new elites, a motley group of business tycoons, politicians, movie stars, professors, judges, and so forth. The new social elites are not very conscious of their status, but firmly committed to parliamentary democracy. The arrival of mass consumption has also dissolved some of the older patterns of group collectivism and made the average German rather individualistic, intent upon personal success and material possessions, and pragmatic rather than idealistic—or ideological. It is small wonder, then, that the age of ideological commitment and fanaticism in Western Germany has given way to a more distant, general identification with a particular party because of its candidates, its general image, or specific bread-and-butter issues.[14]

The programmatic differences between the major parties also bear out this thesis. In subjects as loaded with heated controversy as foreign policy and defense, the two major parties today are substantially in agreement. What little dissension is left, such as between the "Gaullists" and "Atlanticists," or on relations with Eastern Europe, generally does not separate the major parties, but may create opposing factions within each of them. The economic and social policies of CDU/CSU and SPD, while differing somewhat in matters of emphasis and degree, are also so close as

[13] For the first years of the Federal Republic, elaborate breakdowns of the voting behavior of different socio-economic groups can be found in Juan Linz, *The Social Bases of West German Politics* (unpublished Ph.D. dissertation, Columbia University, 1959). For the most recent material see Egon Klepch, Günther Müller, and Rudolf Wildenmann, *Die Bundestagswahl 1965* (n. p. 1965).

[14] See on this aspect of European societies the special issue of *Daedalus* (Winter 1964) entitled "A New Europe," as well as *Germany: Yesterday and Tomorrow*, pp. 126-43, and Dahrendorf, *Gesellschaft und Freiheit*. For a comparative perspective with emphasis on the party system, see Otto Kirchheimer, "Der Wandel des westeuropaeischen Parteisystems," *Politische Vierteljahresschrift*, VI (1965), 27ff.

to be in substantial agreement. The Socialist plans for the nationalization of basic industries, for example, were abandoned as early as 1952, and their commitment to free enterprise and competition has never been in doubt since then. There is very little apprehension among German businessmen today about the consequences of a possible Social Democratic election victory.

What the SPD seems to be saying in effect with every election is that it can do anything and will do anything the voters have found attractive about the CDU/CSU; and, in fact, the SPD will do it better. Real dissension between the parties seems to have been transferred to program details and peripheral issues. Here the CDU/CSU has understandably campaigned time and again on its record of performance in office, telling the voter, as it were, "Don't upset the apple cart. You never had it so good." The Social Democratic opposition, with equal logic, has pointed to such weak spots as the lagging of educational reforms, insufficient road construction, or inadequate provision for public health and welfare in the midst of affluence. The Social Democrats promised the voters prompt action on these problems and an updating of what the SPD regards as obsolete concepts and practices.

III. PARTY GOVERNMENT IN THE FEDERAL REPUBLIC

The establishment of a well functioning two-party system goes a long way toward the achievement of responsible party government. To complete the mechanism, however, there has to be a well integrated merging of the representative processes and institutions with the processes and agencies through which the major parties make their decisions about policies and leaders. A closer examination of the functioning of executive-legislative relations in the Bonn Republic will show the manner in which party government has come to function in Bonn.

Constitutional and Statutory Provisions

The evidence that the framers of the Bonn Constitution intended to set up a system of responsible party government is quite strong, in spite of some minor indications to the contrary. Not only does the Bonn Constitution accord a prominent place to political parties, in contrast to the Weimar Constitution which mentions parties only negatively, but the Bonn document also avoids almost all the uses of plebiscites and referenda by which the Weimar Constitution sought to bypass the authority of the party politicians in the *Reichstag*. More important still, the Basic

Law of the Bonn Republic very deliberately destroyed the powerful position of the presidency of Weimar, which had been the rallying point of the bureaucratic and authoritarian state and which had tempted the party leaders at crucial moments to leave governmental responsibility to the presidential emergency powers. The Bonn Constitution instead shifted the center of political power unambiguously to the chancellorship, the parliamentary executive of the federal government. If there was any need to confirm the tendency of the Bonn Constitution toward party government, such confirmation was soon supplied by the severe criticisms raised by conservative constitutional lawyers, disturbed by what they called the "emasculation of the State" and the "mediatization of the people" in the new Constitution. The Basic Law of Bonn, these critics pointed out, turns over a monopoly of power to the political parties who control the electoral process, the *Bundestag* and its deputies, the upper house, the *Bundesrat,* and the state governments, and who select the Federal President and even the Justices of the Federal Constitutional Court.[15]

Further evidence of the prominent role of political parties is given in the Electoral Laws and also in the Standing Orders of the *Bundestag.* The Electoral Law is a mixture of single-member district plurality and proportional representation, with the latter element enabling the parties to hand-pick at least half of the *Bundestag* deputies through regional lists. The parties' influence over the nomination of candidates for the electoral districts is also considerable. The Electoral Laws and the Constitution show a bias in favor of large, moderate parties and against small, as well as extremist, parties. Two extremist parties, the Communists and a neo-Nazi group, in fact, were outlawed in proceedings before the Federal Constitutional Court. The Standing Orders of the *Bundestag* clearly favor the organized parties over the individual deputy in the debates, in committees, and in the introduction of bills. This restraint on the individual deputy is complemented by the party discipline traditional in German legislative practice.[16]

The Bonn Constitution also placed due weight on executive preponderance in legislation and public finance. As in Great Britain, the bulk of important legislation is introduced by the Government which enjoys

[15] For a representative passage, see Werner Weber, *Spannungen und Kräfte im westdeutschen Verfassungssystem* (Stuttgart: Vorwerk Verlag, 1958), pp. 15ff.

[16] For details, see especially Gerhard Loewenberg, "Parliamentarism in Western Germany: The Functioning of the Bundestag," *American Political Science Review,* LV (March 1961), 93-95, and the sources cited there. See also Dolf Sternberger, *Die lebende Verfassung* (Meisenheim: Westkultur Verlag, 1956), and the relevant documents in James K. Pollock and John C. Lane, *Source Materials on the Government of Germany* (Ann Arbor: Wahr's Publishing Co., 1964), pp. 51-82.

every advantage in debate under the Standing Orders of the *Bundestag.* The few bills originating in the *Bundesrat* also go through the hands of the Government before they reach the floor of the *Bundestag.* In budgetary matters the *Bundestag* is not allowed to increase expenditures proposed by the Government or to add new spending proposals of its own. Thus it is the Government that proposes and the *Bundestag* which disposes. It should be mentioned, however, that the constitutional relationship between Government and *Bundestag* also includes notions of separateness and independence more reminiscent of the older French than of the British tradition. The organization and the leadership of the *Bundestag* parties, in particular, is carefully separated from the Cabinet Ministers of the Government coalition. The Standing Committees of the *Bundestag* give the role of the legislature the weight that its infrequent plenary sessions may not possess.

The framers of the Bonn Constitution went even farther than the establishment of parliamentarism in their concern for the establishment of stable party government, since they could not know in 1948-49 that the breakthrough toward a well defined two-party system was so near. Fearful of a repetition of the unstable coalition governments of the Weimar Republic, they decided to establish an especially strong position for the Federal Chancellor by means of the so-called "constructive no-confidence vote," a device adopted earlier by one of the West German states. This constitutional provision requires the election of a successor before a chancellor can be overthrown, thereby placing the burden of responsibility for maintaining governmental stability upon those who would topple the Government in office. More important still, the other Cabinet Ministers were made dependent not on the confidence of a majority of the *Bundestag,* but on the confidence of the chancellor, who alone "determines and is responsible for the guidelines of Government policy." [17] This concentration of authority and responsibility in the office of the chancellor, it soon turned out, was quite unnecessary for the functioning of stable party government, though it has played a considerable role in fashioning the particular kind of party government which developed.

The Rise of "Chancellor Democracy"

What no one among the framers of the Bonn Constitution had foreseen was the rise of Adenauer's "Chancellor Democracy," an almost unbeatable political combination of strong party leadership, spectacular electoral successes, and Konrad Adenauer's good fortune of leading his

[17] See articles 64, 65, and 67 of the West German Basic Law.

country from the depth of defeat and international contempt back to international status and acceptance in the Western Alliance. Adenauer's control over his party and the appeal of his stature and policies to a majority of the voters alone would have assured him the dominant position as chancellor. His constitutional position further strengthened his hand against coalition partners and dissident groups in his own party. In fact, the many CDU/CSU back-benchers swept into the *Bundestag* on the coattails of Chancellor Adenauer made his domination over small coalition partners, his own party, and especially over his own Cabinet rather oppressive.[18]

For the reasons given above, the waning of Chancellor Democracy after 1959 implied considerable disorganization in the West German power structure. Even though his party had wanted him to retire to the largely honorific office of Federal President as early as 1959, it took four more years until Konrad Adenauer could be forced to withdraw in favor of his successor, Ludwig Erhard. After the intrigues of the old Chancellor's rivals within his own party and of the FDP had failed to dislodge him, the *Bundestag* CDU faction, worried about a series of electoral setbacks, finally prevailed upon him to announce his retirement at the age of 87. By that time one wing of his party had already begun to conduct its own foreign policy along Atlanticist lines, while he was still desperately trying to save his good relations to Gaullist France.

Konrad Adenauer's successor found it very difficult to step into the shoes of *"der Alte."* Not only could he hardly hope to duplicate the association of Adenauer's name with the return of Germany to the position of international status, but he also had to wrestle with entrenched interests in his party and in the Government which Adenauer had easily dominated. It was probably Ludwig Erhard's biggest tactical mistake not to accept the chairmanship of the CDU upon his confirmation as chancellor. When Erhard turned it down, Adenauer himself ran for reelection in 1964, and since then, the new chancellor has had to cope with no fewer than three obstreperous party chairmen of his Government coalition: Konrad Adenauer, CDU party chairman; Franz Joseph Strauss of the Bavarian CSU; and Erich Mende of the FDP. Had Erhard succeeded in getting a popular majority at the polls in 1965, he would have been in a much stronger position in his Government and party. With 47.6 per cent of the vote, he failed to improve his situation and may well continue to be unable to restrain his old CDU party chairman from public

[18] On the concept of Chancellor Democracy, see also Robert Neumann, *European and Comparative Government* (New York: McGraw-Hill Book Company, Inc., 1960), pp. 422-24, 442-44, 717-18; and *Germany: Yesterday and Tomorrow*, pp. 249-65.

interference in his foreign policy. Chancellor Erhard's relations with the FDP and CSU during the formation of his first post-election cabinet in 1965 likewise showed his weak position.

Erhard's failure to be a strong party leader is particularly significant in the contrast he presents to Adenauer. An ebullient orator where the "Old Man" was dour and economic with words, Erhard is indeed lacking in toughness and a sense for the political jugular, as Adenauer has always hinted of Erhard and other Protestant CDU leaders. Ludwig Erhard, in fact, had been very critical of Adenauer's political cynicism and of the high-handed conduct of then-Defense Minister Franz Joseph Strauss (and leader of the Bavarian CSU organization), in the *Der Spiegel* affair. Upon taking office, the new chancellor went out of his way to promise fairness and decency to his colleagues and coalition partners in the Government and even to the Opposition. He made a point of showing his democratic approach in contrast to the style of his autocratic, patriarchal predecessor. Erhard has also hinted at a different conception of executive-legislative relations: he would like to be a "People's Chancellor" (*Volkskanzler*), a plebiscitary executive who directly appeals to the people over the heads of party and *Bundestag*. His appeal to popularity with the voters is evidently supposed to supply the political strength he lacks in dealing with groups in his own party and around him.[19]

Actually, the plebiscitary note in the political system of the Federal Republic is nothing new. For Adenauer it already supplied the chief support of Chancellor Democracy, although the "Old Man" rarely needed to circumvent his own party. In the federal elections, the recurrent confrontations of Adenauer or Erhard for the Government and Erich Ollenhauer or Willy Brandt for the Opposition, have long overshadowed the real object, the election of *Bundestag* deputies. In this, too, the British model has been closely approached.

As for the dialogue between Government and Opposition, the SPD has not been timid about putting up attractive candidates for chancellor, or, indeed, a "shadow cabinet" ready to offer alternative leadership when needed. Neither have the Social Democrats neglected to put forth alternative policies or to change their line when it seemed necessary to gain popular approval. In fact, they have pursued a policy of "constructive opposition" which, rather than merely obstructing the progress of government business, frequently led them to participate in the shaping of important legislation and of institutions such as the new German army. Yet the price for having been in the Opposition at the federal level ever since the be-

[19] Regarding Erhard's concept of executive-legislative relations, see *Germany: Yesterday and Tomorrow*, pp. 268-70.

ginning of the Federal Republic appears to be high in terms of human frustration. Many promising talents in the SPD have wandered off after years in the *Bundestag* and sought administrative posts in Berlin or in one of the State governments the SPD controls. Willy Brandt himself, the candidate for chancellor in 1961 and 1965, refused to play the role of Opposition Leader in the *Bundestag* after each election and preferred to return to his position as Lord Mayor of Berlin. Such a withdrawal from national politics need not imply a permanent loss, however, since the federal organization of the SPD regularly features in its "shadow cabinet" state party figures of proven attractiveness and success with the voters.

Party Government or Party State

In summary, then, "party government" in the Federal Republic indeed seems to have come a long way from the "party state" of Weimar. The similarities to the British model are considerable: the two-and-a-half party system, the confrontation of the plebiscitary party leaders, the patterns of cabinet dominance in legislation and budget-making, the pervasive influence of the major parties. On the other hand, there are noticeable dissimilarities including, in particular, the anomalies introduced into parliamentary government by the position of the Chancellor, "constructive no-confidence," and the habit of executive compartmentalization, which prevent the West German Cabinet from developing the inimitable intimacy and solidarity of the British Cabinet. This disparity is further underlined by the patterns of ministerial recruitment which by and large bypass men of parliamentary accomplishments and instead cultivate expertise and functional particularism. Thus, neither the chancellor nor most cabinet ministers, nor even many members of the "shadow cabinet" of the Opposition are true parliamentary leaders rooted in the parliamentary parties or factions. German political parties do not even have parliamentary secretaries to tie the cabinet to the organization of the governing coalition's parliamentary parties. Given this traditional tendency of German executive leadership and legislative independence, it is perhaps not such a bad idea to leave to the chancellor alone the authority and responsibility of determining the "general guidelines of governmental policy" in responsibility to the *Bundestag*.

In closing, one might also mention the widespread notion that the *Bundestag* is getting less powerful, less effective, and perhaps also less respected. Chancellor Adenauer showed his disdain repeatedly by not informing the *Bundestag* on matters of foreign policy with the regularity it deserves. Attempts to enhance the prestige of the *Bundestag* by broadcasting some of its more significant debates over the radio have met with modest success. Another frequent criticism is that lobbying by organized interests is so prominent as to undermine the authority of the *Bundestag* as a representative institution. However, here too one is reminded of the criticism of the "eclipse of the British Parliament," or of the House of Commons. West Germany is hardly the only Western democracy where the prominent role and image of parliamentary institutions has waned, or at least undergone some change. Yet in Germany, such an eclipse of parliament may be more alarming in view of the brief time the *Bundestag* as an institution has been rooted in the public mind. Nevertheless, even a decline of the importance of the *Bundestag* would not diminish the central role of party government in the Federal Republic of Germany.

Suggestions for Further Reading

Fromme, Friedrich Karl, *Von der Weimarer Verfassung zum Bonner Grundgesetz* (Tübingen: J. C. B. Mohr, 1962).

Heidenheimer, Arnold J., *The Governments of Germany,* 2nd ed. (New York: Thomas Y. Crowell Company, 1966).

Loewenberg, Gerhard, "Parliamentarism in Western Germany: The Functioning of the Bundestag," *American Political Science Review,* LV (March 1961), 87-102.

Merkl, Peter H., "Comparative Study and Campaign Management: The Brandt Campaign in Western Germany," *Western Political Quarterly,* XV (December 1962), 681-704.

———, "Equilibrium, Structure of Interests and Leadership: Adenauer's Survival as Chancellor," *American Political Science Review,* LVI (September 1962), 634-50.

———, *Germany: Yesterday and Tomorrow* (London: Oxford University Press, 1965), Chaps. 8 and 9.

Neumann, Sigmund, "Germany" in *Modern Political Parties,* ed. Sigmund Neumann (Chicago: University of Chicago Press, 1956).

Plischke, Elmer, *Contemporary Government of Germany* (Boston: Houghton Mifflin Co., 1961).

Pollock, James K. and John C. Lane, *Source Materials on the Government and Politics of Germany* (Ann Arbor: Wahr's Publishing Co., 1964).

Treue, Wilhelm and Wolfgang Treue, *Parlamentarismus in Deutschland, Entstehung und Entwicklung* (Bonn: Bundeszentrale für politische Bildung, 1963).

Weber, Werner, *Spannungen und Kräfte im westdeutschen Verfassungssystem* (Stuttgart: Vorwerk Verlag, 1958).

THE LEGISLATIVE PROCESS IN THE U.S.S.R.

Jeremy R. Azrael

Essays on the legislative process ordinarily seek to describe and analyze the role of legislative institutions within the broader political system. Frequently they are addressed to the so-called "crisis of parliamentarism" —the multidimensional threat to parliamentary supremacy that is posed by such developments as the growth of mass society, the emergence of a self-aggrandizing military-industrial complex, the rapid progress of science and technology, and the rise of an administrative state. In the Soviet context, however, these conventional themes are of dubious analytical utility. To put the case summarily, the "legislative branch" of government plays only a marginal role in Soviet political life, and the idea of a "crisis of parliamentarism" is meaningless in a political system where parliamentary supremacy has never existed—or, more accurately, where it has existed only in name.

I. PARLIAMENTARY SUPREMACY: DOCTRINE AND REALITY

Such a qualification is necessary because the *doctrine* of parliamentary supremacy *is* an integral part of Soviet constitutional theory. Thus, Article 30 of the Soviet Constitution explicitly designates the Soviet "parlia-

JEREMY R. AZRAEL *is Associate Professor in the Department of Political Science at the University of Chicago. His primary field of teaching and research is Soviet politics and he has lived and travelled extensively in the U.S.S.R. He is a contributor of numerous articles to professional journals and the author of* Managerial Power and Soviet Politics.

ment," the so-called Supreme Soviet, as "the highest organ of state power in the U.S.S.R." Similarly, Article 32 provides that "the legislative power of the U.S.S.R. is exercised exclusively by the Supreme Soviet." And Articles 48 and 64 stipulate that the federal executive power, including both the so-called Presidium of the Supreme Soviet (a kind of collective president) and the Council of Ministers or cabinet, is directly responsible to the legislature.[1] In point of fact, however, neither these provisions nor the equivalent provisions pertaining to the organization and distribution of power at the republican and local levels of the system have ever had real operational significance. That they should exist at all is somewhat ironic in view of Marx's and Lenin's insistence that socialists should discard the "bourgeois" concept of "separation of powers," but their interest as examples of ideological "deviationism" is diminished by their practical irrelevance.[2]

The Political and Parapolitical Functions of the Soviets

Far from exercising sovereign power, the Supreme Soviet has never played an appreciable role in the Soviet decision-making process. With a few minor exceptions of recent vintage, its "lawmaking" activity has been confined to the endorsement—usually *ex post facto*—of decrees in whose preparation it has had no meaningful voice. Moreover, this endorsement has never been preceded by serious deliberation or debate and has invariably taken the form of unqualified approval. It suffices merely to report that the Supreme Soviet is only in session for a few days a year, that these few days are almost entirely occupied by official speeches, and, finally and most indicatively, that the Supreme Soviet has never witnessed a negative vote or even so much as an abstention. According to official sources, of course, this remarkable unanimity testifies to the mono-

[1] See Herbert McClosky and John E. Turner, *The Soviet Dictatorship* (New York: McGraw-Hill Book Company, Inc., 1960), Appendix II, pp. 617-32, and John N. Hazard, *The Soviet System of Government,* rev. ed. (Chicago: University of Chicago Press, 1960), Appendix, pp. 207-30, for the text of the present Soviet Constitution. This Constitution, which was adopted in 1936, is slated for extensive revision in the near future. However, the revisions are unlikely substantially to affect the provisions here in question or to require any basic changes in the generalizations about Soviet parliamentary life that are advanced in the pages that follow. Likewise, the more detailed descriptions of Soviet parliamentarianism that appear in the two books cited are likely to retain their validity, and interested students are urged to consult both McCloskey and Turner and Hazard for excellent treatments of the structure and functioning of the Supreme Soviet and its local counterparts. Our own discussion draws extensively on these works.

[2] See, for example, Lenin's *State and Revolution,* Collected Works, XXV (Moscow: Foreign Languages Publishing House, 1964).

lithic solidarity of Soviet society and the universal support that the Communist regime enjoys among the Soviet people. In fact, there is no doubt that what it actually signifies is the purely nominal and ritualistic character of the Supreme Soviet's legislative functions. And, what is true of the legislative functions of the Supreme Soviet at the center is true also of the legislative functions exercised within their particular areas of jurisdiction by the various lower level soviets (i.e., the republic-level, provincial, city, and district soviets).

Where there is an appreciable difference between the Supreme Soviet and its local counterparts is in the role of the standing organs that represent these bodies when they are not in session—to wit, the so-called *executive committees* and *permanent commissions*. Thus, whereas the "executive committee" of the Supreme Soviet, or as it is now called, the Supreme Soviet Presidium, plays virtually no independent role in the policy process, the executive committees of the local soviets play a significant part in the administration and direction of certain local enterprises and communal services. Similarly, whereas the permanent commissions of the Supreme Soviet are only nominally analogous to the legislative committees with which we are familiar in the West, the permanent commissions of the lower level soviets do appear to play a significant "watchdog" role and may even initiate a certain amount of local legislation. Even at the local level, however, the permanent commissions are only marginally involved in the policy process and the executive committees operate quite independently of the local soviets to which they are ostensibly responsible. In essence, they are merely low level adjuncts of the centralized ministerial system, and it is provable that the only thing that has prevented their formal incorporation into the latter is a lingering reluctance to discard all pretense of commitment to the Marxist-Leninist idea of a complete fusion of legislative and executive authority. Accordingly, despite certain salient differences between the pattern at the center and at the "peripheries," it can be said both of the Soviet political system as a whole and of each of its constiuent territorial units that the "legislative branch" of government is almost completely devoid of effective political power.

To stress the powerlessness of Soviet parliaments is not to deny that these bodies serve some important political or parapolitical functions. The very stress on parliamentary supremacy in official constitutional theory suffices to invalidate any such suggestion, and the elaborate institutionalization of parliamentary forms makes it clear that the soviets are useful to the regime in a variety of ways. For one thing, the soviets provide the leadership with a ceremonial sounding board for important statements of policy and purpose, as well as with a highly visible forum for prosecuting the unending campaign of "criticism and self-criticism" which is so integral a part of Soviet life. In addition, the soviets provide an arena for giving status rewards to particularly diligent "activists" on the various "fronts" which comprise Soviet society, while simultaneously recruiting new "activists" and opening up new "fronts." Again, by lending the appearance of reality to the fiction that the regime is at once popularly based and genuinely representative, the soviets help disarm both foreign and domestic criticism. In this connection, the fact that the soviets are composed so as almost perfectly to replicate the ethnic, sex, and other demographic differences in society stands the regime in particular good stead. It is not every parliament, after all, that can boast so high a proportion of women, or workers, or members of minority groups; and it is not every observer who can discern that parliamentary recognition is not necessarily correlated with political representation. Moreover, just as the soviets create an illusory sense of meaningful political representation, they also create an illusory sense of meaningful political participation. Thus, there is little question that the operations of the soviets and the elaborately organized plebiscitary elections whereby their members are selected provide some of the population with an illusion of effective access to the policy process—an illusion which, in turn, strengthens political consensus and support.

It is doubly important that these functions be acknowledged at the present time because it is only when they are understood that one can properly evaluate the effort to "revitalize" the soviets that has been so prominent a part of recent Soviet politics. This effort has taken many different forms and has found expression in the recall of certain soviet delegates by their constituents, the rejection of certain candidates at the polls, the criticism of executive committees which fail to convene sessions of local soviets on schedule, the introduction of minor revisions in legislative proposals after "hearings" before the permanent commissions of the Supreme Soviet, the organization of more and more public auxiliary bodies attached to local soviets, and—most strikingly—the bruiting about of suggestions that electors be offered a choice of candidates instead of having no option other than to vote for or against a single nominee. In all of these instances what is involved is an effort to enable the soviets to perform their various legitimation, communication, and mobilizational functions more effectively. What is really at issue is a desire on the part of the ruling elite to make the soviets more effective "transmission belts" or better "schools of communism," as official parlance has it, and attempts to depict these measures as steps toward the "liberalization" or "democratization" cannot bear close scrutiny. As before, so now, the soviets and the population they ostensibly represent are deprived of almost all effective voice in the formulation and implementation of state policy, and this situation is unlikely to change in the near future.

II. DYNAMICS AND SOURCES OF SOVIET LAW

Who then does participate in the legislative process in the U.S.S.R.? What structures and what groups in the Soviet political system do play a meaningful role in the making of law—that is, in the formulation of "principles, regulations, and policies prescribed under the authority of the state or nation?" [3] Instead of going on to a more detailed examination of the soviets as such—instead, for example, of expatiating on the relationship between the two chambers of the Supreme Soviet, the reasons for the existence of a unicameral system at the subnational level, the rules and procedures governing parliamentary debate, and other similar topics —the remainder of this essay will be addressed to these two questions. Because the primary focus of political analysis is the organization and distribution of power and because the soviets are largely powerless, it seems appropriate to move from matters of form to matters of substance and to inquire into the actual dynamics of Soviet politics and the real sources of Soviet law, broadly defined. To repeat, who actually does participate in the legislative process in the U.S.S.R., given that the nominal legislators and the vast majority of their constituents do not?[4]

Exercise of Political Power in the Stalinist Period

The "classical" answer to this question is, of course, that virtually no one except the dictator and the members of his immediate entourage exercises appreciable political power. Moreover, there is no doubt of the fundamental validity of this answer where the Stalinist period is concerned. To be sure, some devolution of power occurred even under full-fledged Stalinism. Indeed, it could not have been otherwise, for no single individual or small group can possibly exercise a complete monopoly of power in a complex modern society covering one sixth of the earth's

[3] *The American College Dictionary* (New York: Random House, 1959), p. 691, *s.v.* "law," definitions 1 and 2.

[4] The assertion that the legislators do not participate in the actual legislative process must be qualified insofar as the soviets are comprised of leading members of the various strategic elites in Soviet society. However, to the degree that these men have power or influence, it is not because they are legislators, and their power and influence are not expressed in their performance of the role of soviet delegate.

surface. In any such society, some decisions have to be delegated to middle and lower echelon officials, and even those decisions that are reserved to the central leadership must rest in large part on the advice and judgment of technical experts and administrative specialists. Because they alone possess the "relevant facts," such experts and specialists inevitably control many of the critical "premises" on which adequate decisions must be based, and from time to time such control is bound to be utilized to effect official policy choices and aggrandize political influence.[5] However, if one can exaggerate the concentration of power that obtained under Stalin, it is nonetheless true that the Stalinist system was an unprecedentedly close approximation of the totalitarian "ideal-type"—that is, of a type of political system in which there are no institutional or societal restraints on the exercise of central power.[6]

Under Stalin, the politicization of society reached unprecedented lengths, and virtually all secondary associations and groups were converted into political "transmission belts," harnessed to the goals and purposes of the dictatorial regime. Hypercentralization was the norm in all spheres, and the dictator made every effort to guarantee that no one who enjoyed a measure of delegated authority was in a position to translate that authority into political independence. Authority was organized in "parallel, competing bureaucracies" which merged only at the top and were purposely assigned vaguely defined and overlapping spheres of jurisdiction. While the *principle* of "collegial administration" had long since been replaced by the *principle* of "one-man management," in practice virtually every "one-man manager," whether plant director, army commander, or university rector, had to share his authority with a party secretary and a secret police official who were responsible to different superiors through independent chains of command and who felt free —indeed, obliged—to intervene in virtually all of the given institution's affairs. This entire system, in turn, was subjected to constant arbitrary terror and a relentless "permanent purge" with results that fully justify calling it a system of "institutionalized cross-espionage, fear, and mutual-suspicion." [7] As such, moreover, it was by no means confined to the lower and middle levels of authority. On the contrary, the members of the rul-

[5] See Herbert A. Simon, *Administrative Behavior* (New York: The Macmillan Company, 1961), for a fuller elaboration of the terminology and line of arguments applied here.

[6] See Zbigniew K. Brzezinski, *Ideology and Power in Soviet Politics* (New York: Frederick A. Praeger, Inc., 1964), Chap. I, for a fuller elaboration of the totalitarian "ideal-type" thus conceived.

[7] See Merle Fainsod, *How Russia Is Ruled,* 1st ed. (Cambridge: Harvard University Press, 1953), for a thorough description of the Stalinist system. Our brief summary makes use of Fainsod's terminology with some slight modifications.

ing elite were at least as vulnerable to sudden arrest as their subordinates, and Stalin went out of his way to cultivate rivalries and conflicts among his top lieutenants, thereby maximizing his own power and insuring that politics was confined to competition for his grace and favor.

The insecurity and subservience (not to say servility) that Stalin inspired among even his closest associates is now well known, thanks *inter alia* to his successor Khrushchev's "revelations." In this connection Khrushchev's reports of the constant humiliation that Voroshilov endured at Stalin's hands and of the pleasure that "the Leader" took in examining his lieutenants to see if they had "shifty eyes" are particularly revealing.[8] They leave no doubt that the atmosphere in the Kremlin was that of a despotic oriental court. For present purposes, however, one of Khrushchev's less lurid and less familiar stories is even more relevant because it relates directly to the policy process as such. We refer to Khrushchev's report of a Council of Ministers' meeting at which Stalin suddenly proposed a production plan that ran directly counter to the advice of his industrial ministers, and then, having watched the ministers vote unanimously in favor of his proposal, openly gloated over his success in keeping his subordinates in their "proper" places.[9] No doubt such scenes were not regular occurrences in that Stalin was ordinarily probably somewhat less imperious in his approach. However, what is of concern here is not Stalin's leadership style, but the fact of his unchallenged leadership; not the tact with which he treated his top aides, but his readiness to ignore or dismiss their advice and his ability to do so with complete impunity. Given this kind of dictatorial power, it is clear that even the upper stratum of the Soviet ruling elite enjoyed only intermittent and highly contingent access to the policy process, and there is no question that the law which emerged from this process came very close indeed to expressing the arbitrary will of a single, omnipotent sovereign.

The Reemergence of Politics After Stalin

It was, of course, inevitable that Stalin's death would leave a huge vacuum of power at the very core of the Soviet system. The demise of the absolute dictator was bound to touch off a major realignment of forces within the ruling elite and to unleash intense pressure for the redress of accumulated grievances. In short, the situation was ripe for change, and it is not surprising that the period following Stalin's death

[8] See Leo Gruliow, ed., *Current Soviet Policies,* III (New York: Columbia University Press, 1960), 187, 196.

[9] *Izvestia,* June 29, 1963, p. 4.

witnessed a marked growth in the political assertiveness of major social groups and a sharp increase in official responsiveness to popular claims and demands. Nevertheless, though this reemergence of conventional politics represented a fundamental and dramatic change, and one whose momentum has yet to be exhausted, its scope must not be exaggerated. The bulk of the population remained politically inarticulate and unorganized while effective access to the system's power processes remained very highly circumscribed. In the final analysis, almost all major decisions continued to be made by a small circle of Stalin's ex-lieutenants, and the ability to exert a significant influence on critical policy choices remained confined to the leading members of four strategic elites: the secret police, the managerial elite, the officer corps, and the full-time party functionaries or *apparatchiki*. Moreover, by 1955 it was evident that a countertrend had set in, and the next several years saw a substantial reconcentration of power and a gradual curtailment in the access of all groups except the party *apparatchiki* to the power-political arena.

The party *apparat* had, of course, traditionally occupied a position of political primacy within the Soviet system. It had acquired this status while Lenin was still alive, and it was above all thanks to his control of the party *apparat* that Stalin had been able to succeed to Lenin's mantle and to aggrandize autocratic power. However, as he moved closer to his goal, Stalin had sought simultaneously to reduce his dependence on the *apparat* and to enhance his direct control over the other major power structures in the system. Only in this way could he hope to attain total domination, and the war and postwar years consequently witnessed an almost uninterrupted rise in the relative authority of the state bureaucracy and the secret police. This process had apparently not yet gone far enough to satisfy Stalin, who seems to have been planning a further downgrading of the *apparat* at the time of his death, but it had nonetheless gone quite far—far enough that by 1953 the *apparat* appeared to be merely one of a number of coordinate and nearly coequal instruments of rule.[10] Moreover, while Stalin's death gave the *apparatchiki* more room to maneuver, it was by no means certain that they would be able to recoup their position and reestablish their traditional primacy under the new regime. On the contrary, it was apparent that most of the major elite groups in Soviet society favored a further curtailment in the authority of the *apparat,* and the manner in which power was divided at the apex of the system, among Stalin's immediate heirs, was clearly calculated to reinforce the pressure that these groups exerted.

[10] For the developments here at issue, see, among others, Leonard Schapiro, *The Communist Party of the Soviet Union* (New York: Random House, 1960), Chaps. 24-29.

As is well known, Stalin's heirs affected a division of power along essentially bureaucratic lines, with Khrushchev emerging as First Secretary of the party, Malenkov as premier and head of the state machine, Beria as head of a newly re-consolidated secret police apparatus, and so on. This alignment of forces, in turn, made it almost inevitable that conflict within the ruling elite would exacerbate the already considerable tension among the regime's principal instruments of rule and cast a number of top leaders in the role of spokesmen for bureaucratic groupings that were inimical to the aspirations of the *apparatchiki*. Indeed with the conspicuous exception of Khrushchev, who clearly had an overriding interest in the maintenance and enhancement of *apparat* primacy, virtually all of the top leaders now found themselves in institutional positions that forced them either to surrender all hope of playing an independent power-political role or else to assume a more or less vigorously anti-*apparat* posture, for only such a posture would enable them effectively to mobilize the support of their principal "constituents." Accordingly, when the "collective leadership" which had been established after Stalin's death disintegrated, Khrushchev was in a somewhat isolated position, and it was uncertain that the *apparat* would be able to hold its own, let alone reclaim its former authority. In the event, however, Khrushchev was able to play his rivals off against each other until his own dominance was assured, and his success in this regard was, *ipso facto,* a success for his supporters.

Apparat *Primacy and Collective Leadership*

Although the period 1953-1958 witnessed major challenges to *apparat* primacy from the side of the secret police (Beria), the state bureaucracy (first Malenkov and then Bulganin), and the armed forces (Bulganin to some extent and, above all, Zhukov), all of these challenges failed. Aided by their still unrivaled organizational resources and their control over the symbols of legitimacy (a critical variable in any succession struggle), the *apparatchiki* were able not only to contain their opponents but to move more and more onto the offensive. Slowly but surely, they reasserted their sovereignty within the power-political arena, and the end result of their self-aggrandizement was a massive extension of the political and administrative hegemony of the party machine. Suffice it to say in this regard that the successive stages of the post-Stalin succession struggle culminated in a drastic political emasculation of the secret police, a complete dismantling of the system of centralized economic ministries (the system from which the managerial elite had derived its power), and a substantial purge of the officer corps in a context characterized by much increased emphasis on the importance of political and ideological—as distinct from professional—criteria in the determination of military organization and policy. In short, by 1958, the record revealed that in a contest with the party *apparatchiki* the other key elite groups in Soviet society were apt to fail not only as counterelite or power-political "constituency groups," but even as "veto groups" where their own most vital interests were at stake.[11] In doing so, it clearly ran counter to the expectations of those who had confidently predicted in 1953 that the Soviet system would undergo a rapid evolution toward a system of "countervailing power" or even toward genuine political pluralism—that is, toward a polity in which the decision-making process is characterized by extensive bargaining among truly autonomous groups representing discrete institutional and professional interests. However, if the outcome of the succession struggle did not confirm the more optimistic projections of the "pluralists," it left room for doubt regarding the validity of claims that the "natural" configuration of Soviet political life is one-man dictatorship or monocratic (autocratic) rule.

Developments subsequent to Stalin's death clearly indicate that the Soviet political system embodies a strong *tendency* toward monocratic rule. The rapid breakdown of the initial "collective leadership" testifies to the operation of this tendency and there is little question that each of the chief competitors in the succession struggle aspired to autocratic power. Certainly there can be little doubt that Khrushchev sought to aggrandize such power following his victory in the succession struggle. This seems clear, for example, from the way in which he treated his erstwhile rivals, for the evidence strongly suggests that Khrushchev wanted not only to expel the leaders of the so-called "anti-party group" of 1957 from the party (a desire that he ultimately satisfied) but also to bring them to trial on capital charges. These charges, moreover, were to pertain not only to crimes committed under Stalin but also to the crime of "conspiracy to seize power"—a new crime which was put on the books at Khrushchev's behest in 1958. What Khrushchev sought from such a prosecution was clearly not only to retaliate against former opponents but also to deter future opposition and to create an atmosphere of terror within the current ruling elite. While he was anxious to observe legal forms, his goal was to rehabilitate the "ritual of liquidation" as a procedure for settling leadership disputes. Moreover, at the same time

[11] See Wolfgang Leonhard, *The Kremlin Since Stalin* (New York: Frederick A. Praeger, Inc., 1962), for a good account of the post-Stalin succession struggle.

that he sought to terrorize his closest colleagues and lieutenants, Khrushchev also began to propagate a new, Khrushchevian "cult of personality" and to pursue organizational and personnel policies that were clearly designed to maximize his own authority and power.

As during the succession struggle proper, Khrushchev now adopted tactics similar to those that Stalin had used in his quest for absolute power. In particular, he made a systematic attempt to reduce his dependence on the party *apparat* and enhance the authority of other power structures. For one thing, he repeatedly tried to bypass the party Presidium in his policy initiatives, going out of his way, for example, to "leak" plans and proposals that were still under discussion and had not yet been approved. In the same vein, he sought to convert plenary sessions of the Central Committee into hortatory mass meetings in which the voice of the *apparatchiki,* who comprised the bulk of the Central Committee's membership, was drowned out by the voice of hundreds of technical specialists, state officials, and "rank and file" workers and peasants. Similarly, he developed an increasingly active personal secretariat, headed by his son-in-law Adzhubei, whom he eventually tried to co-opt into the party Secretariat proper. Again, he himself took over the premiership in addition to the first secretaryship of the party and even went so far as to have himself appointed to the new post of supreme commander-in-chief of the armed forces. Having thus enhanced his direct control over the state bureaucracy, he proceeded not only to sponsor a progressive recentralization of governmental and economic administration (which he had radically decentralized in 1957) but also, and even more importantly, to divide the previously "monolithic" party *apparat* into separate agricultural and industrial committees whose secretaries (now twice as numerous as before and perforce less powerful) were increasingly relegated to the status of low and middle level economic controllers.

All of these measures had a distinct dictatorial cast, and they were rendered the more ominous by the fact that they were accompanied by a marked acceleration of the "permanent purge." At all levels there was a systematic "renewal of cadres," and thousands of new men who owed their positions to Khrushchev were catapulted into high office. However, for all his exertions, Khrushchev's attempt to consolidate absolute power ended in defeat. Although he seemed to be on the verge of an autocratic breakthrough on a number of occasions, especially in late 1962 and again in late 1963, Khrushchev was consistently checked in the event. And when it finally became clear that he would neither moderate his personal ambition nor revamp a number of policies that seemed certain to eventuate in major fiascoes for the regime, he was decisively checkmated.[12]

Khrushchev's ouster clearly suggests that the tendency toward one-man dictatorship that continues to operate within the Soviet system is not irresistible. Indeed, the "lesson" of October 1964 may be that one-man dictatorship cannot be attained so long as the would-be dictator is unable to resort to terror as a technique for controlling his colleagues within the ruling elite. Likewise, the relative stability that has characterized the Soviet leadership since Khrushchev's ouster suggests that "collective leadership"—for it is precisely such leadership that appears to obtain—may be a more viable system of rule within the Soviet context than most analysts would previously have supposed. At the same time, however, it remains true that Khrushchev almost succeeded in his drive for autocratic power. And it must be stressed that there is no guarantee against a breakdown in the present system of "collective leadership" and a consequent reactivation of the tendency toward one-man dictatorship.

Barring a very rapid growth in the procedural consensus which seems to be developing within the Soviet ruling elite, there seems no reason whatever to dismiss the possibility of a bitter and violent succession struggle in the near future. Signs of severe tension within the new leadership have been recurrent, and future developments may yet reveal that the solidarity that seems to exist within the Presidium is largely illusory. Should this in fact prove to be the case, there are as yet no institutional or societal restraints that would preclude the possibility of a younger and more ruthless Khrushchev type from successfully doing what Khrushchev tried but ultimately failed to do—i.e., from aggrandizing absolute power by liquidating his rivals, transforming the party Secretariat into a personal appendage, and using the techniques of "permanent purge" and perpetual reorganization in order to prevent the consolidation of insulated pockets of authority and power. The costs of such a process would, no doubt, be unprecedentedly high, but it would be premature to conclude that they could not be imposed or that their imposition would entail a breakdown in the system. Moreover, even if October 1964 did introduce a new stage in the evolution of the Soviet system, the ouster of Khrushchev and the emergence of a relatively stable "collective leadership" do not necessarily signify an extensive diffusion of power.

[12] For a fuller discussion of the developments treated in this and the preceding paragraph, see Merle Fainsod, "Khrushchevism in Retrospect," *Problems of Communism*, XIV: 1 (January-February 1965), and Richard Lowenthal, "The Revolution Withers Away," *ibid.*

In the first place, it must be stressed that Khrushchev was ousted through a conspiratorial palace coup, participation in which was limited to a handful of top leaders. While the details of Khrushchev's deposition are still shrouded in mystery, it seems clear that the circle of conspirators was confined to members of the party Presidium and a few key officials in the state bureaucracy, military establishment, and security apparatus. To be sure, once the conspirators made their first overt move against Khrushchev, other participants were drawn in, and constitutional or quasi-constitutional forms were observed to the extent of immediately convening a session of the 200-odd man Central Committee to which Khrushchev was allowed to appeal. However, the available evidence leaves little doubt that the real function of the Central Committee was to ratify an irreversible *fait accompli.* While the fact that procedural norms were observed is itself of some significance as an index of political change, it is doubtful that Khrushchev would have been allowed to appeal to the Central Committee if there had been any doubt as to the outcome of his appeal. Thus, at the same time that it testifies to the possibility of effective resistance to autocracy within the system, October 1964 also testifies to the highly elitist and exclusivist character of Soviet politics.

It is true that the Brezhnev-Kosygin government has given the various strategic elites in Soviet society a greater voice in the policy process. However, this is exactly what one would anticipate in the case of a new and as yet unconsolidated regime, and the present situation need not last. Moreover, even now effective access to the ultimate decision-making arena remains very strictly circumscribed. At best, it is only the top cadres of the various strategic elites who exercise decisional prerogatives on any other than a purely intermittent and particularistic basis, and the party *apparat* (which was quickly reunited after Khrushchev's ouster) continues to exercise an extensive power-political hegemony. Indeed, the party Presidium is now, even more than before, a veritable *inner sanctum* of leading *apparatchiki.* Thus, of the five men who have been promoted to the party Presidium since Khrushchev's ouster, four are men who have spent their entire careers in the party *apparat.* To be sure, the new premier Kosygin has made his career primarily in economic administration, but he is nonetheless a peculiarly "unmanagerial" manager who has always enjoyed the particular favor of *apparat*-dominated factions and groups. And, apart from his promotion, none of the personnel changes sponsored by the new regime suggest a break in the pattern of *apparat* primacy.

The Role of Administrators and Managers

Where there has been a marked change is in the amount of operational autonomy enjoyed by state officials and economic executives within the areas of their particular professional competence. However, this autonomy is designed to have a purely instrumental character, pertaining exclusively to the execution of centrally determined policies. Moreover, it is more likely now than ever before to retain precisely such a character. To an ever increasing extent, the men in whom administrative and managerial authority are vested are true professionals who are apolitical in their outlooks and are committed to implementing established policy in a more or less unquestioning fashion, and these men are unlikely to engage in extensive power-political maneuvers or seek to aggrandize personal power. While the growth of professionalism is often cited as a factor foreshadowing the erosion of totalitarianism, it can also facilitate central control, and past experience suggests that in the Soviet Union this is peculiarly likely to be the case. Furthermore, should practice confound this prognosis, it seems likely that the autonomy which has now been granted can and will be revoked without undue difficulty and that we will once again witness a rapid proliferation of *apparat* surveillances and control. Certainly, at a minimum, there seems no reason to anticipate anything approaching a "managerial revolution," let alone a managerial revolution that would eventuate in the acquisition by society of any substantial capacity for political self-determination. Although these two processes are often linked together, they have no logical connection, and a case can be made for the party *apparatchiki* being considerably more receptive to popular claims and demands than either the economic managers or any other major elite group.[13] Be that as it may, however, there is no likelihood of society's soon attaining a significant voice in the policy process.

III. PROSPECTS FOR THE FUTURE

The ouster of Khrushchev has not entailed any fundamental change in the political status of the non-elite groups and broad popular groupings of Soviet society. Now, as before, they are primarily objects of political manipulation rather than initiators of political action, and their claims and demands upon the political system remain unorganized and, from a

[13] For a fuller elaboration of these issues, see Jeremy R. Azrael, *Management and Politics, USSR* (Cambridge: Harvard University Press, 1966).

liberal-democratic point of view, unrepresented. Moreover, it is by no means certain that the new regime—or its successors—will not once again revert to a policy of intensive social mobilization. Such a policy was, of course, part and parcel of the Stalinist system and it occupied a prominent place in the Khrushchev system as well, albeit it was pursued without recourse to mass terror. Thus, Khrushchev was the author of a multitude of measures assigned to undermine the authority of the family, to eradicate religious "survivals," to eliminate all forms of private property, and to restrict sharply the sphere of personal privacy. These measures, which included the prosecution of a violent anti-religious campaign, the confiscation of a great deal of peasant-owned livestock and land, the institution of a far-flung network of boarding schools, and the creation of a variety of parapolice and parajudicial "public organizations" to administer a kind of organized vigilante justice, are too often overlooked in discussions of the political dynamics of the "Khrushchev era." Likewise, their significance is too often ignored in projecting future trends.[14]

It is true that many of Khrushchev's mobilizational policies have been suspended or revoked by the new regime. However, a number have been retained and it is not unlikely that others will be resumed in the not too distant future. Most of the policies in question are firmly rooted in Marxist-Leninist ideology. They follow logically from the proposition that the Soviet Union is about to realize full-fledged communism. This proposition, in turn, continues to occupy a central place in the party program and is hence likely to have an important influence on future policy. This is true, moreover, irrespective of whether or not the Soviet leaders are ideological true believers. Whatever their beliefs, they all have immense vested interests in structures and procedures which incarnate ideological principles and can only be justified and rationalized in ideological terms. This point once noted, however, it is important to go on to note that one can query whether the erosion of genuine ideological commitment has in fact proceeded as far as many analysts believe. Certainly, for all his much vaunted "pragmatism," Khrushchev had a strong fundamentalist streak (viz., for example, his policy of confiscating peasants' private property in the midst of a massive agricultural crisis), and the fact that various of his successors have criticized him precisely for his excessive pragmatism may suggest that the new regime contains an

[14] See Jeremy Azrael, "An End to Coercion?" *Problems of Communism,* XI: 6 (November-December 1962) and "The Party and Society," in Alan Kassof, ed., *Prospects for Soviet Society* (forthcoming; 1966), for a fuller discussion of the policies here in question and their implications.

even higher admixture of ideological militants. Moreover, such militants are unlikely soon to disappear.

While the younger members of the ruling elite are better educated than the present leaders, the educational system of which they are products is massively dedicated to the inculcation of ideological militancy, and the recruitment process through which they have been selected for elite positions continues even today to place very heavy stress on ideological and political criteria. To be sure, despite the regime's best efforts, cases of apoliticism and "technocratism" have become increasingly common among young party cadres, but there is good reason to believe that they are still the exception rather than the rule. Fairly extensive contact with Soviet youth has persuaded the present author that the regime's socialization and recruitment programs have operated successfully enough for most of the members of the emergent ruling elite to qualify for all practical purposes as "new Soviet men," attuned to the "imperatives" of modern technology but determined to maintain the traditional primacy of politics over economics and to base policy on ideological principle and the tenets of Marxist-Leninist doctrine. This determination could waver as the men in question acquire more responsibility, but it is unlikely to disappear. Its psychological roots are often extremely deep, and responsibility is as likely to reinforce ideological conviction as it is to generate ideological agnosticism. Promotion is no certain source of critical acumen, and the tendency toward doctrinaire thinking that is characteristic of the men concerned may well be strengthened by the growing weight of institutional commitments and more intensive involvement in the party's on-going effort to legitimate its political sovereignty. That this quest is likely to encounter more and more obstacles does not necessarily mean that it will be pursued less vigorously, and it could mean precisely the reverse. History knows counterreformations as well as reformations, and in the Soviet Union the forces of ideological orthodoxy and organizational monolithism are well disciplined and occupy positions of vast strength.

In spite of the many factors that are operating to prevent Soviet society's acquiring a significant capacity for political self-determination, the dramatic changes that have ensued since Stalin's death should serve as a caution against excessive pessimism. There is, after all, no doubt that the past decade has witnessed many important victories for the anti-totalitarian forces within Soviet society, including, to name but a few, the elimination of mass terror, the cessation of "bacchanalian" planning, the allocation of many more resources to consumer welfare, and the spread of a multidimensional cultural "thaw." Moreover, there is no doubt that in some cases the term "victory" can be taken quite literally. That is to say, the changes in question have been wrested from a reluctant or recalcitrant regime by social groups (most notably, the liberal intelligentsia) that have backed their demands with sustained pressure and have shown great internal cohesiveness and solidarity in the face of official counterpressure. However, many of the changes that have ensued have been sponsored by the regime itself for the sake of its own interests. These changes, in turn, point more to the modernization of totalitarianism than to liberalization or democratization. Furthermore, many of the other changes have proved highly precarious when subjected to determined assault from above. Such militancy became more and more prevalent during the "Khrushchev era," and it may well prove common in the future.

There are those who argue that freedom is bound to grow at an ever quicker tempo. However, such arguments find little confirmation in past history and are often based on dubious premises. While freedom has grown, it has also declined, and it is well to remember that the freedom that has thus far emerged in the Soviet Union is essentially negative freedom—freedom *from* rather than freedom *to*. As such it is by no means illusory or nugatory, but it must be appraised for what it is and from a perspective that recognizes not only that benevolent dictatorship is nonetheless dictatorship but also that benevolence may actually serve to render dictatorship more effective and more stable. The "thaw" (using the term in the wide sense) may be the prelude to a genuine spring, but Russian springs are notoriously late-coming and winter tends to be the longest, and, as it were, the characteristic season. As men, all we can do is hope that the political winter will at long last yield, as nature's winter always, finally, does. As analysts, we must, I think, be somewhat skeptical, if not precisely pessimistic.

To conclude, over the long run society may acquire a really significant capacity for political self-expression and self-determination, and when it does it may be aided in realizing this capacity by the existence of the parliamentary forms and constitutional provisions that were described at the outset of this essay. Forms do have a way of taking on content, and there may come a time when it will be meaningful to discuss the legislative process in the Soviet Union in more or less conventional terms. This is a remote prospect, however, and it will require decades, not years, before the operation of the "legislative branch" of the Soviet government will acquire real political salience or representative government and parliamentary supremacy will be anything more than a hollow constitutional myth.

Suggestions for Further Reading

Carson, G., *Electoral Practices in the USSR* (New York: Frederick A. Praeger, Inc., 1955).

Conquest, R., *Power and Policy in the USSR* (New York: St. Martin's Press, 1961).

Daniels, R. V., *The Nature of Communism* (New York: Random House, 1963).

Fainsod, Merle, *How Russia Is Ruled,* rev. ed. (Cambridge: Harvard University Press, 1963).

Friedrich, C. J. and Zbigniew Brzezinski, *Totalitarian Dictatorship and Autocracy,* 2nd. ed. (Cambridge: Harvard University Press, 1965).

Hazard, J. N., *The Soviet System of Government,* rev. ed. (Chicago: University of Chicago Press, 1960).

Leonhard, W., *The Kremlin Since Stalin* (New York: Frederick A. Praeger, Inc., 1962).

McCloskey, R. and J. Turner, *The Soviet Dictatorship* (New York: McGraw-Hill Book Company, Inc., 1960).

Scott, D., *Russia's Political Institutions,* 2nd. ed. (New York: Frederick A. Praeger, Inc., 1961).

Senate Committee on Government Operations, *National Policy Machinery of the Soviet Union,* Report by the Subcommittee on National Policy Machinery, 86th. Cong., 2nd. sess., 1960 (Washington, D.C.: Government Printing Office, 1960).

THE ROLE OF THE EUROPEAN PARLIAMENT IN AN EMERGING EUROPEAN COMMUNITY

Leon N. Lindberg

In the Spring of 1965 the Commission of the European Common Market (European Economic Community) proposed to the six member governments[1] that they should take a series of major steps in the direction of further economic and political integration. These steps would have involved: (1) The adoption of a system for pooled financing of a common agricultural policy for all six countries, covering price supports, import controls, export subsidies, structural improvements, and involving an annual expenditure of between $600 million and $1 billion a year; (2) approval of an independent financial resource for the supranational Commission, which would have given it greater autonomy from national controls; and (3) granting the European Parliament a real power of control and supervision over the expenditures of the Community which would result from adoption of the first two steps.

These proposals were the occasion for French President de Gaulle to initiate his famous boycott which plunged the European Community

[1] France, Germany, Italy, Netherlands, Belgium, and Luxembourg.

LEON N. LINDBERG *is Associate Professor of Political Science at the University of Wisconsin. He was a Research Associate at the Center for International Affairs, Harvard University, and his main field of teaching and research is the political and economic integration in Western Europe. His publications include articles in scholarly journals and* The Political Dynamics of European Economic Integration.

into crisis from June 30, 1965, to January 30, 1966.[2] That de Gaulle found much in these proposals to object to is perhaps not as surprising as the fact that they were in general supported by all of the other governments, by most interest groups and political parties (even in France), and by that portion[3] of public opinion that pays attention to such matters.

Extended powers for the Parliament were thought to be necessary because of the fact that if the proposals were accepted vast amounts of money could be spent by a "technocratic" supranational Commission and a Council of Ministers representing the governments, but without any parliamentary control whatsoever. This situation resulted from the fact that in creating the European Economic Community and the European Atomic Energy Community (EEC and Euratom) and their predecessor the European Coal and Steel Community (ECSC), these six countries had in effect transferred vast decision-making powers from national systems to a European Community system. National parliaments thus lost whatever degree of direct control they had had over such matters, for it turned out to be very difficult for any individual parliament to hold its ministers responsible for what they did in the European Community Council of Ministers, where decisions had to be based on compromise and give and take. A European Parliament had been established to fill this gap, but over the years more and more criticism of the inadequacy of the powers and duties assigned to it was voiced in the national parliaments, in the European Parliament, and in elite and general public opinion. To many observers the entire European Integration movement, which had so captured the imagination of Europeans and Americans alike, appeared gravely compromised by this absence of accountability

[2] For an analysis of the crisis see Leon N. Lindberg, "Integration as a Source of Stress on the European Community System," *International Organization,* XX: 2 (1966).

[3] In a study entitled "Public Opinion and Europe of the Six" based on a sample survey carried out in 1962 the following percentages were reported on the question, "How often do you think about the problems of European Unification?"

	Germany	Belgium	France	Italy	Luxembourg	Netherlands
Very often	15	8	7	11	6	13
Sometimes	28	22	26	18	21	32
Rare	33	30	33	21	36	32
Never	21	38	32	28	33	22
No answer	3	2	2	22	4	1

Source: *Sondages: Revue Française de L'Opinion Publique,* No. 1 (1963), p. 46.

or popular control over the growing authority of the supranational institutions it had brought forth.

This essay will attempt to explore the problem of parliamentary control in the European Community by analyzing the nature of the European Parliament as a legislative body: its unique characteristics, its accomplishments and failures, its relationship to national parliaments, and its future possibilities.

I. INTRODUCTION

The European Parliament is the legislative assembly of the European Community—the collective name for the three experiments in transnational economic integration in which the so-called Western European Six have been engaged since 1950. Its 142 seats are allocated to the member states in rough proportion to their populations.[4] The members are chosen from the ranks of the legislatures of the member states and are nominated by the legislatures. In general, care has been taken to assure that each delegation shall include members of all parties in rough proportion to their strength in the national legislatures.[5] Though chosen by the national parliaments, the members are not legally bound by any instructions from the parliaments or the governments. They consider themselves to be "representatives of the people of the Community," and, in general, they behave as such.

According to the three Treaties which established the European Community, the Parliament is given a diffuse role in the operation of the Communities. It must be consulted by the EEC and Euratom Commissions, the ECSC High Authority, and the Council of Ministers before the latter takes decisions; it receives reports from the several Commissions, debates them, and can force the Commissions to resign; it can debate any

[4] Thirty-six each from Germany, France, and Italy; fourteen each from the Netherlands and Belgium; and six from Luxembourg.

[5] *Belgium:* Christian Social Party—6, Belgian Socialist Party—6, Party of Liberty and Progress—2. *France:* Union for a New Republic (UNR)—15, Popular Republican Movement (MRP)—3, Socialist Party (SFIO)—6, Seven minor parties to the center and right—12. *Germany:* Christian Democratic Union/Christian Social Union (CDU/CSU)—18, Social Democratic Party (SPD)—14, Free Democratic Party (FDP)—3, Democratic People's Party (DVP)—1. *Italy:* Christian Democracy (DC)—28, Italian Social Democratic Party (PSDI)—2, Three right wing parties—5. *Netherlands:* Catholic People's Party (KVP)—5, Anti-Revolutionary Party (AR)—1, Christian Historical Union (CHU)—1, Labor Party (PvdA)—5, People's Party for Freedom and Democracy (VVD)—2. *Luxembourg:* Christian Social Party—3, Socialist Party—2, Democratic Party—1. Source: Murray Forsyth, *The Parliament of the European Communities* (London: Political and Economic Planning, 1964), pp. 29-30.

issue and freely criticize member governments; and it can demand answers to oral and written questions. Furthermore, the members, in an effort to increase the importance of their role in the Communities, have declared their goal to be that of turning it into a real federal parliament of Europe. To achieve this goal they have lobbied vigorously for an increase in their powers and have urged that they be elected directly by the people of the several member states.

In its day-to-day operation, the European Parliament resembles national legislatures more than it does other international assemblies. If one were to visit the "House of Europe" in Strasbourg and observe a session, one would note a distinct similarity with a national legislature. Members attend regularly, debating a whole range of problems typical of a modern industrialized state, and debating them in relation to concrete items of legislation rather than to abstract generalities and platitudes. Members are seated not by national delegations, but around a hemicycle by political party affiliation—Socialists, Christian Democrats, Liberals, and UDE.[6] These political parties have steadily increased their internal cohesiveness and their authority to direct the work of the parliament at the expense of the national delegations. Much of the work of the parliament is carried on in fourteen specialized subject-matter committees which prepare studies, reports, and resolutions and attempt legislative oversight of the Community's executives.[7] One usually finds members of the several Commissions and often national Ministers of Foreign Affairs, Economics, or Agriculture sitting on the front bench responding to questions from interested members and participating in some debates. Legislative business is conducted in a self-consciously Com-

[6] The UDE is the European Democratic Union and is made up exclusively of French Gaullists (UNR). The other groups are multinational.

	Belgium	France	Germany	Italy	Luxembourg	Netherlands
Christian-Dem.	6	3	18	28	3	7
Socialist	6	6	14	2	2	5
Liberal	2	12	4	5	1	2

Source: Murray Forsyth, *The Parliament of the European Communities* (London: Political and Economic Planning, 1964), pp. 29–30.

[7] The fourteen specialized subject-matter committees include: political foreign commerce, agriculture, social, internal market, economics and finance, transports, energy, research and culture, sanitary protection, budgets and administration, judicial, as well as the committee for cooperation with the developing countries and the committee of associations. *Annuaire-Manuel de L'Assemblee Parlementaire Europeenne,* 1964-1965.

munitarian atmosphere. The life of the parliament centers around the committees and the transnational groups. Committee chairmen and rapporteurs typically open debates. Few of the MP's taking part in the discussions speak as representatives of national interests, or they apologize if they do so. Spokesmen of the political party groups wind up debates and usually introduce party resolutions which have been hammered out in caucus.

In most of the above respects, the European Parliament differs from such other international parliamentary assemblies as the Consultative Assembly of the Council of Europe, the Assembly of the WEU, the Nordic Council, or the Consultative Inter-Parliamentary Council of Benelux. As Forsyth points out:

Important developments in the nature of international assemblies have taken place. Put concisely, the most dramatic development has been from assemblies of little independence and no power to a type of assembly with a large amount of independence and "limited but real" powers; from assemblies which are little more than international discussion centers to a type of assembly which can claim, with justification, to have some, if by no means all, the characteristics of a national parliament. In terms of the institutions which have emerged since the war, this line of development can be seen running most clearly from the Consultative Assembly of the Council of Europe . . . to the present European Parliament. The other European assemblies all have their own individual characteristics but . . . they can all be placed at one stage or another along this main line of development. . . . It can be said quite firmly that they all stand much closer to the end represented by the Consultative Assembly . . . than to that represented by the European Parliament.[8]

Since the European Parliament is more similar to national legislatures than to international assemblies in its general operation and in the motivations of its members, it is most useful to compare it to the former.

II. THE EUROPEAN COMMUNITY AS A POLITICAL SYSTEM

That the European Parliament is distinct from other international assemblies can be explained in part by the nature of the system to which it is attached. The far-reaching web of commitments into which the Six have entered distinguishes the European Communities from most other international organizations in that its executives can make binding decisions

[8] Forsyth, *op. cit.*, pp. 2-3.

directly affecting the economic life of the member states. What is the nature of this system?

The Nature of the European Community

In discussions of the European Community, it is common to distinguish sharply between "economics" and "politics" and between economic integration and political integration, and to say that the European Community concerns only the former. Using a broader definition of politics and the political, I reject this notion. The European Community is certainly political if one perceives politics as having to do with how legitimate or authoritative decisions are made in a society and how advantages and disadvantages are distributed.[9] In establishing the Communities, the member states agreed to form a customs union and an economic union (and eventually a political union) where agricultural, commercial, monetary, and tax policy would be made by a common decision-making process cutting across national boundaries. This involves a definite distribution of values, advantages, and disadvantages in a legitimate fashion, and, therefore, there seems to be little to be gained by implying that the Community does not have to do with politics. It can most profitably be thought of as a new kind of political system where some policies are decided entirely on the national level (defense), some entirely at the Community level (tariffs and quotas), but where more and more the two levels intertwine.

To develop common policies, the member states created a special institutional system which has permitted the evolution of a unique form of bargaining and decision-making that resembles the mechanisms of domestic politics more than the operation of classical international politics. This institutional system includes the three supranational commissions (the EEC and Euratom Commissions and the ECSC High Authority), bodies whose officials actively develop complex economic policy relatively autonomously of national government control. Policies thus developed are proposed to the Councils of Ministers for approval or rejection. Though the Councils of Ministers consist of delegates explicitly representing the national governments, they too have developed a Community spirit which is reflected in their members' general commitment to agree and in their attitude, "We are condemned to succeed."

Out of the bargaining that takes place within and between the Commissions and Councils come decisions and policies that far transcend the

[9] See David Easton, *A Systems Analysis of Political Life*, (New York: John Wiley & Sons, Inc., 1965).

scope of traditional international agreements. They are the kinds of decisions normally made exclusively at the domestic level. Examples of such decisions are the common agricultural policy which covers export and import systems as well as price supports and subsidies. These decisions are of such a nature as to have a significant impact on national systems by contributing to policy and structural change, thus penetrating into national political life and changing group expectations and behavior.

The crisis occasioned by de Gaulle's boycott of the Common Market beginning June 30, 1965, supports the notion that integration has succeeded rather than failed (though it could fail because of de Gaulle), for de Gaulle would not be so hostile if he did not perceive that integration had gone so far as to restrict French freedom in pursuing her own national interests. De Gaulle's attack on the EEC Commission indicates that he sees it as a real and serious threat to be coped with. Further evidence supporting the notion that the European Community has evolved into some kind of a legitimate political system can be found in the vehement outcries against de Gaulle's boycott which came from the five partners as well as from business, labor, and agricultural interest groups.

On the other hand, the crisis made it clear that the European Community is still only an incipient political system distinguished from more mature ones by the nature of its membership, its decision-making processes, and the diversity of political identification among most Europeans. Moreover, the system is still precarious, and, although it is unlikely to break up completely, it could come to resemble a traditional international organization, rather than continue to develop in a truly transnational direction.

The argument up to this point has been that the European Parliament should be analyzed as being of the genus "legislatures," and that it operates in a functioning political system of a unique nature, but one that is still incipient and precarious. What I want to do is to analyze the role of the European Parliament as a legislative body in this system, but to do so poses a methodological problem, for, while my frame of reference will be national legislative bodies, we must try to go beyond the usual assumptions of empirical studies and theories of legislative behavior. These have concentrated by and large on the ways in which legislative bodies have influenced the processes whereby decisions are made and scarce resources are distributed among competitors in the political arena. What such studies take for granted is the continued existence of a more or less stable and legitimate political community. In an examination of the European Parliament this is precisely what cannot be taken for granted.

III. THEORIES OF ALLOCATION AND THEORIES OF SYSTEMS-PERSISTENCE

What I have in mind here is a distinction between political theories of allocation and political theories of systems-persistence. Theories of allocation ask such questions as: How are decisions made? How is power distributed and put to work in the selection of public policies from a number of alternatives? Who receives the benefits from political activities? [10]

Theories of party politics, interest groups, legislative behavior, political leadership, administrative organization, coalitions, voting behavior and the like seek to understand varying parts of the allocative processes. They deal with those structures or practices through which the outputs are influenced, formulated and implemented and that thereby determine the way in which the valued things of the society are allocated.[11]

Political theories of allocation have provided the dominant direction for political research in general as well as for research in legislative institutions and processes. Students of the legislature have typically asked questions about the lawmaking functions of the legislature and about the role of the legislature in controlling or influencing the executive in its formulation and administration of public policy. Relatively little attention has been paid to the role of legislative institutions in the building up and maintenance of the political system itself. Here we are interested in such questions as: How is it that a political system as such is able to persist through time? What is the role of the legislature, of representative institutions, in increasing the capacity of a political system to cope with the stresses of economic, social, and political change?

To clarify this point, one may ask what role the United States Congress played in integrating the American political community? How did the attitudes, values, and expectations of Senators and Representatives change as they continually interacted in the capitol? How were the norms of acceptable behavior established? How did party control and activity develop? These are only rhetorical questions, for to my knowledge students have failed to give adequate answers. I suggest that it would be fruitful to try to answer these and similar questions.

There is a status quo *bias built into allocative research when it is untempered with an appreciation of the systemic conditions under which*

[10] Easton, *op. cit.*, p. 474.
[11] *Ibid.*

the allocations are taking place. It leaves the impression that the pie must always remain the same and even that the allocative processes change for reasons that are explicable solely in terms of the system itself. To escape this bias, we need a theoretical framework that helps us understand how the very pie itself comes into existence and changes in its basic content or structure. . . . Where the system itself is threatened with destruction, as in highly unstable systems, allocative theories, although relevant, no longer suffice.[12]

I submit that it is important to ask about both allocation and persistence in seeking an understanding of or in guiding research on most any legislative institution. But it is clearly crucial to do so in the case of the European Parliament, for it was a dominant purpose of the original architects of the European Community institutions, as it has been of the members of the European Parliament itself in the years since 1952, to use these institutions for the purpose of promoting the construction of a new federal or quasi-federal system among the six members of the Community. And, as we have seen, this is a goal that has its opponents as well as its supporters. For the members of the European Parliament this has led to a persistent paradox inherent in the possibility that behavior appropriate to the goal of contributing to the system's capacity to persist may not be conducive to increasing or stabilizing their role *vis-à-vis* political allocations.

It will be the purpose of the analysis which follows to consider the performance and potentialities of the European Parliament with regard to these two types of roles—allocation and systems-persistence—keeping in mind that the distinction between them is an analytical one and that many of the things that the European Parliament does can well be allocated to both categories. We shall be interested in such questions as: What tools does the European Parliament possess in each of these areas? With what success has it amended or increased its allocative role? How has it contributed to the persistence of the system? Which role seems most salient or appropriate, given the nature of the system in which the European Parliament finds itself? Has the European Parliament made maximum use of its potentialities?

IV. THE ALLOCATIVE ROLES OF THE EUROPEAN PARLIAMENT

The two allocative roles most commonly attributed to legislatures are lawmaking and control of the executive in its formulation and execution

[12] *Ibid.*, p. 475.

of policy. Before considering the European Parliament on these dimensions, one should be aware that existing national parliaments differ widely in how and if these roles are fulfilled in practice.[13] Variations may be explained in terms of three sets of interrelated independent variables: the general nature of the political system of which the legislature is a part, the internal structure and system of rules of the legislative body (e.g., standing subject-matter committees, seniority system, and question period), and the behavior patterns and role conceptions of the legislators (e.g., kinds of debates conducted and attitudes towards representative function).

The United States Congress is one of the few legislatures where these three sets of variables interact in such a way as to allow it to exercise considerable lawmaking and control power. The relevant variables in this case include the absence of executive responsibility to the legislature, the presence of standing subject-matter committees, the relative lack of party discipline, and the general independent role assumed by Congressmen. In most European countries, on the other hand, parliaments neither make laws nor exercise effective control over the executive. This situation may result from the presence of highly disciplined legislative parties that merely ratify policies formulated by the cabinet (Great Britain, Benelux countries, and to a lesser extent West Germany), from the formal dominance of the executive in the system (Fifth French Republic), or from the existence of many undisciplined parties reducing the government to inaction rather than a position of parliamentary control (Fourth French Republic). Thus, as the above discussion indicates, certain prerequisites in the political system, the internal legislative structure, and the legislators' behavior are required if the legislature is to play a major part in the allocative process in the political system.

One bright note in the allocative role played by national legislatures, however, can be found in the indirect influence exerted by some, and most strikingly by the British House of Commons, through the publicity engendered by its debates and the use made of the question period. This is the so-called "lyrical function" of parliament.[14] It can affect decision-making if there are interesting, heated, and stimulating debates which

[13] For a general discussion of legislatures in Western nations see K. C. Wheare, *Legislatures* (New York: Oxford University Press, 1963); Roland Young, *The British Parliament* (London: Faber & Faber, Ltd., 1962); David Thomson, *Democracy in France* (New York: Oxford University Press, 1952); Arnold J. Heidenheimer, *The Government of Germany,* 2nd ed. (New York: Thomas Y. Crowell Company, 1966); Alfred Grosser, "The Evolution of European Parliaments," *Daedalus* (Winter 1964).

[14] For a discussion of the lyrical function see Samuel H. Beer and Adam Ulam, *Patterns of Government,* rev. ed. (New York: Random House, 1962), p. 143. This discussion is based on Walter Bagehot, *The English Constitution,* first published in 1867.

provide some controversy and are reported in the press and brought to the attention of interest group and opinion leaders. Her Majesty's Loyal Opposition plays an important part in making debates and questions[15] in Commons both coherent and controversial and thus more likely to be absorbed by the interested public. In fact, the debates in Commons have been described as a permanent election campaign keeping the electorate informed about the attitudes and activities of the major parties. To insure their stay in power, leading political actors, seeing legislative debates from this perspective, have to reckon with what is said in Commons when formulating and administering policy.

Turning to examine the allocative roles of the European Parliament against this background, one finds that, despite all of its interesting features, it lacks even the formal trappings of any lawmaking power or of control over the executive. Its role in the allocative processes of the European Community is certainly less than that of any parliament in a developed democratic system. The crucial variable here is the partial and incipient nature of the system of which it is a part. To the extent that there is legislative control in the system, it is exercised by national legislatures acting upon their respective negotiators in the Council of Ministers' deliberations. The powers and duties of the European Parliament permit it to approach but not achieve control of executive activity. It has no power to pass legislation or to levy taxes. And, although in recent years it has made every effort to increase its influence over the Community's budget, it still remains relatively ineffectual in this area.[16] Its opinions must be solicited but need not be taken into account by the executive. The following estimate of a recent observer confirms the analysis of earlier students of the Parliament.

As far as the advisory powers of parliament are concerned, honesty requires to admit that they rarely influence the course of events. To be sure, the Council consults Parliament on most of the Commission's proposals. But the parliamentary recommendations do not carry much weight, as the Council—as a Community institution—is under no compulsion to justify its actions before the Strasbourg assembly.

The Commission of course is. But even so, it is more the exception than the rule that the Commission alters its proposals to the Council because of the advice of Parliament. If it does amend its proposals during the course of the negotiations in the Council, more often than not this

[15] For a discussion of the role of the question period in the House of Commons, see D. N. Chester and N. Bowring, *Questions in Parliament* (London: Oxford University Press, 1962).

[16] Walter Yondorf, *Europe of the Six: Dynamics of Integration* (unpublished Ph.D. dissertation, University of Chicago, 1962), Chap. VI.

is done in order to obtain the required unanimity or majority in the Council. And who can blame the Commission? A decision requires the agreement of all or a majority of the Council members, not of the members of Parliament.[17]

The control it does have is over the Commissions, which it can dismiss, and not over the Council of Ministers, but it is the latter that makes the final and binding decisions. This ability to dismiss the Commissions is the only formal weapon in the Parliament's arsenal.

But it is a weapon without weight. It lacks deterrent power because under present circumstances it is just about unthinkable that it will ever be used. For even if the Strasbourg Parliament does force the Commissioners to resign, it does not know who might come in their place, nor can it influence their selection. The governments appoint the new Commission; in theory they do this in common agreement, but in reality each government appoints the Commissioner(s) of its own nationality. The political life of a Commission member therefore, if he wishes to be reappointed after a four year term of office, is not so much in the hands of the European Parliament as in those of his own government.[18]

Furthermore, since the Commissions symbolize the pro-integration dynamism in the system, and the Councils the reluctance and resistance of the national governments, and since the great majority of the members of the Parliament are basically committed to integration as against nationalism, the Parliament has almost always supported the Commissions regardless of the content of their proposals:

The Commission has been able to count on the Assembly's support at all times: when it comes to a confrontation with the Council of Ministers, when any of the long-range goals of the Community seem threatened, and even when the Commission has been unwilling to change its proposals along the lines urged by the Assembly. The only way it [the Assembly] can hope to play a significant role in Community affairs is by supporting the initiatives of the Commission and by urging the Member States to continue to delegate authority to it.[19]

The difficulty in exercising control is further compounded by the complex nature of the policy proposals developed by the Commission.

[17] "The European Parliament: The Great Leap Forward," *Common Market,* V (July 1965), 134.

[18] *Ibid.,* pp. 133-34.

[19] Leon N. Lindberg, *Political Dynamics of European Integration* (Stanford: Stanford University Press, 1963), p. 260.

The specialized subject-matter committees were developed to overcome this problem. These fourteen committees spend a total of from 260 to 300 days a year in meetings in an effort to influence policies adopted by the Commission before they submit proposals to the Council.[20] Although these committees have some influence, they find it difficult to compete effectively with the expertise of the Commissions. Their role is further limited by the absence of publicity given to committee proceedings. In general, the Commissions have cooperated with the committees, for they have found it useful to solicit the support of the Parliament against the Council. But they have resisted any commitment to consider themselves bound by committee reports or by parliamentary resolutions. "Thus the role being played by the EPA *vis-à-vis* the Commission is analogous to that of a pressure group. It represents one source of opinion and pressure among the many to which the Commissions must remain sensitive." [21]

If, as we have seen, the European Parliament lacks formal powers, can it still exercise influence through something akin to the "lyrical function" of the British House of Commons? What features of its internal practices and rules might be useful for this purpose? Up to now how effectively have these been exploited? The "lyrical function" works in Britain because important political actors listen to what is said, and because what is said is nearly always coherent. What has the European Parliament achieved in these areas?

The "Lyrical Function"

The European Parliament has sought to oblige important actors to listen in three ways: (1) by urging the Council to submit all issues for its opinion, not only those matters formally specified by the Treaties; (2) by pressuring the Council to meet with the Parliament and the Commissions in an annual colloquium, a sort of grand general debate on the "state of Community"; and (3) by directing questions to the Council and Commissions, thus seeking to oblige them to provide information, justify or defend past actions, or define what they propose to do in the future.[22]

[20] For details see Elena Bubba, "Six Ans d'Activite du Parlement Europeen," *Revue du March Commun,* LXXIII (October 1964), 431-37.

[21] Lindberg, *op. cit.,* p. 88.

[22] It has sought to make its support for the Commission against the Council indispensable in an effort to get some prior influence over the substance of the proposals the Commissions make to the Council. Although these efforts have not met with much success, as we saw above, the technique may become more important should the Commission become weaker in the future.

In response, the Council has agreed to consult the Parliament in all important Community problems, to give some sort of "supporting reasons" when it does not comply with its resolutions, and to present an Annual Report on the activities of the Council which can be followed by oral questioning and a debate. The colloquium, first held in 1957, has evolved into a sometimes exciting confrontation on the "burning issues" of the day in which ministers frequently speak on behalf of their respective governments, giving a "defense" of their European policies.

Many observers, with British practice in mind, have stressed the potentiality inherent in the device of written questions directed to the Commissions and to the Council. Indeed, it appears that the European Parliament has made increased use of these over the years, the total number of questions asked rising from twenty-nine in 1958-59 and eighty-four in 1959-60 to 184 in 1962-63 and 160 in 1963-64. But a closer look behind these impressive figures reveals a less optimistic picture, for as the chart below indicates, 10 per cent of the members asked between 74 and 83 per cent of the questions, with fully 90 per cent asking few or no questions.

Table I

The Number of Representatives Asking Questions, by Session[a]

Sessions and total number of questions	Number of reps. asking at least one question	Percentage of reps. asking at least one question	Percentage of questions asked by 5 per cent of reps.	Percentage of questions asked by 10 per cent of reps.
58–59 (29)	19	13%	58%	—[b]
59–60 (84)	36	25%	49%	74%
60–61 (130)	43	30%	53%	77%
61–62 (101)	46	32%	61%	78%
62–63 (184)	40	28%	67%	83%
63–64 (160)	47	32%	65%	76%
Total 686				

[a] In calculating the number of representatives asking questions I included all the representatives involved in joint questions.

[b] This was not calculated because of smallness of figures.

Source: *Annuaire-Manuel du Parlement Europeen*, 1958–1964.

Furthermore, the same men from the same countries consistently asked the majority of questions. (Vredeling of the Netherlands has asked more questions than the combined delegations from either Italy, Belgium, and Luxembourg.) Only the Netherlands' representatives have consistently made extensive use of written questions, asking 37 per cent of the questions, though they make up only 10 per cent of the membership.

Table II

Nationality of Questioner, by Session

	Percentage of Total Questions Asked[a]					
Session	Netherlands	Germany	Italy	France	Belgium	Luxembourg
58–59	45	20	10	14	14	0
59–60	45	16	15	21	7	0
60–61	30	24	10	28	9	.7
61–62	47	17	12	15	13	2
62–63	41	19	15	13	18	.5
63–64	35	31	22	16	9	1
Total	37	21	14	17	11	.8

[a] The percentages add up to more than 100% because they were calculated on the basis of all men participating, even in cases of joint questions. In other words, 27 men might ask 25 questions.

Source: *Annuaire-Manuel du Parlement Europeen*, 1958–1964.

One must conclude therefore that the technique is of little appeal to the Parliament as a whole. The imbalance in the use of written questions may be explained in part by different role conceptions held by the members. It may also be the product of the diversity of attitudes of the six governments toward the desired role and function of the various European institutions. Whatever the reason, it seems clear that the great majority of the European legislators does not perceive its role to be one of overseer of executive activities.

If the "lyrical function" of the legislature is to be developed, not only must the key actors pay attention to the debates but they must make sure that the debates are coherent. Probably the most important characteristic of the European Parliament with respect to its effort to make its debates as coherent as possible is the system of political groups: Christian Democrats, Socialists, and Liberals. These groups try to make what is said in Parliament coherent by simplifying and organizing debate, and by working to create solid blocs of members with common positions. Were they successful in this latter task, the Commission and the Council of Ministers would be more likely to take the debates into account when developing and implementing policy. In general, however, progress in the direction of detailed group resolutions in matters of economic policy has been very slow. Only in the Socialist group has there been real progress, and even then only in a few fields such as agriculture and antitrust policy. Success, even when measured in terms of the ability to speak as a unit in debate at all, regardless of the content of the resolution or statement (and most have been very vague), has been less than spectacular. A rough tally of group resolutions between January 1963 and January 1965 yielded the following figures.

Table III

Frequency of Group Statements, by Type of Issue

Issue	Socialist	Christian-Democrat	Liberal
Social	100	75	25
Operation of Community Institutions	81	37	43
Economic Questions	80	47	41
External Relations	75	83	41
British Membership	100	100	50

But the legislators have become accustomed to working in a transnational context where they try to hammer out supranational party policy positions on the basis of mutual compromise. According to Yondorf:

The emergence of political groups changed the character of the Assembly from an assemblage of national delegations into an integrated European parliament. In the process, national dividing lines were blurred—although not eliminated—and increasingly replaced by an image of the welfare of the Community as a whole. This view of the whole has encouraged the party groups to develop an ever more coherent approach to the problems of integration.[23]

It would thus appear that with regard to allocation, the European Parliament has made its greatest progress in the area of the "lyrical function"—that is, the exercise of indirect influence by forcing holders of actual power to pay attention to what it says. But the "lyrical function" assumes something more than convincing the power holder to meet with you or to entertain your questions. It assumes that the general public or specialized publics are paying attention to the confrontation that ensues. One of the major findings about public opinion in these countries is that while there are large majorities in each country favorable to European integration, relatively few people have

[23] Yondorf, *op. cit.*, Chap. VI, p. 34.

much information about it.[24] Furthermore, even fewer pay much attention to the activities of the various institutions, and the fewest appear to be familiar with the Parliament among all the European institutions. This lack of attention and information is due partly at least to the very technical nature of most of the issues with which the Community institutions are concerned, and partly to the fact that the national systems still have a virtual monopoly of the symbolic and dramatic content of politics.

What can the "lyrical function" amount to in this sort of situation? Is there any incentive to listen carefully to an institution with no formal powers and no effective sanctions? Can there be a truly relevant clash of opinions when there is no formal opposition, no political parties to organize the electorate accordingly, and no elections at issue? One key link that might have been developed to overcome some of the above difficulties—namely, that between the European Parliament and the national parliaments, which can influence their respective governments—has been sorely neglected. There is no reason to modify Haas' findings in 1958 that:

In jurisdictional and organizational terms, the outstanding parliamentary artificiality of the Assembly remains its inability to bind the parent legislatures, to administer its own composition, to control its two executives meaningfully, or to coordinate the debates and votes of the national parliaments. . . . In the absence of these powers the Assembly's routine work takes place in a vacuum; the national legislatures remain free to act as they did before; there is no evidence that they defer in any way to the resolutions of their delegates in Strasbourg.[25]

The European Parliamentarians

One of the more troubling developments has been the gradually widening gap between the European Parliament and the national parliaments. Members of the European Parliament must devote so much time to their committee work and to the numerous plenary sessions that they are in danger of losing influence in their national parliaments. It is indeed ironic that the harder they have worked to control—that is, the more they have acted like legislators—the more they are in danger of losing their effectiveness at home, without any apparent compensa-

[24] See, for example, L'opinion publique et l'europe des six," *Sondages*, no. 1 (1963), pp. 7-13, 42-45.

[25] Ernst B. Haas, *The Uniting of Europe* (Stanford: Stanford University Press, 1958), p. 413.

tion of an accrued role with respect to the emerging supranational system. Activities that conduce to building up the "lyrical function" as well as other allocative roles are not necessarily conducive to making that role relevant. It may be that the heavy work load assumed by European Parliament members and the specialization in European affairs that this involves is dysfunctional in the long run. It has not markedly increased its impact on Community allocations and it could hasten isolation. Perhaps there should be only a few career "European" legislators in each national party's delegation, with the remainder serving shorter periods and then returning to the national parliaments, thus presumably helping to transmit to the national systems the effects of European Parliament participation on attitudes, expectations, and symbols.

There is also some evidence that these men are often looked upon with a certain amount of suspicion by their colleagues and by their constituents at home, being suspected of having "lost touch with reality." It may become harder and harder to get ambitious and able men to serve in the European Parliament if these trends continue. Even today one is frequently told by national MPs, perhaps spuriously, that the European Parliament is made up largely of second-raters who have no ambition to shape events and who look upon the European Parliament as a pleasant, well paid sinecure. The degree of consensus they achieve has been possible precisely because nobody is paying any attention at home, and has more to do with the pleasures of sociability in Strasbourg than with a real rapprochement of national views.

Yet we can hardly chastize too severely the European Parliament and its members for failing to work to coordinate the efforts of national legislatures to control or oversee the European integration activities of their respective governments, for only two of the six legislatures (Netherlands and Germany) have themselves made any real effort to do so at the national level. And the German *Bundestag* alone has actually tried to directly influence in advance the decisions taken by its ministers in the Council of Ministers.[26] Nevertheless, given the present situation in the Community and the uncertainties about the future, it seems undeniable that if there is to be legislative control of the Community system, it must be based on national parliamentary activity.

[26] For details, see J. M. Houben, *Les Conseils de Ministres des Communautes Europeennes* (Leyden: A. W. Sythoff, 1964). That this should be the case is not in itself surprising, for all legislative bodies, even the United States Congress, find it very difficult indeed to actively attend to all the complexities and technicalities of the kinds of policy matters that are subsumed by the "welfare state," and these are the very stuff of the European Community.

It is thus particularly unfortunate that the European Parliament has not tried to develop further its communication and cooperation with the national parliaments with a view to perhaps developing together new techniques of legislative control or supervision.

Instead, the characteristic response has been to call for an increase in the formal powers of the European Parliament and for direct election of its membership. Such proposals are superficially attractive but are in my view subject to criticism on the grounds that their chief impact would most likely be to further widen the gap between national parliaments and the European Parliament. In the first place, it is highly unlikely that it will be possible for the European Parliament to increase its formal powers, especially in view of the recent crisis in the Community. Nor is there any reason to assume, given the nature and pace of the integration process, that a European Parliament with formal powers could wield them effectively. As Henry Kissinger observes:

The decline in the role of the European national parliaments has been apparent for decades. In no European country—not even Great Britain—does parliament exercise an effective control over the formulation or the conduct of foreign policy. Party discipline has become so pervasive that in European parliaments the majority almost always ratifies the decisions of the cabinet. And where the party system is ineffective either because the parties are weak or because there are too many of them—the result is paralysis of government rather than parliamentary control. These conditions are likely to be magnified by all-European elections. The need to effect a consensus comprising Schleswig-Holstein and Sicily and Scotland and Bavaria will surely tempt demagogic appeals.[27]

Direct election (even if only of a part of the membership) without an increase in formal powers that can be effectively utilized seems ill advised. It might well tend to finalize the divorce between the European Parliament and the national political systems. Europeans are not likely to go to the polls in large numbers to elect European representatives who can only make speeches and not influence events or perform other services. Nor are able and ambitious men likely to stand for such an office.

Thus, European parliamentarians, those who go to Strasbourg and those who serve only in the national capitols, find themselves confronted by several paradoxes that threaten to doom them either to frustration or to possibly self-defeating efforts to increase the formal

[27] Henry Kissinger, *Troubled Partnership: A Re-Appraisal of the Atlantic Alliance* (New York: McGraw-Hill Book Co., 1965), p. 242.

role of the European Parliament. Since they represent six nationalities, come from thirty different political parties, embody diverse political styles, and exhibit widely different expectations of the legislative role, it is not surprising that they should have difficulty coming to grips with the amorphous Community system. Our analysis suggests that there are two related strategies that they might pursue: (1) using the European Parliament as a forum for the coordination of the control activities of national parliaments, and (2) making the "lyrical function" more effective by trying to focus public and elite attention on what goes on in the European Parliament. Both of these strategies would seem to depend on breaking through the general public indifference toward the European integration process, of which we have spoken, and both bring us back to a point made earlier in the essay—namely, that the system is incipient and precarious. Indeed, these are the characteristics of the system that seem to remove it from the grasp of the legislators. This situation seems to indicate that future legislative control depends ultimately upon pushing on with the process of integration,[28] extending the area of common policy-making, and thus changing the attitudes, the expectations, and the focus of attention of more and more people. There is some evidence to support this prescription from experience in the field of agriculture, the one area in which common policy-making has gone relatively far in the direction of a real all-European policy. Here agricultural interest groups have been actively involved, and have changed from a traditionally conservative, nationalist orientation to a strong support for further integration. This has happened as more and more key policy decisions have been taken in the Community system and as a Community administrative system has been set up. Significant strides have thus been taken in the direction of breaking through the indifference of the "consumers" of European agricultural policy—most strikingly with farm leaders, markedly but more gradually with the farmers themselves. Interestingly enough, it has been the agricultural debates of the European Parliament that have drawn the most attention, at least for the specialized public represented by farmers and farm leaders.[29] These debates perhaps came closest to approximating real debate and, contrary to the usual pattern, did not result in a resolution adopted by quasi-unanimity. A farm bloc or "green front" emerged, championing higher agricultural prices and greater guarantees to farmers, and was opposed by a consumers bloc in favor of low food prices and

[28] Or on withdrawing from it and thus restoring national control.

[29] Of the 687 written questions asked in the European Parliament from 1950 through 1964, almost one-fourth (158) concerned agriculture.

reduced subsidies. A "lyrical function" for the Parliament thus was made possible with regard to the common agricultural policy. I wrote in 1963 that:

the energy with which agricultural groups from all countries have sought to influence the Assembly is impressive; in terms of the future, it suggests that the practical effectiveness of that body will vary in relationship to the extent that groups channel their expectations and demands through it.[30]

Thus, control-minded, pro-integration legislators have an incentive to push their governments in the direction of further integration, and to continue to support those institutions in the Community system that contribute the most dynamism to the integrative process. Can they also use the European Parliament in some more direct way to help build up this emergent system—that is, to contribute to what we have called systems-persistence?

V. THE EUROPEAN PARLIAMENT AND SYSTEMS-PERSISTENCE

Since there are practically no studies dealing explicitly with the systems-persistence role of political institutions, the present analysis cannot be set in the context of the existing literature. Instead, the abstract systems analysis model developed by Professor David Easton will be used as an instrument to generate a series of questions to guide us in an exposition and evaluation of the potential contribution the European Parliament might make to systems-persistence. This will be done largely by inference, for Easton says very little about legislatures *per se*. Hence the analysis that follows must be treated as tentative and speculative.

Stresses and Supports in Political Systems

Easton posits that all political systems are subject to a variety of stresses. A major source of such stress is cleavage resulting from intense social diversity. A system can maintain itself in the face of such stress in three general ways that seem relevant to representative legislative institutions: (1) by stimulating *specific support* for the system; (2) by contributing to *structural mechanisms* for reducing diversity; and (3) by creating or stimulating *diffuse support* for the system.[31]

[30] Lindberg, *op. cit.*, p. 259.
[31] Easton, *op. cit.*, Chaps. 16 and 17.

The concept of specific support refers to favorable attitudes and predispositions toward the political system which are stimulated by outputs (decisions) that are perceived by the members of the system to meet their demands. "Structural mechanisms for reducing diversity" refers to institutions and procedures which allow for the expression of ethnic or national diversity, but in a way that effectively moderates the stress of conflict.

Systems may respond by structuring their regime so as to permit maximal expression for cultural variations through a federal type system, rules may be included to depoliticize or denature issues, and norms may encourage overlapping group membership. Through representative structures, broadly conceived, varied and effective avenues may be provided for groups to express and negotiate their differences so that no group feels entirely excluded.[32]

Finally, political systems can respond by stimulating diffuse support, by which is meant:

a reserve of support that enables a system to weather the many storms when outputs cannot be balanced off against inputs of demands. It is a kind of support that a system does not have to buy with more or less direct benefits. . . . Members may get satisfaction, for example, from the promise of the future greatness for their system and even some gratifications from being made to feel an important part of a larger historic process that calls for present restraint on behalf of future benefits.[33]

The European Community would seem to be an especially good example of a system operating within an extremely diverse social environment. This diversity is reflected in national, linguistic, historical, religious, and cultural differences. It follows that anything the European Parliament or any other institution of the Community can do to contribute to the stress-reducing capabilities of this incipient and still precarious system will be of profound importance for the future of the Community.

At the outset we can eliminate the category of specific support from our consideration, for on the basis of our analysis of its allocative role we have concluded that the European Parliament has not contributed much to meeting demands by influencing the decision-output of the European Community system.

[32] *Ibid.*, p. 266.
[33] *Ibid.*, p. 273.

As regards structural mechanisms and diffuse support, we can derive from Easton six general hypotheses about the role a representative institution might play in helping the system reduce stress due to social diversity:

1. Representation can itself reduce conflict by providing an opportunity for diverse interests to meet, discover the nature of their differences, and possibly find some ways to reach compromise agreements.

2. Representative institutions may promote the overlapping of groupings as in coalition-type political parties. These would serve systems-persistence by cutting across cleavage lines, thereby reducing the intensity of stress.

3. Representative institutions may contribute to the development of new norms of conflict resolution incorporating "the ideal that disputes should be conducted in terms such that the participants never forget that they must continue to live together as continuing members of a common political system. . . ." (A Systems Analysis of Political Life, *p. 259.*)

4. Representative institutions might stimulate diffuse support by seeking to instill in their own members and to communicate to the outside a sense of legitimacy for the system's institutions and the actors who run them.

5. Representative institutions might stimulate diffuse support by defining and transmitting in their debates and other activities a concept of a "general interest" or "common good" for the political community as a whole.

6. Representative institutions might stimulate diffuse support by working to arouse or nurture a sense of mutual political identification and by instilling the feeling among their members that they are a part of an interdependent system.

The Extent of Systems-Persistence in the European Parliament

While the European Parliament seems at least relevant to these hypotheses, not much is really known on these dimensions, with the exception of the role of the supranational political groups. The potential contributions which the Parliament might make, however, seem to be substantially vitiated by its isolation and artificiality. It may be true that the mere fact that, through the European Parliament, national parties are represented and associated with the decision-making process may provide at least a minimum of assurance that a number of channels for expression of viewpoints and differences are held open. This may also help legitimize the system that is emerging by easing somewhat the anxieties of many that the emerging system was totally devoid of any democratic accountability—or even visibility—in its decision-making process. The internal processes whereby the political groups hammer out common positions, the various subject-matter committees prepare studies and reports, and the plenary sessions meet to debate the full range of national and international issues might all serve to heighten the sense of mutual awareness and responsiveness among the individuals involved, for as Easton points out:

In system of multiple nationalities, if the relevant members feel that each group recognizes, respects, and is willing to consider seriously the major needs and demands of others, the probability of eliciting support for a common community is increased.[34]

But the conflict-reducing impact of representation cannot be expected to do much to stabilize the system if only those who are already in favor of the system go, if there is relatively little turnover in membership, and if parties representing 25 per cent of the electorate in France and 40 per cent in Italy are systematically excluded.

We have some evidence suggesting that what takes place in the Strasbourg conference hall, the lobbies, the caucus and committee rooms, and the political group offices has contributed to the development of new norms of conflict resolution, to a sense of legitimacy in the institutions (especially the Commissions), to a concept of a Community "general interest," and to a sense of mutual identification. But this effect has been necessarily limited to those who take part and that has been a restricted number. Furthermore, as we saw in the section on the allocative role, relatively little has been done to systematically communicate the results of the European Parliament's interactions back to the parliaments from which these men came. (There well may be an impact that operates through some informal processes, but we have no studies that would confirm it.) The European Parliament, indeed, seems in danger of becoming a "House Without Windows," [35] a group of men absorbedly playing an intricate and exciting secret game with

[34] Easton, *op. cit.*, p. 250.

[35] A nickname given to the French National Assembly during the Fourth Republic. See Constantin Melnik and Nathan Leites, *The House Without Windows* (Evanston: Row, Peterson, & Co., 1958), p. 31.

little regard for its impact or relevance for a generally apathetic outside world.

The one facet of the systems-persistence role of the European Parliament upon which we have a substantial body of research is the development of transnational political parties.[36] As we have seen, its internal operations are controlled by transnational political party organizations to the almost total exclusion of the national delegations. The fact that it has been possible for at least some of the political party groups in the European Parliament, notably the Socialists, to increase over time their internal consensus, both procedural and substantive, is strong evidence of the role of the European Parliament in helping to promote inclusive, coalition-type parties. Though the Liberals and Christian Democrats have been less successful, they continue to make the effort. Even when efforts to achieve party consensus have failed or are attained at a very low level of specificity, the cleavages that remain do not tend to occur on strictly national lines. In 1958 Haas concluded that:

Doctrinal consensus has developed significantly. . . . Largely as a result of the increased opportunities to criticize meaningfully and continuously the activities of a true administrative agency, the Socialist deputies of six nationalities began to function as a supranational political party, showing a consistent record of successful internal compromise, deference to each other's wishes, alternating leadership, and willingness to de-emphasize issues on which a unanimously endorsed doctrine proved unobtainable. . . . The group . . . of Christian-Democratic deputies shows less doctrinal unity but functions smoothly as a general support for any "European" policy. . . . The Liberal group shows no such unity and is rarely cohesive on concrete policy issues. Nevertheless, all three groups have developed into a permanent parliamentary elite conversant with the problems of integration and respected as such in their home legislatures.[37]

It seems clear that this party development has also provided some of the other systems-persistence roles suggested by Easton—for example, the development of new norms of conflict resolution.

The truly vital development is the growth of a code of conduct considered appropriate to supranational legislators: the right to be continually consulted by executive agencies, to put forward programmes not clearly

[36] See especially Haas, *op. cit.*, Chap. 11; P. J. G. Kapteyn, *L'Assemblee Commune de la Communaute Europeenne du Charbon et l'Acier* (Leyden: A. W. Sythoff, 1962).
[37] Haas, "Challenge of Regionalism," *International Organization*, XII (1958), 453.

and previously declared to be national policy, to organize, investigate, and criticize on the basis of opinions and convictions developed as a result of contacts with ideologically kindred but nationally different colleagues. To make such a development possible there has to be an institutional medium in which the appropriate convictions and codes could be developed. . . . One aspect of the code is the habit of intra-party compromising which has been developed by both Socialists and Christian-Democrats into a fine art.[38]

Furthermore, the Socialists and Christian Democratic group secretariats are trying to serve as liaison bureaus between their member national parties in an effort to encourage policy coordination with the goal of establishing the basis of European constituency parties. This is a most important development for it seems to run contrary to the otherwise marked trend toward isolation. If significant lines of communication and transaction are opened up between the political groups and party organization and party membership at the national level, it could be of vast significance for the persistence of the European Community system. We have substantial reasons for thinking that political parties play crucial roles in integrating political communities. For example, in his perceptive comparative study of federalism, William Riker found that the one variable which was consistently related to the degree of centralization or peripheralization of a federal system, and the one institutional condition that determined the success of the "federal bargain," was the nature and structure of the party system prevailing at the two levels of the system.

The federal relationship is centralized according to the degree to which the parties organized to operate the central government control the parties organized to operate the constituent governments. This amounts to the assertion that the proximate cause of variations in the degree of centralization (or peripheralization) in the constitutional structure of a federalism is the variation in degree of party centralization.

The exact nature of this causal connection can best be examined by asking how to measure the federal relationship according to partisan variation. . . . There are . . . two kinds of relationships between parties at the two levels: 1) the degree to which one party controls both levels of government; and 2) the degree to which each potential governing party at the national level controls the partisan associates at the level of constituent governments.[39]

[38] Haas, *op. cit.*, p. 438.

[39] William H. Riker, *Federalism: Origin, Operation, Significance* (Boston: Little, Brown, & Co., 1964), pp. 129, 131.

The evolving relationship between political groups in the European Parliament and political parties at the national level seems to stand at the extreme of peripheralization according to the above criteria, but this situation may well change if and as the European integration process continues. It is at any rate a particularly relevant dimension both for political actors, who would shape the future of the European Community system, and for scholars who would chart its dynamics.

VI. CONCLUSION

It has not been my purpose in this paper to criticize the members of the European Parliament or to suggest that it has played no important role in European integration. It has been, rather, to suggest that under the present circumstances a shift of emphasis may be called for. It does not seem that the optimistic expectations that a federal United States of Europe was on the near horizon will be realized. Not only are present accomplishments still precarious and the future obscured, but it has become more and more clear that much remains to be done before a real "community" of common purpose and identification is achieved. The ability of the European Parliament to contribute to such a "community" and its ability to further parliamentary control and oversight of the integration process are closely intertwined and will in my view be measured in terms of its achievement as a transmission belt between an emerging European system and the still dominant national systems.

Suggestions for Further Reading

Easton, David, *A Framework for Political Analysis* (Englewood Cliffs, N.J.: Prentice-Hall, Inc., 1965).

__________, *A Systems Analysis of Political Life* (New York: John Wiley & Sons, Inc., 1965).

Forsyth, Murray, *The Parliament of the European Communities* (London: Political and Economic Planning [PEP], XXV: 478 [March 9, 1964]).

Grosser, Alfred, "The Evolution of European Parliaments," *Daedalus* (Winter 1964).

Haas, Ernst B., *The Uniting of Europe: Political, Social, and Economic Forces, 1950-1957* (Stanford: Stanford University Press, 1958).

Houben, P. H. J. M., *Les Conseils de Ministres des Communautes Europeennes* (Leyden: A. W. Sythoff, 1964).

Lindberg, Leon N., "Integration as a Source of Stress on the European Community System," *International Organization,* XX (1966), 2.

———, *Political Dynamics of European Economic Integration* (Stanford: Stanford University Press, 1963).
Lindsay, Kenneth, *European Assemblies* (London: Stevens, 1960).
Stein, Eric, "The European Parliamentary Assembly: Techniques of Emerging Political Control," *International Organization,* XIII (1959), 233-54.

THE GENERAL ASSEMBLY OF THE UNITED NATIONS

Battleground of Interests

Charles O. Lerche

Were the United Nations a world government, the General Assembly would be its legislative arm. Analogically, as the body in which all members are represented and in which decisions are made on the broadest possible basis of participation, the General Assembly bears a striking resemblance to the House of Representatives in the United States or, perhaps more accurately, to the House of Commons in Great Britain. The impression of "legislativeness" is heightened by the practice of registering decisions by roll-call votes, culminating a process replete with much of the other paraphernalia of legislative proceedings.

Yet we must constantly remind ourselves of a basic fact: the United Nations is not a world government, and the General Assembly—for all its external similarities to national deliberative bodies—is not a true legislature. It is an extremely interesting and important body with a continuing role to play both within the workings of the United Nations itself and within the broader context of world politics. But it must be considered in its own terms, as a unique manifestation of international relations, rather than in any comparative study of legislative processes.

In one important way, however, the General Assembly does fit into the general legislative pattern. Like any collegial body that incorporates,

---

CHARLES O. LERCHE *was Dean of the School of International Service at The American University. He was a frequent contributor to professional and scholarly journals. His books included* The Uncertain South, The Cold War . . . and After, America in World Affairs, *and* Concepts of International Politics (*co-author*).

however imperfectly, the principle of constituency representation, the General Assembly has been from its birth a battleground of conflicting interests. Political cross currents have racked it for two decades. At times it has been effectively stalemated; at others it has been a powerful instrument of action. If, as is often argued, the lower house of a more or less equitably apportioned legislature in a democracy reflects fairly accurately the state of politics at any moment, then the same general point can be made about the General Assembly.

It is this proposition which constitutes the basic hypothesis on which this discussion is grounded. We argue here that the General Assembly can best be appreciated as the international system in microcosm, and that the broad trends in the evolution of world politics since 1945 can be found in the operations of the United Nations and especially in its largest organ. On this basis we will be in a position to hazard some judgments about the future place of the General Assembly both within the United Nations and on the world scene in general.

I. THE CHANGING ROLE OF THE GENERAL ASSEMBLY

We should, however, begin with theory. The General Assembly, as the direct descendant of the Assembly of the League of Nations, borrowed its organizational principles and its original dynamic from the parent body. Both assemblies, furthermore, owe their place in their respective bodies to nineteenth-century experience; the "conference" of all members to decide general policy and handle fiscal and administrative matters was a standard feature of the public international unions that played so large a role in the nonpolitical sphere of international relations a century ago and, for that matter, do so today.

But the experiences of the First World War and the influence of Woodrow Wilson added a new dimension to the League Assembly, and this idea was also carried over in the Charter of the United Nations. The Wilsonians conceived of the Assembly of the League as being truly representative not of *governments* but of *Peoples*. Essential to the Wilsonian idea of "public diplomacy" was the deliberate introduction of mass opinion—what a more sophisticated age calls "consensus"—into the decision-making process on international issues. Although the entire League structure was supposed to be responsive to the wishes of peace-loving men everywhere, it was in the Assembly, where every national group was to be represented, that the moral judgments of the citizenry were to find their clearest expression.

The General Assembly was built on the same principle. Universality of membership, equality of voting power, and the grant of a broad scope of competence by the Charter clearly identified the Assembly as the one spot in the entire United Nations structure where public opinion, formulated through national channels, was to have full opportunity to be expressed. The entire range of economic and social activity to be carried on by the United Nations was placed under General Assembly supervision. The framers of the Charter attempted to extend the old Wilsonian concept into the new body. In this effort they were aided by the obvious fact that the United States in 1945, far from being the reluctant and eventually negative outsider of 1919, was ready and anxious to play a leading part.

But the men of Dumbarton Oaks, Yalta, and San Francisco had learned a hard lesson from the experiences of the League years. The Council and Assembly of the League had been established as coequals with neatly overlapping spheres of competence, especially in political-security problems. Given the conditions of the inter-war era, it speedily became apparent that the mechanisms for registering national opinion on highly emotional questions were so effective that creating a supranational synthesis of opinion for League action was impossible. A universal assembly, particularly one with a *liberum veto,* was not a workable instrument for enforcement of peace and restraint of aggression. The ignominy of the Ethiopian and Spanish cases proved that point beyond cavil.

Therefore, "realism" prevailed at San Francisco. Although the General Assembly was authorized to discuss any question within the scope of the Charter, it was forbidden to deal with any matter of political or security import that was on the agenda of the Security Council. Thus, the maintenance of peace in actual operational situations was to be the monopoly of the Security Council, the much smaller body on which only the Great Powers were to hold permanent seats and in which they alone were protected by the veto. A second inhibition on General Assembly action was more subtle: Assembly resolutions could take only the form of recommendations to members, while the Security Council was given the authority—under certain circumstances—to reach decisions binding on all members.

The "Town Meeting" of the World

The General Assembly was thus differentiated from the Security Council in a distinctly pejorative way. The "town meeting of the world" was free to discuss almost any subject under the sun—except important political problems of war and peace. Its conclusions, furthermore, were not even in a technical sense to be binding upon its membership. The Assembly was left free to debate, to exhort, and to pass resolutions expressing the sense of the body, but it did not (and does not today) have even a shadow of formal coercive authority.

It can be argued, of course, that in a body primarily designed to generate and express a supranational consensus of individual opinions a grant of coercive power was not only unnecessary but perhaps dangerous. World public opinion is its own sanction; the strength of consensus is not in the armies it can mobilize, but rather in the moral choice it forces and the isolation it imposes on those who defy it. The UNESCO Charter contends that wars begin in the minds of men; the General Assembly was founded on the principle that wars are finally won only in the minds of men and it is bound to attempt to win its victories only on such battlefields.

In any case, this has been the framework within which the General Assembly has been obliged to proceed. Lacking Charter authority to make basic political-security decisions, it has been limited at any moment to the amount of active consensus it has been able to command. At times this has been considerable, and the role of the General Assembly has bulked large; at other times, however, deep and multiple divisions have made Assembly debate an exercise in futility.

One final point should be made here. In constitutional law and in political logic, the General Assembly is the special province of the small members of the United Nations. With every member represented and casting just one vote, it is in the General Assembly that the principle of "sovereign equality" finds its clearest expression. Counting sovereign heads is the only effective way of reaching decisions in the General Assembly, and in this game the smaller members, since they are so numerous, enjoy a great advantage. The large members, especially the superpowers, have been bemused from the era of the San Francisco Conference itself by the determination of small states to make common cause against them.

The history of the United Nations clearly reveals not only the small-state orientation of the General Assembly but also the effect of General Assembly dominance in the organization. The Security Council, as everyone knows, has labored (at least until very recently) almost impotently under the handicap of deep division among the permanent members. The General Assembly, led at first by the United States but subsequently by active and self-assertive small-state spokesmen, has instead played the controlling role in almost all United Nations activity on behalf of international peace and security. Opinions can and do differ about the wisdom or the effectiveness of United Nations peacekeeping efforts under the aegis of the General Assembly, but no one can challenge the fact that by and large they have borne the marks of small-state policy and distinct anti-Great Power bias.

Should recent developments prove to be harbingers of a trend toward the restoration of the Security Council to its original eminence, the role of the General Assembly might contract, at least in the political field. But it would nevertheless remain primarily the instrument for expression of whatever small-state consensus might exist. Under such circumstances the General Assembly might find new areas in which to exert itself, but fifteen years of freedom from Great Power control have definitely left important and probably permanent imprints.

II. THE GENERAL ASSEMBLY AND THE COLD WAR

What the evolution of the General Assembly might have been had there been no cold war is a fascinating speculation. Had the Great Powers carried their wartime unity over into policing the postwar world and had the General Assembly been given the opportunity to develop according to its Wilsonian image as the voice of the people of the world—disinterested, peaceful, moral—certainly the history of the United Nations would have been different. But the General Assembly was never permitted to focus primarily on issues of other than immediate political significance. It was from the outset caught up in the political struggles of the cold war.

The framers of the Charter—and, indeed, all serious students of international affairs—agreed that any general international organization was not an effective instrument for prosecution or control of Great Power conflicts. Collective enforcement of peace was most efficaciously undertaken on the basis of Great Power consensus implemented through whatever institutional mechanisms were at hand. Thus, as everyone realizes, the veto: if the Security Council, as the enforcement arm of the United Nations, could not muster Great Power unanimity, it was better for everyone that it remain impotent rather than tear itself apart in a struggle among its key members. This is to say that the irrelevance of the Security Council in the Soviet-American struggle was intentional and even desirable rather than a measure of weakness and failure of the United Nations mechanism.

What was true of the Security Council was in theory doubly true of the General Assembly. Insulated by Charter provisions from short-term political crises and peculiarly subject to small-state influence, the General Assembly, one would suppose, should have been permitted to remain outside the tight orbit of Soviet-American vituperation and conflict. But this, unfortunately, was not to be. The General Assembly, as well as virtually all the rest of the United Nations system, was put intensively through its cold war paces during the first decade of its existence.

Responsibility for bringing the cold war to the General Assembly must be shared by the two major protagonists, but the United States must bear the lion's share. In 1945 and 1946 Americans were so certain that their conflict with the Soviet Union was "total" and absolute that it was literally unthinkable that any arena of East-West contact was to be considered immune to the prosecution of the cold war. If the Soviet-American conflict gambled for such high stakes and if the United Nations were the key element in American foreign policy—as postwar rhetoric often insisted—then it was no more than just for the battle to be carried to the floor of the General Assembly, particularly since the United States was so neatly stopped in the Security Council.

We must recall that there were victories (of a sort) to be won in General Assembly debates in those early days. Under the grip of a strict bipolar construct of the cold war, according to which everyone who was not for the United States was against it, Washington was able to force a sizeable number of issues to roll calls in which the communist side received no more than six to nine votes. That these roll-call votes were only occasionally followed up by any sort of concrete action was viewed in Washington as regrettable but essentially irrelevant. What really counted was the repeated establishment of the point that communist policy commanded the support of only a very small number of states and therefore was immoral and illegal.

Between 1946 and the beginning of the Korean War, the General Assembly thus found itself maneuvered into being not only a battleground but also an instrument of the cold war. By and large, all the advantages of this early period lay with the United States. Washington had the votes: its control over the Latin Americans, the Western Europeans, the free Asians, and the other noncommunist members made it quite certain that Moscow would always be caught in a hopeless minority position. Although these votes were primarily prestige victories with no realistic political consequences, they at least made it possible for the United States to invoke the sacred principles of majority rule and to portray the Soviet bloc as obstinately obstructing the unified will of the rest of mankind. This dogmatic classification sufficed to control the General Assembly until the Korean War brought about the first major changes in the status of the Assembly and forced the surfacing of hidden cleavages.

American policy makers were delighted with the way the United Nations functioned in the early weeks of the Korean War. Thanks to the absence of the Soviet delegate, the Security Council proved to be an amenable and responsive instrument, and resistence to communist aggression in Korea was quickly transformed into a collective enterprise in the name of the United Nations. The United States did not deceive itself; for all its brave words about "collective security" and "police actions," the Korean War was a cold war operation of the United States with the United Nations functioning at its side.

Of course, the euphoria was short-lived. The Soviet delegate quickly returned to the Security Council and resumed his routine of successful obstructions. The best laid plans of the United States seemed to be about to go for naught; the Korean War could be continued under existing Security Council directives, but there was no way to bring it to a successful conclusion or to extract political advantage from it so long as Soviet obstinacy could tie the Security Council's hands.

Uniting for Peace Resolutions

It was at this juncture that the United States engineered what was honestly conceived as a major coup: the "Acheson Plan" that led to the Uniting for Peace Resolutions in 1950. This arrangement put the General Assembly into the middle of the political-security picture, for a time gave the United Nations a distinct and effective cold war role, and seemed almost as if it provided the route around the veto for which the United States had been seeking for so long.

Uniting for Peace provided that the General Assembly could assume jurisdiction—when necessary and upon a strictly emergency basis—in a political-security question on which the Security Council was deadlocked by a veto or other procedural block. This major change in the scope of the General Assembly's competence was brought about not by amendment to the Charter, but simply by a change in the Assembly's own rules for procedure. The letter of the Charter was scrupulously preserved in the sense that the Assembly, no matter how binding the language in which it phrased its resolutions, was still legally confined to make *recommendations* only, rather than empowered to issue *directives.*

It goes without saying that the Soviet Union objected strenuously to the passage of the Acheson proposals; Moscow argued that the fundamental theory of the United Nations had been drastically (and illegally) modified and that so long as a question remained on the agenda of the Security Council, the General Assembly had no right to consider it. The

Soviet's fears were well taken: the veto protected communist interests in the Security Council, but there was no such guarantee in the General Assembly. To give the Assembly an action dimension in the cold war was to add a sometimes effective weapon to the American arsenal.

But, as was indicated above, the United States had the votes in 1950. The Acheson plan passed by a vote of 52 to 5, with only two abstentions, and the subsequent direction of the Korean War passed into the hands of the veto-free General Assembly.

Again, we must distinguish between American rhetoric and American political reality. There was much official self-congratulation at the fact that the majority of peace loving states had been given the controlling voice and a way around the veto had been found. In reality, however, what pleased the United States was the fact that the only organ of the entire United Nations system that seemed to have any action competence in 1950 had been brought effectively under American control. Washington now had the ability to produce a virtually automatic majority on any question, and also to generate the two-thirds majority necessary to sanction Assembly action in "important" matters—obviously including cold war questions. For a few weeks it seemed as if the fundamental problems of the General Assembly (and, indeed, of the United Nations) in a cold war environment had been solved to the satisfaction of the American people.

It was during General Assembly discussion of the Korean problem, however, that the initial invalidation of this assumption took place with the formal secession of India and some of its associates from the ranks of the "free world" and the creation of a "neutral" or at least "non-aligned" stance on cold war issues. This was a major contretemps: India took away enough votes from the United States-led coalition to make the automatic two-thirds majority no longer seem solid and predictable. The United States found itself in the unprecedented position of no longer being able to call for a vote in full confidence that overwhelming majority approval of the American position would be forthcoming. Instead, Washington found it necessary for the first time to engage—however tentatively—in the parliamentary game of coalition-building on a *quid pro quo* basis, to logroll, and to look with great care to its support.

Even so, by the time the Korean affair had run its course, neutralist secessions had so far diluted the once automatic two-thirds majority in support of any American position that Washington could be certain only of enough votes to beat back neutralist proposals of which it disapproved. On one occasion, an Indian-sponsored resolution on prisoner repatriation was defeated by the United States with only the Latin American bloc,

China, and the Philippines in support. The American press hailed this as a "victory," but it was rather a grim harbinger of the future.

The end of the Korean episode thus found the United States more or less disillusioned with the same General Assembly for which it had had such high hopes, while the Soviet Union—grown cynically experienced in its hopeless minority position—found considerable amusement in the way the United States from time to time contemplated the Frankenstein monster it had gone so far to create. The American attempt to use the General Assembly as an arena of Great Power conflict had come to grief almost at its very outset, and the forces of neutralism—still unable to dominate the Assembly—had at least brought both major powers to something of a standstill.

Membership and Expansion of the General Assembly

Great Power concern with the General Assembly for the next few years centered around questions of membership. The original membership of the United Nations was basically Western-oriented, and even the new neutral bloc led by India was prone to cast at least its disagreements in terms familiar to Western ears. But outside the organization, and beginning to demand entry, were other states whose basic commitment to Western (and anticommunist) values was not so certain. An increase in United Nations membership was obviously in the offing, and both Great Powers sought to develop policies on admission that reflected their controlling preoccupation.

The Soviet Union generally favored any admission that would further dilute the American-led majority—that is, either a communist or a nonaligned state. The United States, naturally enough, was primarily concerned with holding its already none too secure position, and attempted to confine admission only to those states that could be counted on to support American cold war policy. The result was predictable: admissions up to 1955 were few and relatively unimportant, while outside the gates the lines of those awaiting entry grew steadily longer.

It was the dissolution of colonial empires and the creation of dozens of new states that dissolved the impasse. Washington and Moscow finally came to the obvious conclusion that arrangements for admission would have to be made and that they could come about only on the basis of a package deal. According to the strict logic of bipolarity, any such arrangement would profit the communists relatively more than the West and should therefore be avoided by the United States. By 1955, however, there had been a marked retrogression from bipolar thinking in the United

States—this was, after all, the year of the Geneva summit conference—and little confidence was felt any more in the prospect of making the United Nations General Assembly an effective anti-Soviet weapon.

As a result, the 1955 package deal on admissions was arranged, and the great evolutionary change in both the composition and the dynamics of the General Assembly was launched. Sixteen new members were admitted in one group. Four (Ireland, Italy, Portugal, and Spain) were pro-Western; four (Albania, Bulgaria, Hungary, and Rumania) were in the Soviet bloc; eight (Austria, Cambodia, Ceylon, Finland, Jordan, Laos, Libya, and Nepal) were either formally or effectively uncommitted. The logjam was broken: from 1955 onward, expansion of membership was steady as the contemporary General Assembly was created piece by piece.

For the next decade, admission of a new state to the United Nations was all but automatically consummated immediately after it assumed the trappings of sovereignty from the former colonial power. So far had the Great Powers moved from their earlier positions of exclusion that more members were added between 1955 and 1964 than had originally signed the Charter in 1945. Both the United States and the Soviet Union competed in welcoming new members and in extending to them the fullest courtesies of the organization.

The Soviet position was easier to understand. Almost without exception the new members were explicitly (often stridently) nonaligned in the cold war. Moscow had long ago concluded that its only chance of escape from a hopeless position of absolute numerical inferiority lay in winning a sizeable slice of the nonaligned world to its side. The Soviet Union therefore welcomed all new nonaligned members as potential recruits or, at the very least, as nonadditions to the American-led bloc.

The United States adopted its pro-new-member position for somewhat broader and more complex reasons. By 1955 its control of the General Assembly had vanished forever: Washington could never again count on a two-thirds vote on command. But the larger pattern of world politics was asserting itself in the General Assembly and, indeed, in the whole United Nations system. Nonalignment was a major fact of political life by the late 1950s; bipolarity became an empty concept as the third world became a significant participant in international politics. A successful foreign policy for the United States demanded that nonalignment be met squarely.

To put the matter in cold war terms, Washington reasoned that if the Soviet-American struggle did in fact come down to a competition for the support and favor of the nonaligned world, the United States had certain advantages in such a competition and was well equipped to emerge victorious. Let the Soviet Union court the neutrals all it wished; in the final analysis, the United States had both more to give and better terms of cooperation.

The era of rapid expansion ended in 1964, not because of any Great Power change on admissions policy, but simply because the world had all but run out of candidates for admission. Only a handful of divided victims of the cold war—such as Germany, Korea, and Vietnam—and the few remaining colonial territories had not yet won admission. The change that the decade of admissions had brought about in the United Nations can be best seen in a simple statistical comparison of the General Assembly before and after: in 1945, of a total membership of fifty-one, thirteen states could be classified as "non-Western"; in 1965, of 114 members, no less than sixty-one were "non-Western." The General Assembly of today is a significantly different political entity from what it was twenty years ago.

III. BIG AND SMALL STATES: SHIFT OF POWER AND VOTES

In a loose and imprecise way, what has happened to the General Assembly since 1955 may be compared to the transformation undergone by a number of the state legislatures in the United States after reapportionment on the "one man, one vote" principle. The Great Powers and their respective entourages, the principal beneficiaries of the existing order of things, had controlled the General Assembly up to 1955—or at least had been rather effective in preventing the Assembly from responding to any other than traditional political concerns. Once the logjam of admissions was broken, however, and once the dozens of new states began to make their appearance in the Assembly, the effective dynamic of the organization became more reflective of the new members and less an echo of the political preoccupations of the erstwhile Establishment.

Of course, the analogy with domestic reapportionment breaks down sharply in terms of the interests represented. Historically, in the United States it has been the rural areas that have held a disproportionately large share of legislative power as contrasted with the under-represented urban areas. Reapportionment has therefore led to a more sympathetic hearing for the issues of particular concern to what one might call the "developed" areas of America. In the United Nations, however, the reverse is true. The United Nations was cast in a distinctly Western mold and was so constructed as to be more effective in dealing with the concerns of the Western state system. The vast majority of the new members, however, have not only been underdeveloped (at least in comparison with most of the original signatories of the Charter) but have also assumed general positions on many issues basically opposed to Western values. Thus, the General Assembly's equivalent of reapportionment has led to a greater voice for the world's rural areas.

What have been the more apparent consequences of this great shift of power and votes in the General Assembly? There are many, and here we will be able to discuss only several of the more important ones.

Consensus-building Bloc Politics

Probably the most obvious—and yet perhaps the most significant—change in the operative dynamics of the Assembly in the past decade has been the great increase in the number of free-moving participants in the consideration of questions. A Great Power-dominated world (and a Great Power-dominated General Assembly as well) would be marked by the limitation of effective participation in problems to the smallest practical number of states, all of them functioning under Great Power leadership. The "new" General Assembly no longer meets this criterion; on any issue, other than those of the most minor importance, large numbers of states will participate, most of them as fairly independent factors. This is to say not only that the raw number of participants in General Assembly decisions has increased—a crude quantitative factor easily verifiable from the total number of votes cast on roll calls—but also that the number of *relevant* participants has likewise increased. To put it simply, a larger proportion of the total membership is significant today than ever before in the history of general international organization.

This has led to the development of another analogy with a Western legislature: the appearance of consensus-building bloc politics as the norm of decision in the Assembly. "Bloc politics" can be used as a shorthand phrase, but only with caution. Except for a few clusters of states that hang closely together, true blocs are difficult to isolate in the contemporary General Assembly. Instead, the student finds a situation reminiscent of the case with the House of Representatives of the United States Congress, in which there are what might be called "single-issue blocs" that hold together only for the voting of a specific issue and that re-form on a different basis around other leaders on other questions. Thus a given small state may vote on one question as an African state, on another as a Commonwealth member, on still another as a nonaligned power, and on a fourth as an economically underdeveloped state.

Widespread effective participation and freewheeling voting by nonaligned states have placed a heavy burden on those states that aspire to leadership in the Assembly. Building an effective majority (of two-thirds) has often required that the United States, for example, go to infinite pains to win votes to its side, almost one government at a time, with each one demanding something in the way of a consideration. This is not to minimize the ability of the United States to obtain the necessary majority; generally, whenever Washington has felt it worth the effort to construct an effective majority, it has been able to do so. In part this has been because the kind of political lobbying intrinsic to constructing a consensus is native to American political genius, in part because the United States remains (for financial reasons if for no other, and there are many others) the most significant and powerful single member of the United Nations, and in part because the United States has used considerable discretion in forcing issues to a vote. But even so, on a limited number of issues (of which the admission of mainland China is the best known) the United States has lost bit by bit its ability to control the decisions of the General Assembly, and the outcome of a vote now depends on the freely cast votes of dozens of small states.

New Issues on the Agenda

Another consequence of the change in the character of the General Assembly has been the change in the major items on the agenda of discussion. During the first decade of its history, the General Assembly dealt primarily with questions familiar to classical international politics, questions that grouped themselves under such standardized headings as security and well-being. The mass influx of new members—the bulk of whom, we will recall, are non-Western and therefore more or less out of sympathy with Western political concerns—has led to the rise of a family of new issues, issues new to international politics but also issues that the established states of the Western political system would prefer never to raise. For ten years the new General Assembly has been talking about (and voting on) questions with no lengthy history but of great contemporary and future significance.

Probably the best known of these new issues are anticolonialism and economic development, although of course each shows a multiplicity of forms. The General Assembly's central concern with anticolonialism, since the breakup of empires in Africa triggered the rash of new African states, symbolizes perhaps most clearly the change that has occurred in the United Nations since 1955. From the point of view of an established power like the United States or any of its major NATO allies, General Assembly discussion and passage of resolutions condemning imperialism cannot help but seem rather digressive. For the United States the major issue of the age is still the threat of communism, and Washington has not yet been completely successful in incorporating any anticolonialist hypothesis into its cold war posture. On the contrary, experience seems to indicate that the Assembly's excessive concern with the dangers of neocolonialism tend to play directly into Soviet hands. Communist propaganda is able to disport itself freely with anticolonialist clichés, while the United States has found itself openly embarrassed by the problem.

While the Soviet Union has attempted to use the anticolonialist syndrome of much of the General Assembly as an instrument for the creation of a pro-Moscow voting majority, the same cannot be said for the issue of economic development. Here the Soviet Union and the United States—along with the other economically developed states of Europe and Anglo-America—have found themselves willy-nilly on the same side, arrayed against the packed ranks of the economically unfortunate. "Economic development" is a phrase with many meanings, but within the context of contemporary General Assembly politics, it signifies the determination of the bulk of the non-Western members to obtain unconditional assistance from the developed states until one by one they reach the point of "takeoff."

It has been in the General Assembly and its subsidiary bodies that the issue of economic development—the confrontation between the rich and the poor, the West and the non-West, the North and the South—has received its most explicit formulation. Indeed, no issue more sharply illustrates the metamorphosis through which international poltics has passed as a result of the increase in the cast of characters. When the United States launched the concept of development assistance with President Truman's 1949 Point IV program, it was clear that the extension of economic aid of any sort was an act of grace by the donor and that the scope, duration, and nature of each program was clearly to be kept under its control. By 1963, when the United Nations Conference on Trade and Development (UNCTAD) convened in Geneva, all the underdeveloped states of the world were in agreement that development assistance was an obligation owed them by the rich societies simply because they are rich, and that bascially it is the recipient countries who should have the deciding voice in determining the content and nature of the aid programs. The developed states divided sharply in response to this position, with some agreeing and others merely shaking their heads in confusion and disbelief.

Not only do the new members of the United Nations insist on development assistance, but they further demand that it be extended free of any political considerations ("strings") and that preferably it be funneled through United Nations institutions. Here, since in economic and social matters the General Assembly's voting system prevails, the emerging and nonaligned world could control the way in which Western-sponsored development funds and programs would be expended and carried out. On this point the major donor nations—the United States and the Soviet Union—have proved adamant, and only a tiny fraction of the aid funds from either of them do go through United Nations channels.

What these new issues—and many others could be cited—really signify in terms of the development of the General Assembly as a more or less legislative body may be briefly stated: in an historic era in which the traditional index of national power—military strength—has been sharply downgraded by technological stalemate, and in an organization in which consensus is the only effective instrument of action, those states that have been simultaneously the molders and the beneficiaries of contemporary consensus have placed their impress on the General Assembly. In any international body founded on the principle of sovereign equality and one state, one vote, there is a natural tendency for the largest group to cluster and to wield consolidated power. This can only be the small states who are the playthings of the Great Powers in noninstitutionalized international politics, but who become the master of the scene in organizations because of their voting power.

The Forum of Small States

So we may postulate that in the General Assembly from the very beginning there has been a drift toward dominance by a coalition of small states (a trend clearly identifiable in the history of the League of Nations as well). We have seen how the exclusionary policies of the Great Powers on questions of membership slowed—but did not interrupt—this process up to 1955, and how the next decade unleashed the dynamic in full force. It happened, however, that the bulk of the new members were, in addition to being small, also non-Western, anticolonialist, and underdeveloped. This distinct variation was thus added to the distinct anti-Great Power bias one finds in any large international organization.

This distinction may be put in perhaps overprecise terms. Great Powers look upon international organizations—particularly upon bodies like the General Assembly—as only a part of their overall box of policy tools, and a rather limited and specialized part at that. From the viewpoint of a Great Power, a large international assembly offers little opportunity for affirmative action and is therefore better suited for protecting interests than for promoting new ones. Smaller states, however, have fewer alternatives. Since their major concerns tend to lie in the direction of inhibiting and limiting Great Powers' freedom of action as necessary preliminaries to making positive decisions of their own, small states tend to place greater stock in Assembly procedures, resolutions, and votes.

Dag Hammarskjöld put the point with great delicacy in 1960 in reply to Soviet attacks on his role in the Congo operations:

> *It is not the Soviet Union, or, indeed, any other great powers who need the United Nations for their protection;* it is all the others. *In this sense the organization is first of all* their *organization, and I deeply believe in the wisdom with which they will be able to use it and guide it.*[1]

In an era when the General Assembly was the dominant element of the entire United Nations structure, when the Secretary-General referred to "the United Nations" he was, in fact, referring to the Assembly; when he spoke of "all the others," he was really speaking of the small-state coalition in the Assembly for which Mr. Hammarskjöld was so efficient an instrument.

Indeed, no organizational issue more clearly symbolizes the Great Power-small state cleavage in the General Assembly than the evolution of the office of the Secretary-General. It is a very complicated story, as well as an extremely interesting one, but it can only be briefly summarized here.

In general, the Great Powers looked upon the office of Secretary General as fundamentally a technical one: more than a "chief clerkship," but still one with little political significance. The Charter of the United Nations had given the Secretary-General considerably more independence of decision than his League predecessor had ever enjoyed, but nevertheless his political role was undefined. The Great Powers preferred that it be kept that way; whatever political initiatives were made in the United Nations they intended to make themselves.

Thus it was that the first Secretary-General repeatedly found himself involved in Great Power controversies during the first decade, for this was the stuff of General Assembly discussion. It was not until the watershed year of 1955 that the office began to change character, and not really until the Congo crisis in 1960 that it reached fruition. This is to say that the role of the Secretary-General was clearly a function of the change in the composition of the General Assembly.

[1] For the full text of the late Secretary-General's reply to personal attacks made by former Premier Khrushchev see *The New York Times,* October 4, 1960.

Between the Suez crisis of 1956 and the Congo affair that began in 1960, the evolving small-state bloc in the Assembly seized upon and was seized by Dag Hammarskjöld in what was obviously mutual fulfilment. The latter years of the 1950s saw the clear creation, expression, and application of a "United Nations presence" in one major political-security question after another. In all of these, the crucial element was the bloc of between twenty and forty small states in the General Assembly that clearly inspired the Secretary-General to take the many initiatives he did and upon which he relied heavily for support.

Mr. Hammarskjöld quickly became an eloquent spokesman for the non-West on issues of anticolonialism and development, but he also led the fight for a steadily increasing role for the General Assembly on such questions as arms control. Here was a clear case of a more or less official sanction of the small states' interest in hobbling the Great Powers. On any matter that touches the symbolism of sovereignty and military power so intimately as arms control, enough major powers naturally want to keep control of events substantially in their own hands. They especially do not wish to allow small states with a military significance near zero to have anything to say about arms control and limitation. But ever since the mid-1950s, the General Assembly has insisted that it is the body which must finally ratify and approve whatever arms control measures may be worked out, and the Eighteen Nation Disarmament Conference in Geneva is a vindication of that position: more small and nonaligned states participate than do major or committed powers.

By 1960, the General Assembly had become the hunting ground of the small states, rather loosely organized under the leadership of the Secretary-General. The small-state bloc had, as suggested above, a dual purpose: first, to restrain and inhibit the cold war powers in as many ways as possible so as to reduce the likelihood of an explosion; second, to advance their own special purposes as effectively as possible. The Great Powers did not welcome this development, especially since their own frustrations led them to give more credence to small-state claims than they otherwise might have done.

The United States, less embarrassed by the new developments than the Soviet Union, has not yet formulated any clear response of its own. The nonaligned bloc has only seldom taken positions clearly contrary to American policy, and the United States has generally been scrupulous not to offend the emerging-nation group. Washington retains much of its former ability to maneuver and build an effective majority on issues of major importance. This is not to say that the United States has not been annoyed and on occasion resentful of the behavior of the nonaligned group; accusations of "irresponsibility" and "selfishness" directed at the neutral leaders have appeared frequently in the American press and obviously reflect official opinion—at least the opinion of some officials. But no concerted American plan for dealing with the anticolonial majority has yet appeared, even though much interest in some scheme of weighted voting has been shown on an unofficial basis.

The "Troika" Proposal of 1960

The most overt Great Power assault on the domination of the General Assembly by the small-state coalition speaking through the Secretary-General was one of the most misunderstood events of recent history: Premier Khrushchev's ill-fated "troika" proposal of 1960. Official and journalistic comment in the United States immediately condemned the Soviet idea as a direct attack upon the integrity of the Secretary-General (which it was) and as a shameless attempt to pander to the anticolonialist prejudices of the small-state majority in the Assembly (which it obviously was not). As such, the United States never gave the troika any serious consideration.

As Americans saw the troika in 1960, its purpose was to dilute the power of the Secretary-General by making his office representative of the three basic points of view in world affairs: the communist, the Western, and the nonaligned. Washington professed great fears that the unsophisticated, inexperienced, and gullible nonaligned states would be seduced by Mr. Khrushchev's wiles and that they would desert Dag Hammarskjöld and flee to the perilous embrace of the Kremlin.

Actually, the troika had no appeal to the nonaligned majority of the Assembly, and they proved the point by remaining steadfast in support of Mr. Hammarskjöld. Mr. Khrushchev was offering them one-third of the Secretary-General, but why should this appeal to them when they already had virtually all of him? True, Mr. Hammarskjöld was a Swede, and therefore a Westerner, but his role was special, as was his country's. In a few months, furthermore, the Assembly was to complete the cycle by selecting U Thant of neutralist Burma as the new Secretary-General, a man who was to make his primary commitment to the interests of the small-state majority crystal clear on many occasions.

It seems incredible that so experienced a statesman as Premier Khrushchev could have so drastically miscalculated a neutralist reaction. Much more logical is quite another explanation for the troika proposal and the attack on Mr. Hammarskjöld. Mr. Khrushchev was not speaking to the nonaligned small powers, according to this thesis; he was speaking to the

United States. The troika was a Great Power attempt to build a Great Power veto into the runaway majorities in the General Assembly—or at least into the abilities of the small states to implement them. By interposing a Soviet (or American) veto upon an operative resolution of the Assembly, Great Power control of a sort could be maintained.

Cursed as he was by the necessity to cloak his arguments in the ineffable rhetoric of communist statecraft, Premier Khrushchev never broke through to the American consciousness. His message, that the day might well come when the United States as well as the Soviet Union would welcome the protection of some sort of veto over General Assembly or Secretary-General action, never won a hearing in Washington. In 1960 it was still impossible for the United States to conceive of a situation in which a Wilsonian consensus of mass international opinion could be at odds with American policy (or vice versa), and Mr. Khrushchev's troika and his vague cautionary exhortations fell on deaf ears. His proposal collapsed, and sporadic Soviet attempts to revive it have been to no avail.

Yet the United States, by the mid-1960s, was forced to accept the possibility—and in the case of admission of Communist China, the probability—of a genuine international consensus hostile to American policy. For two decades the United States had made a "strengthened United Nations" one of its fundamental foreign policy goals. By 1966 it was facing the question in a particularly acute form: did American national interest call for the creation of a United Nations strong enough to frustrate American policy? Or should the United States do what the Soviet Union had done for twenty years, and use its veto ruthlessly where necessary and possible, and use some other form of obstructionist tactics everywhere to guarantee that the United Nations would remain impotent?

IV. PROSPECTS FOR THE FUTURE

As the intensity of the Soviet-American cold war began to decline after 1962, however, the Great Powers discovered one effective way around the assertive and obstructive General Assembly: a return to the Security Council, at least for issues on which Great Power agreement was possible, on terms that called for the exclusion (or at least the minimization) of small-state participation. In spite of the increase in the size of the Security Council that the Afro-Asian bloc had pushed through in 1965 in order to guarantee their own continued representation on the smaller body, the United States and the Soviet Union—at least when they joined forces—still effectively dominated the Security Council. When a common Soviet-American position on a political-security question was arrived at (usually in highly private negotiations) there was little either the General Assembly or the Secretary-General could do to obstruct the acceptance of this position as United Nations policy.

This development—called "parallelism" in American cold war terms—has shown up in the United Nations on only a few occasions. The major instances have been Cyprus in 1964 and the Kashmir cease-fire in 1965. But even the limited number of examples make the point quite clear: the only way for the Great Powers to escape the biases and interests—and the voting power—of the small-state bloc in the General Assembly is to transfer the effective arena of United Nations participation (at least on political-security questions) to the Security Council. And, for that matter, even here they must concert their efforts if they are to have their way at all.

As a result of this discovery and the exploitation of a steadily increasing area of common interest by the Great Powers, the United Nations may be considered as evolving back toward an approximation of its original concept: a Security Council dominated by the Great Powers dealing with immediate crises; and a General Assembly dominated by the small states concerning itself with long-range questions of human betterment. This is the Wilsonian dream of half a century ago come closer (at least in the Assembly) to realization than ever before and closer than Wilson himself ever dared dream. The General Assembly is an almost universal body, and its consensus is powerful in world affairs. But it is not an especially efficient instrument for coping with immediate security problems—the entire area of "peacekeeping" or "peacemaking"—except when it is operating through an executive head in the person of the Secretary-General. And, as the recent crisis over Article 19 demonstrates, even these operations cannot be continued indefinitely in the face of Great Power opposition.

So we may expect that at least in the next phase of its history, the General Assembly of the United Nations will behave more like the Assembly of 1947 than that of 1957. The metamorphosis will never be complete, of course; there will continue to be issues on which the Security Council will find itself unable to act and the Assembly will try its political hand again. But the special function of the General Assembly will be to reflect and to help shape the new supranational consensus of men and states, a function made considerably easier by nearly universal membership and instantaneous communication. To the extent that the Assembly is able, by its formulations of opinion and its recommendations to members, to shape the future, it will be justifying its role as the "legislative" element in the United Nations. Even if, as has often been the case and will often be the case again, discussion of basic questions reveals only that opinions are hopelessly divided and that no consensus is possible, the real purposes of the Assembly—the representation of mass interests—will still be served. One need not be a pessimist to argue that in this direction lies the true destiny of the General Assembly, rather than in attempts to become the supreme political arbiter of the entire United Nations system.

Suggestions for Further Reading

Bailey, Sidney D., *The United Nations: A Short Political Guide* (New York: Frederick A. Praeger, Inc., 1963).

Cohen, Benjamin V., *The United Nations: Constitutional Developments* (Cambridge: Harvard University Press, 1961).

Gross, Franz B., ed., *The United States and the United Nations* (Norman: University of Oklahoma Press, 1964).

Goodrich, Leland M., *The United Nations* (New York: The Crowell Press, 1959).

__________ and Norman J. Padelford, eds., *The United Nations in the Balance* (New York: Frederick A. Praeger, Inc., 1965).

Hovet, Thomas, *Bloc Politics in the United Nations* (Cambridge: Harvard University Press, 1960).

Nicholas, Herbert G., *The United Nations as a Political Institution* (London: Oxford University Press, 1962).

Stoessinger, John, *The United Nations and the Superpowers* (New York: Random House, 1965).

Wilcox, Francis O. and H. Field Haviland, Jr., eds., *The United States and the United Nations* (Baltimore: Johns Hopkins University Press, 1961).

DECISIONAL STRUCTURES AND COALITION FORMATION IN SMALL LEGISLATIVE BODIES

A Pilot Analysis[1]

Heinz Eulau and Peter Lupsha

I. THE STRUCTURAL ANALYSIS OF SMALL LEGISLATIVE BODIES

An interesting and potentially fruitful development in the study of legislative behavior and institutions during the last few years has been the discovery of the small group as a "link" between the individual and the larger legislative body of which he is a member. The existence of committees, both permanent and temporary, has long been recognized as a means of dividing the legislative labor. But only recently has scholarly

[1] The larger project of which this analysis is a part, the City Council Research Project, is supported by the National Science Foundation under contract GS 496, and is conducted by the authors and their associates under the auspices of the Stanford Institute of Political Studies.

HEINZ EULAU *is Professor of Political Science at Stanford University. He has been a Fellow of the Center for Advanced Studies in the Behavioral Sciences and, most recently, a Visiting Professor at the Institute for Advanced Studies, Vienna, Austria. His books include* The Legislative System (*co-author*), The Behavioral Persuasion in Politics, Class and Party in the Eisenhower Years, *and* Journeys in Politics. *He is general editor of the* International Yearbook of Political Behavior Research *and an associate editor of the forthcoming* International Encyclopedia of the Social Sciences.

PETER LUPSHA *is a Ph.D. candidate in political science at Stanford University and Research Coordinator of the City Council Research Project in the Stanford Institute of Political Studies.*

effort been systematically directed to the study of these formal legislative groups.[2] It has also been discovered that many other groups, some of them semi-formal, others quite informal, contribute to the legislative process. In the Congress, for instance, the leadership cadre[3] or the state delegations[4] are semi-formal groups of considerable importance to the functioning of the legislative body as a whole. Finally, and more difficult to identify, there are such truly informal groups as cliques or friendship groups that are crucial in linking the individual legislator with his colleagues.[5]

As a result of these studies, the legislative structure, and with it the legislative process, appear to be much more complex than earlier macro-analysis suspected. The legislature comes to resemble an elaborate labyrinth of monads, dyads, triads, and other small group formations. These units may have overlapping memberships. Groups of overlapping members constitute further units to which we give such names as "alliance" or "coalition." The sheer description of the legislative institution from the micro-analytical perspective is challenging, complicated, and extraordinarily difficult.

Structural Analysis

Despite the persuasive arguments made in favor of proceeding from the study of functions to the study of structures,[6] it seems to us that the problem is not one of method but of strategy. If functions are easily identifiable and structures are not, an economical research strategy advises us

[2] The pioneer study is Ralph K. Huitt, "The Congressional Committee: A Case Study," *American Political Science Review,* XLVIII (June 1954), 340-65. For a critical appraisal of the literature on legislative behavior between 1961 and 1964, see Heinz Eulau and Katherine Hinckley, "Legislative Institutions," in James A. Robinson, ed., *Political Science Annual* (Indianapolis: Bobbs-Merrill Company, 1966), Vol. I.

[3] See, f.i., David B. Truman, *The Congressional Party* (New York: John Wiley & Sons, Inc., 1959), pp. 94-144, 193-246; Donald R. Matthews, *U.S. Senators and Their World* (Chapel Hill: University of North Carolina Press, 1960), pp. 118-46; Ralph K. Huitt, "Democratic Party Leadership in the Senate," *American Political Science Review,* LV (June 1961), 333-44; Randall B. Ripley, "The Party Whip Organizations in the United States House of Representatives," *American Political Science Review,* LVIII (September 1964), 561-76.

[4] David B. Truman, "The State Delegations and the Structure of Party Voting in the United States House of Representatives," *American Political Science Review,* L (December 1956), 1023-45; John H. Kessel, "The Washington Congressional Delegation," *Midwest Journal of Political Science,* VII (February 1964), 1-21.

[5] See, f.i., Alan Fiellin, "The Functions of Informal Groups in Legislative Institutions: A Case Study," *Journal of Politics,* XXIV (February 1962), 72-91.

[6] For recent discussions of the issues involved, see Don Martindale, ed., *Functionalism in the Social Sciences* (Philadelphia: American Academy of Political and Social Science, February 1965).

to begin with functions. If, on the other hand, structures are more easily identifiable than the functions they perform, structural analysis recommends itself as a first step.

In fact, most contemporary studies of small political or politically relevant groups, whether formal, semi-formal, or informal, are of both a structural and a functional kind. Some research is explicitly concerned with examining the effects of a group's existence, practices, and policies on the functioning of the whole political system or some of its subsystems.[7] In this research, the group is largely treated as an internally undifferentiated unit. Another type of research approaches small political groups as structurally autonomous units—autonomous in the biological sense, as when an organism responds or reacts independently *of* the whole, and not in the legal sense of being independent *from* the whole. In these studies, it is primarily the functional problems of the group itself and the consequences of its members' behavior for the solution of these problems that are of interest.[8]

Strictly structural analysis focuses on the *relations* that exist between group members and that, as a corollary, give shape to the group's structure. Of course, this type of analysis, though intrinsically interesting, is not an end in itself. It may be used to study the functions which a group performs for the larger system, the group's own functional problems, such as its efficiency or integration, or the consequences of group membership on the behavior of its members.[9]

A group does not have a single structure; it has multiple structures. The relations among its members may be analyzed and ordered in terms of several dimensions. A group may have a power structure, a role struc-

[7] See, f.i., Herbert McClosky and Harold E. Dahlgren, "Primary Group Influence on Party Loyalty," *American Political Science Review,* LIII (September 1959), 757-76; Richard F. Fenno, Jr., *The President's Cabinet* (Cambridge: Harvard University Press, 1960); James A. Robinson, *The House Rules Committee* (Indianapolis: Bobbs-Merrill Company, 1963).

[8] For studies concerned with the functional problem of "integration," see Richard F. Fenno, Jr., "The House Appropriations Committee as a Political System: The Problem of Integration," *American Political Science Review,* LVI (June 1962), 310-24; Charles O. Jones, "The Role of the Congressional Subcommittee," *Midwest Journal of Political Science,* VI (November 1962), 327-44; John F. Manley, "The House Committee on Ways and Means: Conflict Management in a Congressional Committee," *American Political Science Review,* LIX (December 1965), 927-39.

[9] Quite often the terms "group" and "structure" are used interchangeably, and structures are treated as if they were collective actors. But structures cannot act; only groups can act. While a group has a structure, by virtue of the fact that its members interact with each other in characteristic ways, a structure is not a group. For "structure" is an analytic concept that refers to the patterns of relationship among the group's members, whereas "group" refers to a concrete unit of interacting persons, whatever the structure of the interactions may be.

ture, a communication structure, a solidarity structure, a status structure, and so on. This is what we mean when we speak of a group's "structural properties." But not all of these structures need to be of equal interest. Just what group properties are to be chosen for structural analysis depends on the theoretical concerns of the researcher, the problems he proposes to tackle, and the uses he wishes to make of structural data.

A group's multiple structures may or may not be interdependent. For instance, a group's status structure and its solidarity structure may overlap or be independent of each other, depending on the value attributed to the particular properties by the group's members. In a group in which status, however defined or measured, is highly valued, the solidarity structure may be underdeveloped. Varying degrees of interdependence between group structures may have different consequences for group functions.

If structures are interdependent, we may ask whether one structure is more "powerful" than the other in shaping the group's political life. For instance, for the analytical purposes of this paper, we shall use the legislative group's "decisional structure" as our primary ordering device —on the very simple, if highly plausible, ground that legislatures are eminently decision-making bodies. As decision-making is the central formal function of a legislative group, we seem on firm ground in looking at its other structures from the standpoint of its decisional structure.

In the next section, we will identify the decisional structures of legislative groups in terms of the relations that exist between its members at the time of voting on controversial issues. The group's decisional structure may be unipolar, bipolar, or multipolar. Setting aside for the moment the operational definitions of these types, we may ask how a legislative group's decisional structure shapes the political process that goes on within the group. In particular, we shall be concerned with the process of coalition formation and certain aspects of members' influence on decision-making.

In legislative groups characterized by division into majority and minority, the formation of coalitions is a crucial aspect of their politics. Coalition is defined here as a purposive or goal-oriented alliance between two or more members of a group for some indeterminate period of time.[10] By way of contrast, a faction is defined as a stable subgroup whose members are closely related to each other over a long period of time. The

[10] This definition is a composite of definitions in William Riker, *The Theory of Political Coalitions* (New Haven: Yale University Press, 1962), p. 12, and William Gamson, "A Theory of Coalition-Formation," *American Sociological Review,* XXVI (June 1961), 373-82.

politics of coalition must take place, therefore, within the context of the group's factional structure. But factions are permeable; not all members are equally committed to supporting them at all times. We shall, therefore, take account of the swinger who shifts his support across factional boundaries from time to time, though he may be more often aligned with one faction than another. We shall raise the question whether the swinger has more influence over the group's decisions than other members, and whether he is looked upon as a desirable coalition partner.

The kind of structural analysis we have in mind has not been seriously pursued in the study of small political groups. In part, this is probably due to the fact that the "small group" as an object of analysis has only recently been brought to the attention of political scientists. Verba and Golembiewski have sought suggestive leads for political science in the large body of small group research produced by sociologists and social psychologists, but this research largely deals with experimental rather than natural-state, institutionalized groups.[11] The study of real-life small political groups is beset by many technical difficulties, especially when these small groups are located in larger bodies like legislatures. Even if the problem of identifying small legislative subgroups has been solved, it is extraordinarily difficult to generate the data out of which a group's multiple structures can be constructed by the analyst.[12]

The City Council Research Project. What we report in this paper represents only a very small part of the data on city councils and city councilmen now being collected by the Stanford City Council Research Project in the ninety cities of the San Francisco Bay region.[13] The data are being collected by means of lengthy interviews with all the members of the city councils, as well as by self-administered questionnaires. The project was stimulated by previous work on legislative behavior at the state level.[14]

[11] Sidney Verba, *Small Groups and Political Behavior—A Study of Leadership* (Princeton: Princeton University Press, 1961); Robert T. Golembiewski, *The Small Group: An Analysis of Research Concepts and Operations* (Chicago: University of Chicago Press, 1962).

[12] See Samuel Patterson, "Patterns of Interpersonal Relations in a State Legislative Group: The Wisconsin Assembly," *Public Opinion Quarterly, XXIII* (Spring 1959), 101-10; Wayne L. Francis, "Influence and Interaction in a State Legislative Body," *American Political Science Review,* LVI (December 1962), 953-60; for an early failure, see Garland Routt, "Inter-personal Relationships and the Legislative Process," *Annals of the American Academy of Political and Social Science,* CXCV (1938), 129-36.

[13] Space limitations do not permit us to present, even in the briefest form, sketches of the demographic characteristics of the cities and their formal governmental structures. Suffice it to say here that in all of the cities used in this analysis councilmen are elected at large in nonpartisan elections.

[14] See John C. Wahlke, Heinz Eulau, William Buchanan, and LeRoy C. Ferguson,

The data used in this paper come from interviews with city councilmen in twenty-nine cities and were collected in four waves between 1962 and 1966. The data are nonrandom for three reasons. First, the councils chosen for this analysis are not necessarily representative of all the councils in our universe of cities. They were chosen only because they are part of the data collection that has been presently completed. Second, we were unable to interview all the councilmen in the cities of this sample, and we have no way of controlling for sampling error. Finally, we have no way of determining the randomness of the responses made by those whom we interviewed. A respondent could refuse to answer one or perhaps all of the sociometric questions that called for giving names. Response failure, just as interview failure, makes statistical testing questionable. Appendix A presents a table summarizing the results of our interview efforts in the twenty-nine cities.

Response failure also complicates our analytic task. In a large random sample, a nonresponse rate of about 10 per cent, as in the present study, is very favorable. If one deals with small groups of five, seven, or nine members, even a single refusal is unfortunate. It is in this respect that the study of small groups in real-life politics is so much more difficult than the study of experimental groups where a missing "subject" can always be replaced by a substitute.

Because of the nonrandomness of the data, we did not subject the distributions to statistical tests of significance. Furthermore, lest we be seriously misunderstood, let us also point out that we are omitting a multitude of considerations that will obviously occur to any student of local government or legislative behavior as possibly relevant. For instance, we shall say nothing about the larger environment in which the councils function, about the formal legal and institutional constraints that channel a good deal of political behavior, about the effects of different kinds of issues, or about the personal needs, skills, and values of councilmen. Those addicted to case analysis will, therefore, dissent from the type of analysis presented here. But we see no alternative, for two reasons.

In the first place, comparative method is the only viable alternative to the experimental method in the study of natural-state phenomena, and it must of necessity ignore much of the rich contextual detail that fascinates the writer of a case study.[15] The comparative analyst can protect

The Legislative System: Explorations in Legislative Behavior (New York: John Wiley & Sons, Inc., 1962).

[15] The requirements of comparative method are specified in Heinz Eulau, "Comparative Political Analysis: A Methodological Note," *Midwest Journal of Political Science,* VI (November 1962), 397-407.

himself from the charge that his neglect of context violates reality in two ways. First, he can introduce *types* of context as controls. In this paper, we shall use the councils' decisional structures as contextual variables in the analysis of coalition politics and influence. Or, second, the comparative analyst can assume that, if he deals with many cases, the context is random—a statistical problem yet to be explored in the study of comparative method.

In the second place, it should be obvious that in a single analysis we cannot deal with everything of possible relevance at once. We shall concern ourselves with certain structural variations. We shall do so not only outside of the total environmental context, but in disregard of particular antecedent or consequent events. Though we are sensitive to the "causal challenge" that faces all analysts of social systems, we prefer to leave the causal door open rather than close it prematurely. Especially when one deals with the endogenous factors of structure, the relationship between independent and dependent variables is most difficult to disentangle and the problems of circularity are multiplied. As Thibault and Kelley succinctly put it in speaking of social interaction:

Each subject's behavior is at the same time a response to a past behavior of the other and a stimulus to a future behavior of the other; each behavior is in part dependent variable and in part independent variable; in no clear sense is it properly either one of them.[16]

II. IDENTIFICATION OF DECISION-MAKING STRUCTURES

Because institutionalized groups like legislative bodies are rather long-lived, their multiple structures are often assumed to be more stable than they probably are. Indeed, the very term "structure" gives the impression of stability and even conveys a sense of rigidity. But these connotative imputations of stability are deceptive. In actuality, a group's structures may be quite fluid even though the group may be very stable as a unit because its members are in continuous interaction. For instance, in legislative bodies, as a group's members seek each other out for mutual support or advantage, the relevant structures change, even if rather imperceptibly. The structures to which interpersonal relations, in all their diversity, give rise only appear as stable as they do because of the process of construction from behavior in which the analyst is engaged.

[16] John W. Thibault and Harold H. Kelley, *The Social Psychology of Groups* (New York: John Wiley & Sons, Inc., 1959), p. 2.

Nevertheless, structures differ in degree of stability and some structures are likely to be more stable than others. In the case of a legislative group, its decisional structure is probably more stable than some of its other structures—say, its role structure or influence structure. The relative stability of a legislative group's decisional structure, we posit, is inherent in the process of legislative decision-making. For in this process there is a point in time when, for all practical purposes, the behaviors involved in decision-making stand still—the point of decision. For at this point, a point of no return, the individual actor must commit himself. And, through his commitment, he defines his position *vis-à-vis* the other actors who are participating in the decision. He must line up with one or another of his fellow decision-makers, or he must oppose them (though he has the option to abstain—an option severely limited by the requirements of the legislative process for commitment). The voting decision is like a single frame in the moving film of decisions that the legislative group must make. It is out of these "stills" that the group's decisional structure emerges.

Considerations like these, even if rarely articulated, underlie the efforts of students of legislative and judicial behavior to identify voting "blocs." [17] Bloc analysis calls for the ordering of a decision-making group's members in terms of their position on legislative roll calls. If, in the course of time, the votes of some actors are more consistently cast with the votes of certain others or in opposition to specified others, we characterize those voting together as a bloc and speak of the group's decisional structure. Of course, if no regular patterns emerge from an attempt at identifying blocs, the group still has a decisional structure. It is, however, a fragmented structure rather than a consensual or factional one.

A legislative group's voting patterns, then, are the most direct and objective evidence of its decisional structure. If each city council's votes were recorded on all issues, conventional roll-call analysis would be the most reliable way to secure the information needed to identify their decisional structures. However, in many councils the vote is not recorded or names are not revealed. As an alternative to roll-call analysis, we therefore asked each respondent the following question about his council's voting behavior:

[17] For a classical article, see Stuart A. Rice, "The Identification of Blocs in Small Political Bodies," *American Political Science Review,* XXI (August 1927), 619-27; for a recent methodological study, see John G. Grumm, "The Systematic Analysis of Blocs in the Study of Legislative Behavior," *Western Political Quarterly,* XVIII (June 1965), 350-62. Studies of judicial bloc voting may be conveniently found in Glendon Schubert, ed., *Judicial Behavior: A Reader in Theory and Research* (Chicago: Rand McNally & Company, 1964).

When the Council is in disagreement on an issue, would you say there is more or less the same line-up here in [*city*]*? I mean, do some members seem to vote together on controversial issues? Who seems to be voting with whom? With whom do you usually vote?*

Our confidence that this question yields reliable information is based on the dual assumption that as councils are small groups, each member is highly aware of the behavior of each other member, and as councils vote *viva voce,* voting positions are common knowledge to all members. Moreover, in order to have an independent check on respondents' perceptual accuracy, we also asked each respondent to name a "second" and possibly a "third" group which he thought voted together. We could and did use this "second-hand" material to check the perceptions of each councilman and to infer actual relations in those cases where councilmen either refused to give names or could not be interviewed.[18]

In order to manipulate the data effectively, the council structures were initially identified by way of sociograms and sociometric matrices. Appendix B presents a number of illustrations of how the data were handled. In the text we use tables. In order to facilitate inspection and comparison, we employ percentages in spite of the small numbers that are at times involved. Each individual councilman is identified by number only, but the number "one" designation is always reserved for the mayor. This procedure was necessary because not giving the mayor a special position in the diagrams, matrices, or tables would do undue violence to the real-life situations which we are trying to depict. We do not think that it represents a breach of anonymity.

Major Types of Decisional Structure

It is possible to organize the voting line-ups reported by the respondents into three major types of decisional structure. In constructing the types, difficulties encountered in classifying certain councils were solved by using the comments which the respondents often made in explaining the voting line-ups. They helped in clarifying the interpersonal patterns that were reported in the direct responses to our question.

Unipolar Structure

Few difficulties stood in the way of identifying the type of structure we call "unipolar." In the councils of this type, each member sees him-

[18] In the final analysis of the entire project, we shall undertake a truly independent check on the reliability of the reported voting patterns by comparing responses with

self allied with every other in decisions concerning controversial issues. Typical comments were: "Our council is pretty solid," "There is pretty much homogeneity," "We all think alike," or "We have unanimity on about all controversial issues," and so on. The respondents were simply unable to identify voting splits or permanent factions. In general, then, if the council never or rarely splits in the voting stage and votes unanimously on all or most controversial issues, its structure is unipolar. But this does not mean that prior to the voting stage all the members are necessarily of one mind. In fact, a good deal of bargaining and compromising may well have taken place.[19] Respondents may take pride in being "independent"; as one councilman put it:

We all express ourselves and try to reach agreement satisfactory to everyone. . . . In a body of people not paid, like we are, we feel quite independent, yet we want to work as a team. We are all interested in what is best for the city, and no one has any particular axe to grind.

Another respondent stated:

We try not to bring an item to a vote until such time as the pros and cons have been ironed out to the point where you wouldn't expect anyone to have to go out of line to support your project. Before you get an item on the table you want the feeling that the council has accepted it to be good, so you can have a unanimous vote. You keep doing things, changing the wording, adding or subtracting things, until that happens.

We can assume that in the councils of the unipolar type the members have numerous and strong ties with each other, a similar ideology, or a profound feeling of solidarity so that group consensus is a pervasive property of their interpersonal relations.

Multipolar Structure

If in the voting stage the council is often split on controversial issues, with shifting memberships in the majority and minority, we speak of a fragmented or multipolar structure. This structure was more difficult to identify than the unipolar, but comments like the following alerted us to its existence:

---

roll call votes for those councils where minutes are available and votes are recorded. Preliminary work along this line indicates that the interview data are highly reliable.

[19] For a theoretical statement about the politics of unanimity, see Heinz Eulau, "Logics of Rationality in Unanimous Decision-Making," in C. J. Friedrich, ed., *Rational Decision* (New York: Atherton Press, 1964), pp. 26-54.

The majority can go any way. On this meat ordinance issue, councilman No. 5 and I thought alike. But I wasn't sure and finally voted with the majority.

It's amazing the way it shifts around. People don't believe me when I tell them, but there's no two or three who stick together.

On this particular council, we just go back and forth all the time. There is no regular line-up.

There are a lot 4:3 votes, but it is always different people. There are no voting cliques on this council. I wouldn't have stayed on if there had been just certain groups and everyone had always voted with his group.

Despite this last councilman's protestation that "there are no voting cliques on this council," the multipolar structures are often characterized by cliques of varying size, depending on the council's size, whose members have close ties with each other. There may, of course, also be isolates, and a council may consist only of such isolates. In the multipolar council as a whole, interpersonal relations are often strained and highly variable. There may be a dominant majority faction, but the opposition may be fragmented into cliques or isolates. These councils find it difficult to come to a majority vote in the final stage of the decision process.

Bipolar Structure

If in the voting stage the council is split into the same majority and minority factions, with certain members voting with each other more regularly than with other members, we speak of a bipolar structure. Bipolar structures were relatively easy to identify, especially those with a 3:2, 4:3, or 5:4 split. As the lines of conflict in these councils are more sharply drawn than in the multipolar councils, respondents seem to find it easier (and perhaps also socially more acceptable) to name their own regular voting partners. The factional split is frankly acknowledged, as in this comment of a minority member:

I would like to say that they [i.e. the majority members] tend to vote together. You can't always be sure they are going to. I sometimes get the feeling that they vote differently on minor matters to demonstrate that they aren't a caucus.

In a bipolar structure interpersonal ties are more or less numerous and strong within the factions, depending on the depth of cleavage that characterizes the group as a whole. In contrast to the unipolar or multipolar situations, the same structural relations presumably exist among the members prior to the voting decision. As we shall point out in the next section, the bipolar structures may be more or less polarized, depending on the number of swingers who are occasionally inclined to cross the factional lines of division. But, in general, it is a permanent majority's decision which usually commits the council as a whole on controversial issues.

Size of Council and Structural Type

While our present sample is limited to twenty-nine out of a potential ninety councils, the distribution of the three structural types suggests that decisional patterns may be related to the size of a council's membership. As Table I shows, none of the larger seven-man and nine-man councils produced a unipolar structure. Four of the five seven-man councils are multipolar, and the two nine-man councils are both bipolar. On the other hand, small size alone does not seem to be exclusively determinative of structure. Of the twenty-two five-man councils as many are unipolar as bipolar, and four are multipolar.

Table I

Types of Decisional Structure and Council Size

Type of Structure	Council Size		
	Five	Seven	Nine
Unipolar	9	—	—
Bipolar	9	1	2
Multipolar	4	4	—
	22	5	2

III. THE SWINGER: AGENT OF POLARIZATION

A council's decisional structure is relatively stable and durable. As we have seen, council members themselves perceive certain voting line-ups and are able to locate themselves and their colleagues in these line-ups. This does not mean, however, that the voting alignments on controversial issues will invariably remain the same. On occasion, certain members may shift their votes from one side of the line-up to the other, thus introducing an element of fluidity into the decisional structure. In fact, if this occurs frequently, one structure may be transformed into another.

The type of synchronic analysis we are making does not permit us to say anything about the process of change from one structure to another. But we had reason to believe that council members with an inclination to shift from one side to another could be identified. Therefore we asked the following question:[20]

When the Council is split over an issue, is there a member, or two, who sometimes votes with one side, sometimes with the other? Who are they?

The "swingers," as we shall call the councilmen who tend to shift sides, are those members who, in their own view or in that of their colleagues, play a role that makes for uncertainty in the decisional structure.

Let us emphasize that taking the role of swinger does not preclude a councilman's regular affiliation with a faction in a bipolar, or with a clique in a multipolar, decisional structure. In other words, the swinger is not necessarily a maverick or dissenter who votes against whatever the majority is for. The swinger merely reserves for himself the option of occasionally voting against those with whom he is usually associated in decisions involving controversial matters. In unipolar structures, of course, there cannot be a swinger as we have defined him, though the unanimous pattern of voting may occasionally be broken. Our analysis will therefore be limited to the bipolar and multipolar councils.

The data attest to the viability of the swinger role. In the twelve bipolar councils, 39 per cent of the members were named, either only by themselves or by others, as swingers; in the eight multipolar councils, 31 per cent were named as swingers (Table II). This finding does not tell us very much, however, for we would expect swingers to be named with relative frequency in both structures. Perhaps we might have surmised that swingers would be named significantly more often in the multipolar structures. But the result is not surprising if we keep in mind that a member in a multipolar group is, almost by definition, a swinger because there are no regular "sides" in vote outcomes as there are in bipolar councils. Hence, our respondents in the multipolar councils were probably hard put to identify swingers. On the other hand, in the bipolar councils, because the lines of conflict there are more clearly defined, the swinger is more immediately visible and more easily recognized by

[20] This question was followed by another: "Why do you think they behave that way?" We are not using responses to this question here.

the members. In the bipolar structure the swinger is the member who occasionally switches sides; in the multipolar structure, he is less a man who shifts sides and more a man who deserts a temporary coalition.

If the swinger is a more central figure in bipolar structures, we should expect that swingers in these structures are more self-conscious of their role than are swingers in multipolar structures. Being a swinger in a bipolar structure is more distinctive than being a swinger in a multipolar structure. As Table II shows, swinger self-nominations are more frequent in bipolar than in multipolar structures. Over one half of the swingers

Table II

Nominations of Swingers by Self and Others in Bipolar and Multipolar Structures

	Structures	
	Bipolar	Multipolar
Total membership	70	48
Named as swingers	27 (39%)	15 (31%)
Of those named as swingers		
By self only	5 (19%)	2 (13%)
By self and others	9 (33%)	3 (20%)
Total by self	14 (52%)	5 (33%)
By others only	13 (48%)	10 (67%)
Total by others	22 (81%)	13 (87%)

in bipolar councils named themselves, while only a third did so in the multipolar councils. One reason for the high percentage of self-nominations in the bipolar setting may be that the swinger in a clearly perceived conflictual situation is not necessarily ambivalent about his role or an ill-informed "independent" voter. Rather, he is a mediator who seeks consensus amid strife and uses his vote in an attempt to moderate the conflict.

Consensus on Swingers

Swinger self-nominations are perhaps indicative of the visibility of the role, but they have low probative value if not reinforced by the agreement of others. However, even if nominations are made by others, they should be consensually validated if they are to tell us something about behavioral reality. If a councilman is named as a swinger by only one other, the probability of his really being a swinger is less than if he were named by several others.

The degree to which a council member's swinger role is inter-subjectively agreed upon can be measured by a very simple device—the number of nominations he actually received in proportion to the number he would have received if all respondents had chosen him.[21] Table XIII in Appendix C presents the individual swinger choice ratios of councilmen in bipolar and multipolar structures. If a ratio of .51 or better is accepted as a criterion for high consensus, it appears that nine of the swingers in the bipolar structures, or 33 per cent of those named, and only one of those named in the multipolar structures, can be considered consensually validated. Evidently, as a consensually validated role, being a swinger makes severe demands on members of conflictual legislative bodies. However, the data suggest a limited confirmation of the hypothesis that the swinger would be more visible in the bipolar than in the multipolar settings.

Our interest is not just in individual swingers, but in the degree of agreement on swingers for a council as a whole, for this may tell us something about the depth of cleavage in bipolar and multipolar structures. To measure council consensus on all swingers, regardless of how many nominations any one swinger received, we simply average the individual choice ratios. The group swinger choice ratio is indicative, then, of the dispersion of nominations in a council. As Table XIII in Appendix C shows, five of the twelve bipolar and only one of the eight multipolar councils have relatively high consensus on swingers. The average group choice ratio for all bipolar councils is .53, for all multipolar councils only .29. In general, then, there is more consensus on swingers in bipolar than in multipolar structures.

Polarization and Consensus

The frequency with which swingers are encountered in bipolar and multipolar structures would seem to be indicative of the degree of polarization that characterizes these structures. Where relatively few swingers, or none, are found, the decisional structure is probably more conflictual than where the presence of many swingers makes for greater fluidity in voting alignments. We shall measure a structure's degree of

[21] The "individual choice ratio" is computed by dividing the number of nominations a councilman received by the number of respondents. For instance, if he received three nominations in a council with five respondents, his choice ratio is .60.

polarization in two ways: first, in terms of the proportion of councilmen named as swingers by others; and second, in the case of the bipolar structures, in terms of the proportions named across factional boundaries.

Table XIV in Appendix C presents the data. Regardless of which measure is used, the councils of either structural type exhibit a wide range of variation in polarization, from no inter-subjectively validated swingers in councils 103 and 401 to 57 per cent in bipolar council 302. With the cross-factional measure for the bipolar councils the polarization of the councils shifts somewhat (because 802's two swingers and two of 302's swingers are not named across factions), but not drastically (rho = .72).

By rank-ordering the bipolar councils, using the cross-factional measure (which is probably the stronger of the two), we can classify them into two subtypes—high bipolar and low bipolar structures. In the aggregate, as Table III shows, there are considerably fewer swingers in the six high bipolar than in the six low bipolar councils. Interestingly, in the multipolar councils the proportion of swingers falls between the two bipolar types. These distributions might suggest that the multipolar structures are more conflictual than the low bipolar structures, but this imputation, based exclusively on the proportion of swingers in different structures, is not justified. As we noted earlier, consensus on swingers may vary a

Table III

Proportions of Swingers in High Bipolar, Low Bipolar, and Multipolar Structures

Type of Structure	Number of Councils	Proportion of Swingers
High bipolar	6	18%
Multipolar	8	27%
Low Bipolar	6	45%

good deal. We would assume that a structure is more conflictual not only where there are few swingers—i.e., where polarization is high—but also where consensus on swingers is relatively high, for a high level of conflict should make for perceptual clarity. In other words, members of the highly polarized councils should be able to be more fully aware of which of their colleagues from time to time vote across more sharply defined factional boundaries. Table IV therefore cross-tabulates the three types of structures in terms of their polarization and their aggregate consensus on swingers. Though four of the twenty councils deviate from the expected pattern, there is a positive relationship between intracouncil conflict and consensus on swingers. This relationship is even more vividly expressed by the "group choice ratio" measure of the degree of consensus on swingers. It now appears that, as we should expect, consensus in the low bipolar structures is somewhat greater than in the multipolar structures, though still considerably less than in the high bipolar structures.

Table IV

Cross-tabulation of Bipolar and Multipolar Structures in Terms of Polarization and Consensus on Swingers

Consensus	Structures		
	High Bipolar N = 6	Low Bipolar N = 6	Multipolar N = 8
High	4	1	1
Low	2	5	7
Group choice ratio	.68	.37	.29

The number of swingers alone, then, is not a sufficient measure of cleavage. Consensual validation of swingers, as a corollary of polarization, is a necessary condition for a conflictual situation to affect a group's decisional process. While voting alignments in a bipolar structure, regardless of the degree of its polarization, may be indicative of the ebb and flow of relatively stable policy cleavages, in the low bipolar and multipolar structures they may be more indicative of shifting cleavages anchored in personal preferences of the members or of pressures brought on the members from the outside.

IV. CO-SPONSORSHIP: THE POLITICS OF COALITION

It is within the context of the decisional structure of their councils that city councilmen, like the members of other legislative bodies, may seek to promote particular projects to solve a variety of municipal problems. What they can or cannot accomplish is likely to be severely limited by the factional alignments, the cross-factional relationships, and the degree of consensus or cleavage that give the decisional structures their particular forms. But whatever the decisional structure, councilmen will seek to maximize support and mobilize a winning coalition in order to achieve their goals. One way of doing this is to interest others in a project and solicit their aid. The politics of coalition begins where the politics of faction ends.

In the course of our interviews with councilmen, they were asked to tell us something about the "two most pressing problems" facing their city, and then presented with this question:

On a key problem such as we just talked about, is there any council member you would especially like to have join you as co-sponsor of a proposal you might have?

Formal co-sponsorship is not as common in city councils as it is in larger legislative bodies, but the pressure to get a proposal or pet project enacted is, and having the support of one or even more others is helpful in lining up the votes that are needed for passage of a proposal. But one would also expect that co-sponsorship as a device of coalition formation will be variously used in different decisional structures. For instance, we would expect that co-sponsorship occurs more often in the more fragmented settings where coalitions *must* be formed to mobilize the majority needed for legislative success (as in multipolar or perhaps low bipolar structures) than in settings where one is confident of a majority's support (as in unipolar structures and on the majority side of high bipolar structures). Or where the legislative situation is perceptually ambiguous (as in multipolar and low bipolar structures) we would expect more efforts to form coalitions to be made than where the structure is more clearly perceived (as in unipolar and high bipolar structures), for engaging in coalitional politics is, in effect, a form of reality testing. Finally, in the more conflictual settings we would expect coalition partners to be sought primarily within factions, with cross-factional choices going from minority to majority members.

Incidence of Co-sponsorship

To measure the occurrence of co-sponsorship in the different decisional structures, we shall employ two measures: first, a "co-sponsor choice ratio," which represents simply the proportion of co-sponsors in any one council of all members of that council, regardless of the number of nominations any one individual member received. Aggregated for all councils of a particular decisional structure type, this gives us an "aggregate co-sponsor choice ratio." We expect this ratio to be highest in multipolar structures, for here the fragmented nature of the decisional structure and perceptual ambiguity with regard to the position of any one member on a proposal should occasion a maximum of coalitional politics. We expect the ratio to be lowest in the unipolar structures, for here the basic consensus that prevails is likely to make the search for support unnecessary. Moreover, proposals introduced here are likely to be noncontroversial since members will not introduce controversial proposals in the first place because of the broad agreement on what is and what is not desirable. Finally, we would expect the bipolar structures to fall between the other two types. While the lines of faction are fairly well marked in these structures, the presence of swingers, especially on the majority side, is likely to make for coalitional activity as majority members seek to hold the majority together and minority members seek to attract the support of a marginal majority member.

Our second measure is even simpler. It is the aggregated average number of co-sponsor choices. Again, for the reasons just stated, we would expect that any one co-sponsor will be more frequently chosen in the multipolar than in the bipolar structures, and more frequently in the latter than in the unipolar structures.

Table V

*Coalitional Activity in Unipolar, Bipolar, and Multipolar Decisional Structures**

Type of Structure	Aggregate Co-sponsor Choice Ratio	Aggregate Average Co-sponsor Choices
Unipolar (N = 45)	.36	1.25
Bipolar (N = 70)	.63	1.48
Multipolar (N = 48)	.67	1.65

* The co-sponsor choice ratios for the individual councils are presented in Table XV of Appendix C.

As Table V shows, our expectations are met. In all three types of decisional structure, the indices point in the hypothesized direction. Although the difference in the aggregate co-sponsor choice ratios for the bipolar and multipolar structures is small, suggesting that coalitional politics in the former is as critical as in the latter, coalitional activity in the multipolar councils seems somewhat more intense—on the average, co-sponsors receive .17 more nominations than in the bipolar councils.

Factions and Coalitions

In conflictual structures it is the existence of more or less stable factions that introduces more or less certainty about voting outcomes. Yet, on any particular proposal, factional alignments may break down. It is for just this reason that councilmen wishing to assure the passage of a proposal will not leave the matter to chance but will actively engage in securing support. But where will they seek this support? In bipolar structures we would expect that majority members will make sure that their proposals are passed by seeking support among their own faction, while minority members will try to form a winning coalition by attracting support from among the majority. The strategic problem for any one member, whether in the majority or the minority, is to secure the co-sponsorship of at least one prestigious member in order to maximize the probability of success. In multipolar structures, coalitional activity is not only to be more frequent, as we have noted, but efforts to win the support of members belonging to other cliques than one's own is for all practical purposes mandatory.

In order to appraise the politics of coalition across factional boundaries in bipolar and multipolar structures, we shall first examine each type separately and then both types comparatively. Table VI presents the co-sponsorship nominations made within and across factional boundaries in the twelve bipolar structures. It is immediately evident that in these structures majority members strongly tend to seek support among

Table VI

*Intra- and Inter-Factional Co-sponsorship Nominations in Bipolar Structures**

(A)

Nominations Given by	Nominations Given to		
	Majority	Minority	
Majority	55% (36) +	10% (6) =	42
Minority	12% (8) +	23% (15) =	23
N =	44 +	21	65

(B)

Nominations Given by	Nominations Given to		
	Own Faction	Other Faction	
Majority (N = 42)	86% (36)	14 (6)	100%
Minority (N = 23)	65% (15)	35 (8)	100%

* The intra- and inter-factional co-sponsorship nominations for each individual council are presented in Table XVI of Appendix C.

members of their own faction. But, surprisingly, minority members also prefer as co-sponsors members of their own faction more often than members of the majority. The contrasts appear even more sharply if we look at the same data as presented in part B of Table VI. Of the nominations made by majority members, 86 per cent are intra-factional choices; and of the minority nominations, 65 per cent are given within the faction. In bipolar structures, it seems, the factional alliances are so strong that there is relatively little room for coalitional politics across factional boundaries. Majority members, of course, need not seek support from among the minority. But minority members, who might be expected to seek out majority members as co-sponsors, are evidently deterred from doing so by the prevailing factional cleavage.

This interpretation is supported by internal analysis of the data. If we control intra- and inter-factional nominations by level of polarization, Table VII shows that the tendency of majority members to seek coalition partners within their own faction is considerably greater in the high bipolar than in the low bipolar councils. Moreover, minority members tend to pick legislative associates more often in the low than in the high

Table VII

Intra- and Inter-Factional Co-sponsorship Nominations in Bipolar Structures, Controlled by Level of Polarization

Nominations by	Nominations Given to			
	High Bipolar		Low Bipolar	
	Majority	Minority	Majority	Minority
Majority	66% (21)	9% (3)	45% (15)	10% (3)
Minority	6% (2)	19% (6)	18% (6)	27% (9)
		N = 32		N = 33

polarized structures. In fact, six of the eight majority choices by minority members occur in the low bipolar councils. In other words, the more clearly defined the lines of cleavage in a factional structure are, the greater is the tendency to seek legislative allies within one's own faction.

Multipolar Structures and Coalition Formation

In the case of multipolar structures, our analysis must be somewhat different because the lines of cleavage are more difficult to identify, as we are dealing with cliques rather than factions. But the multipolar structures can be classified into three subtypes: (1) those where there is a majority faction, but the opposition is split into cliques or individuals—as in a 4:2:1 division; (2) those where there is a strong but not dominant faction—as in a 3:2:2 split; and (3) those where there are only weak cliques or isolates—as in a 2:2:1 structure. Table VIII shows that in multipolar structures, in contrast to the situation in bipolar structures, cross-factional or cross-clique coalitional politics is more widespread, except in the one-faction dominant cases. Here the nominations of co-sponsors are mostly made within the majority faction, similar to the choice pattern in bipolar structures. Where there are only weak cliques,

Table VIII

Intra- and Inter-Factional Co-sponsorship Nominations in Three Subtypes of Multipolar Structures

Nominations	Multipolar Structures with		
	Dominant Faction (N = 8)	Strong Factions (N = 29)	Weak Factions (N = 5)
Intra-Faction	75%	45%	0%
Inter-Faction	25	55	100
	100%	100%	100%

however, choices of co-sponsors go exclusively to members of other cliques.[22] In the structures with strong but not dominant cliques, the nominations are split, about one half being given within a faction or clique and another half across factional or clique lines of division.

If we compare the intra- and inter-factional co-sponsorship nominations given in bipolar and multipolar structures, the contrast in the coalitional politics of these different decisional contexts appears in sharp focus. As Table IX indicates, in the bipolar structures the politics of coalition is predominantly directed toward members of one's own faction; in the multipolar structures efforts at coalition formation are somewhat more strongly concentrated across factional or clique divisions. In other words, it appears that a legislative body's basic decisional structure places powerful constraints on what its individual members can and cannot do

[22] In Table VIII of the text, council 304 has been omitted. The split in this council seemed to be 1:1:1:1:1. If we had classified it, it would have been included in the multipolar category with weak factions and, in regard to co-sponsorship, would have shown eleven inter-factional choices. This would not have changed the result in the table, but it would have unduly influenced the aggregate result for all multipolar structures reported in Table XVI of Appendix C.

Table IX

Comparison of Intra- and Inter-Factional Co-sponsorship Nominations in Bipolar and Multipolar Structures

Nominations	Nominations Made in	
	Bipolar Structures (N = 65)	Multipolar Structures (N = 42)
Intra-Faction	78%	45%
Inter-Faction	22	55
	100%	100%

in pursuing their legislative objectives. Where factions are sharply divided, even minority members do not readily venture to seek legislative allies across factional boundaries. Where the structure is fragmented, coalition politics across lines of cleavage is necessary to mobilize support and form a winning majority.

V. COALITIONAL POLITICS AND THE SWING VOTER

Coalitional politics functions to mobilize a temporary majority in support of a particular proposal. As we have noted, where factional bonds in conflictual decision structures are strong, members of both the majority and minority factions incline to seek legislative associates among their own side. The strategic problems facing members of the majority and the minority are, of course, different. For the former, coalitional politics serves to harness and preserve the effective power of their faction that stems from the principle of majority rule. A majority member can therefore be expected to behave just as he does. His own influence in the council as a whole derives from his belonging to the majority, and continued maintenance of the majority's power is in his own long-range interest as a wielder of influence. We would expect him to seek support among the minority only if and when his own faction fails to go along with him.

For the member of the minority the problem of maximizing his influence is quite different. By virtue of his minority position he is powerless by definition. We would therefore expect him to seek support for a particular proposal among the majority. Yet he does not tend to do so, but rather chooses his legislative allies among his own faction, as does the member of the majority. How can we explain his behavior? In particular, if he were to act rationally, should we not expect the minority member to seek the support of those in the majority who are most likely to defect—the swingers?

The Swinger in Coalitional Politics

The principle of "one man, one vote" presumably guarantees the equality of members in a voting group. If all members have one vote and simple majority voting is the decision rule, then supposedly all enter the voting situation as equals and their free choice decides an issue. In practice, of course, the situation is more complicated. Members of a voting group differ in the quantity and quality of various relevant attributes, such as status, skill, or knowledge, that are likely to effect different degrees of influence over group decisions.

Even if we ignore the variety of personal attributes that make for differential influence, we can make two alternate behavioral assumptions about the influence of the swinger over group decisions. One assumption is that the swinger possesses influence greater than that of others by virtue of the uncertainty of his voting behavior. His vote cannot be automatically counted on, even though he is more often allied with one faction than another. This uncertainty in his behavior, perceived by others, can make his vote a bargaining resource which, if properly managed, provides him with a degree of influence not matched by any other member of the group. Especially in voting situations where both sides are nearly equal in strength, the swinger's support would seem to be highly desirable.

But we can also make the assumption that the swinger may be altogether without influence. Precisely because he is a swinger, his behavior may be a source of distrust. He may be viewed as an unreliable coalition partner, and his support will be disdained. If so, the swinger's vote as a bargaining resource will be nullified by the refusal of the more steady members of a faction to bargain with him.

Our data permit us to examine these assumptions. The first assumption would seem to be plausible if a preponderance of swingers are sought as co-sponsors of a proposal; if not, then perhaps the second assumption is the more tenable one. However, we should also expect that the relationship between being a swinger and being sought after as a co-sponsor would vary from the context of one decisional structure to the other. We would hypothesize, for example, that swingers are less likely to be chosen as co-sponsors where the decisional structure is defined by clearly perceived lines of cleavage. In other words, swingers are more likely to be named as co-sponsors in multipolar than bipolar structures, and more in low bipolar than high bipolar structures.

Table X presents the data. It is immediately evident that of the swingers in the high bipolar structures only a third are sought after as co-sponsors, while in the low bipolar and multipolar structures about two-thirds, more or less, are selected. In terms of total membership, presented in Table XI, we find that the swinger-co-sponsor combination appears most frequently in the low bipolar, less often in the multipolar, and rarely in the high bipolar structures. In other words, the distributions

Table X

Proportions of Co-sponsors Among Swingers in Bipolar and Multipolar Structures

Co-sponsorship	Decisional Structure		
	High Bipolar (N = 6)	Low Bipolar (N = 16)	Multipolar (N = 13)
Chosen	33%	63%	69%
Not chosen	67	37	31
	100%	100%	100%

Table XI

Coalition Politics in Bipolar and Multipolar Councils

Named as	Decisional Structure		
	High Bipolar (N = 34)	Multipolar (N = 48)	Low Bipolar (N = 36)
Both co-sponsor and swinger	6%	19%	28%
Only co-sponsor	56	48	36
Only swinger	15	8	17
Neither co-sponsor nor swinger	23	25	19
	100%	100%	100%

support our hypothesis that swingers are least likely to be picked as coalition partners in high bipolar structures, but in the low bipolar structures being a swinger seems to be less of a handicap. We can only speculate why this is the case. It may well be that the swinger is viewed as a potential co-sponsor in the low bipolar structures because conflict is less intense and perceptual ambiguity is greater than in the high bipolar settings. Hence the swinger is more likely to be seen as a mediator who is acceptable as a legislative partner.

The Swinger as Pivotal Voter

The fact that the swinger is not as often chosen as a coalition partner as one might expect does not preclude, however, that his vote cannot have a decisive influence on a council's decision-making. Especially in decisional structures in which the regular voting alignment is close, as in 3:2, 4:3, or 5:4 situations, a majority swinger may have the decisive say. We stipulate that the swinger is the "pivotal voter" if and when his vote is determinative of the success of a winning coalition. And insofar as his vote is critical, it also commits the voting group as a whole. Two questions may be asked about the swinger's influence: first, regardless of whether or not he is considered a desirable coalition partner, which swinger is in fact the pivotal voter? And second, is a pivotal swinger more likely to be chosen as a legislative associate than a swinger who is not in a pivotal position?

The "power" of members of a voting group in terms of the pivotal votes they cast has been examined in a small number of theoretical studies.[23] These studies have developed theoretical "power indices" based on probability calculations. Implicit in these calculations are two behavioral assumptions: first, that the group is unstructured—i.e., the individual members are in no way aligned with each other before the voting takes place; and second, that voting proceeds randomly, so that the outcome is determined when, in a division under majority rule, the pivotal vote has been cast. Neither of these assumptions holds for the institutionalized groups with which we are concerned. First, the councils are characterized by regular decisional structures and voting practices, so that the search for support takes place within the context of a structured situation; and second, because the councils are divided into factions and cliques, a vote on a particular proposal always represents behavior within or outside of a pre-existing pattern of alignments.

We must also keep in mind that a vote cast by a swinger in opposition to his usual faction may be offset by a vote cast by another swinger in

[23] See L. S. Shapley and Martin Shubik, "A Method for Evaluating the Distribution of Power in a Committee System," *American Political Science Review,* XLVIII (September 1954), 787-92; Samuel Krislov, "Power and Coalition in a Nine-Man Body," *American Behavioral Scientist,* VI (April 1963), 24-26; Glendon Schubert, "The Power of Organized Minorities in a Small Group," *Administrative Science Quarterly,* IX (September 1964), 133-53.

opposition to *his* usual faction. In light of these constraints, therefore, we must measure a swinger's influence over vote outcomes both in terms of his position in the decisional structure—i.e., his membership in the majority or the minority faction—and in terms of the numbers of swingers in all factions. Moreover, we must make the behavioral assumption that in a voting situation where the usual factional alignment breaks down and a temporary coalition is formed, every swinger will in fact shift his vote. Appendix D explains how the "pivotal swinger index" was constructed, and Table XVII presents the influence values of the index for a 3:2 factional situation. If, in reality, not every swinger behaves as the index assumes he will, this will change his index value, but it does not affect the validity of the index as such. Because of the small number of cases involved, we shall not make use of the particular index values in the following analysis, but use them only to identify the pivotal swingers. Suffice it to say that where several swingers are in pivotal positions affecting the outcome of a vote, so that influence is shared, the complex calculations required of the swinger to maximize as much of his share of influence as possible are likely to have a restraining effect on his behavior and make him weigh more carefully the timing and probable effects of his cross-overs.

Our data, presented in Table XII, show that about two-thirds of the swingers in bipolar structures and 77 per cent in multipolar structures could be identified as potentially pivotal voters with varying degrees of influence. In the bipolar structures, there is a slight tendency for pivotal

Table XII

Swingers as Pivotal Voters in Bipolar and Multipolar Structures

Influence	Bipolar Structures			Multipolar Structures (N = 13)
	Majority (N = 14)	Minority (N = 8)	Total (N = 22)	
Pivotal	57%	75%	64%	77%
Not pivotal	43	25	36	23
	100%	100%	100%	100%

swingers to be more frequent among the minority factions. Evidently, in bipolar structures, it may be somewhat riskier for members of majority factions to break away from their usual voting alignments than it is for members of minority factions, for the latter have nothing to lose and everything to gain. But the numbers involved here are so small that we must not make too much of the distributions. The data simply suggest that the probability of a swinger's being an individual pivotal voter or in a group of pivotal voters is quite likely.

VI. CONCLUSION

Research on small political groups raises two general questions: first, how are small groups related to the larger wholes of which they are parts? [24] And second, is it feasible to study problems of politics characteristic of large systems by studying these problems in very small systems? [25] Both questions raise a host of as yet unsolved methodological problems. But if the assumption is correct that human and social behavior is continuous, then small-group structures, functions, and processes may well be considered as isomorphisms of parallel properties in larger systems. This does not mean that the methodological task is simply one of extrapolation from micro- to macro-phenomena, or that it is possible to transfer knowledge gained on one level to the other, for size is itself an important variable. Rather, the task is to treat both small and large systems in a comprehensive, strictly analytic theoretical framework. If this requirement is not met, the result of dealing with small groups *as if* they were large ones can only lead to distorted interpretation.[26]

In many instances, the internal structural arrangements and processes of the small political groups treated in this paper, city councils, may be expected to reflect structural relationships external to the groups themselves; the council's decisional structure and the politics of coalition formation involved may simply reflect the degree of consensus or cleavage that prevails in the larger community, or a change in a council's structure may reflect population shifts and a gradual transformation of community attitudes and norms. We plan to examine these possibilities in later analyses.

However, insofar as internal structural arrangements and processes hinge upon such factors as interpersonal relations of various sorts, per-

[24] The problems involved are discussed in Daniel Lerner, ed., *Parts and Wholes* (New York: The Free Press of Glencoe, Inc., 1963).

[25] No satisfactory treatment of the "micro-macro problem" exists in the literature of political science. But see Stein Rokkan, "The Comparative Study of Political Participation: Notes toward a Perspective on Current Research," in Austin Ranney, ed., *Essays on the Behavioral Study of Politics* (Urbana: University of Illinois Press, 1962), pp. 47-90.

[26] For this sort of distortion, see Ralph K. White and Ronald O. Lippitt, *Autocracy and Democracy* (New York: Harper and Row, Publishers, Inc., 1960).

sonality conflicts, or the variety of role expectations among councilmen that may have been built up almost exclusively within the council chamber, the changing lines of faction or coalition may have significant implications for the content of policy outputs and ultimately for the fate of the larger community itself. Presumably, the councilman's internal and external relations are in continuous interchange. If there is a lag in this interchange, questions about the stability and adaptibility of the political system as a whole may be raised.

These problems are beyond the scope of the present study. If, however, some of the problems within the narrow range of questions dealt with here can be solved, we may be able to move with some confidence to a consideration of the implications of informal structural patterns for the political system as a whole. It is our contention that it is possible to study rather spectacular problems of politics in research sites that do not seem to be as glamorous as large institutions or systems. Yet the choice of such sites facilitates access to and control over data not as easy to come by in larger settings. Needless to say, we are not arguing that the study of large political systems is expendable. We merely plead that the study of micro-politics can be fruitful from the perspective of political theory.

Appendix A: The Sample

Council Number and Type	Number of Seats	Number of Respondents	Number of Response Failures
Unipolar			
105	5	4	1
306	5	5	0
320	5	5	0
402	5	5	0
404	5	5	0
406	5	5	0
419	5	5	0
501	5	5	0
502	5	5	0
Bipolar			
101	5	4	1
102	9	9	0*
103	5	4	1
201	5	4	1
202	9	6	3
302	7	6	1
303	5	5	0
307	5	4	1
407	5	4	1
410	5	5	0
605	5	5	0
802	5	5	0
Multipolar			
204	5	5	0
304	5	5	0
305	7	6	1
309	7	7	0
312	5	5	0
401	7	6	1
405	7	6	1
607	5	5	0
	163	150 (92%)	13 (8%)

* Unfortunately, in Council 102 three of the respondents, all members of the minority faction, refused to answer all or most of the sociometric questions.

Appendix B: Sociograms and Sociomatrices

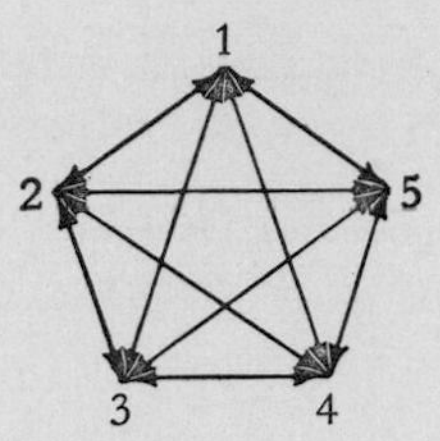

Reciprocal unipolar structure

To:

From:	1	2	3	4	5
1		O	O	O	O
2	O		O	O	O
3	O	O		O	O
4	O	O	O		O
5	O	O	O	O	

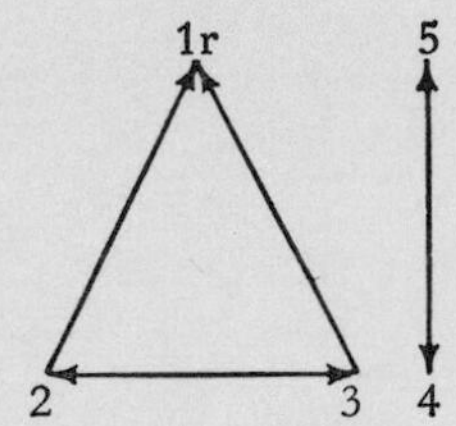

Incomplete bipolar structure

	1	2	3	4	5
1		r	r	r	r
2	O		O	S	S
3	O	O		S	S
4	S	S	S		O
5	S	S	S	O	

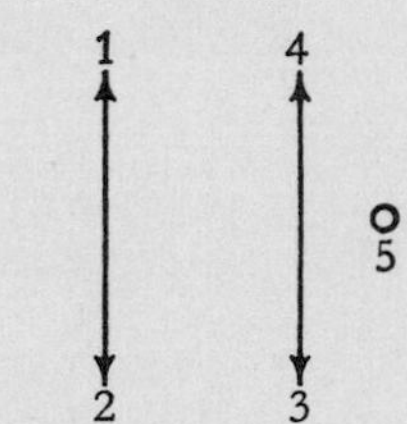

Multipolar structure

	1	2	3	4	5
1		O	S	S	T
2	O		S	S	T
3	S	S		O	T
4	S	S	O		T
5	S	S	T	T	

Reciprocal bipolar structure

	1	2	3	4	5	6	7
1		O	O	O	S	S	S
2	O		O	O	S	S	S
3	O	O		O	S	S	S
4	O	O	O		S	S	S
5	S	S	S	S		O	O
6	S	S	S	S	O		O
7	S	S	S	S	O	O	

Unidirectional choice

Reciprocal choice

r = refused answer
O = names other in *own* group
S = names other in *second* group
T = names other in *third* group

Appendix C

Table XIII

*Individual and Group Choice Ratios for Swingers in Bipolar and Multipolar Structures**

Council Number and Type	N	Individual Choice Ratio for Number = 1	2	3	4	5	6	7	8	9	Group Choice Ratio
High Bipolar											
101	4	—	—	1.0	—	—	—	—	—	—	1.0
102	7	—	—	—	1.0	—	—	—	—	—	1.0
103	4	—	.25	.25	—	—	—	—	—	—	.25
307	4	—	—	—	—	.75	—	—	—	—	.75
410	5	—	.80	—	—	.60	—	—	—	—	.70
802	5	.40	—	—	.60	.20	—	—	—	—	.40
Low Bipolar											
201	4	—	—	.50	.25	.25	—	—	—	—	.33
202	6	—	.17	—	—	.17	.50	—	.33	.17	.27
302	6	.17	—	.67	.17	.83	—	—	—	—	.46
303	5	.60	—	.40	—	—	—	—	—	—	.50
407	4	—	—	.25	.25	—	—	—	—	—	.25
605	5	.40	—	—	—	—	—	—	—	—	.40
Multipolar											
204	5	—	20	—	.20	.20	—	—	—	—	.20
304	5	—	—	—	—	.40	—	—	—	—	.40
305	6	—	—	.17	—	—	.17	—	—	—	.17
309	7	.43	—	—	—	.29	.29	—	—	—	.50
312	5	—	—	—	—	.20	—	—	—	—	.20
401	6	—	—	—	—	—	—	—	—	—	.00
405	6	.17	—	.50	.17	—	—	.34	—	—	.30
607	5	—	—	—	—	.60	—	—	—	—	.60

* Ratios are based on self- and other-nominations. The individual choice ratio is the proportion of nominations received by any one councilman to the number of respondents. The group choice ratio is the average of the individual choice ratios.

Table XIV

*Proportions of Swingers in Bipolar and Multipolar Councils, Proportions of Cross-Factional Nominations in Bipolar Councils, and Polarization Classification**

Council Number and Type	Council Size	Percentage and Rank Swingers		Percentage and Rank Cross-Factional Swingers		Polarization Classification
Bipolar						
103	5	0%	1	0%	1½	High
102	9	11	2	11	3	High
101	5	20	4	20	5	High
307	5	20	4	20	5	High
605	5	20	4	20	5	High
201	5	40	8	40	9½	Low
303	5	10	8	40	9½	Low
407	5	40	8	10	9½	Low
410	5	40	8	40	9½	Low
802	5	40	8	0	1½	High
202	9	44	11	44	12	Low
302	7	57	12	29	7	Low
Multipolar						
401	7	0%	1			
305	7	14	2			
304	5	20	4			
312	5	20	4			
607	5	20	4			
204	5	40	6			
309	7	43	7½			
405	7	43	7½			

* Self-nominations as swinger, unless confirmed by others, have been omitted.

Table XV

Co-sponsor Choice Ratios and Average Co-sponsor Choices in Unipolar, Bipolar, and Multipolar Councils

Council Number and Type	Council Size	Number of Co-sponsors	Choice Ratio	Number of Nominations	Average Choice
Unipolar					
105	5	3	.60	4	1.33
306	5	4	.80	4	1.00
320	5	0	.00	0	0.00
402	5	2	.40	4	2.00
404	5	1	.20	2	2.00
406	5	2	.40	2	1.00
419	5	0	.00	0	0.00
501	5	2	.40	2	1.00
502	5	2	.40	2	1.00
Total	45	16	.36	20	1.25
Bipolar					
101	5	4	.80	5	1.25
102	9	6	.67	15	2.50
103	5	5	1.00	5	1.00
201	5	3	.60	3	1.00
202	9	8	.89	12	1.50
302	7	3	.43	4	1.33
303	5	4	.80	7	1.75
307	5	1	.20	1	1.00
407	5	2	.40	2	1.00
410	5	3	.60	5	1.66
605	5	2	.40	2	1.00
802	5	3	.60	4	1.33
Total	70	44	.63	65	1.48
Multipolar					
204	5	3	.60	3	1.00
304	5	5	1.00	11	2.20
305	7	5	.72	11	2.20
309	7	6	.86	9	1.50
312	5	3	.60	3	1.00
401	7	3	.43	5	1.83
405	7	5	.72	9	1.80
607	5	2	.40	2	1.00
Total	48	32	.67	53	1.65

Table XVI

Intra- and Inter-Factional Co-sponsorship Nominations in Bipolar and Multipolar Structures

Council Number and Type	Nature of Division	Nominations: Intra-Faction	Nominations: Inter-Faction	Total
Bipolar				
101	3:2	100% (5)	0% (0)	5
102	5:4	80% (12)	20% (3)	15
103	3:2	100% (5)	0% (0)	5
201	3:2	100% (3)	0% (0)	3
202	5:4	83% (10)	17% (2)	12
302	5:2	75% (3)	25% (1)	4
303	3:2	57% (4)	43% (3)	7
307	3:2	0% (0)	100% (1)	1
407	3:2	100% (2)	0% (0)	2
410	3:2	40% (2)	60% (3)	5
605	3:2	50% (1)	50% (1)	2
802	3:2	100% (4)	0% (0)	4
	Total	78% (51)	22% (14)	65
Multipolar				
204	2:2:1	0% (0)	100% (3)	3
304	1:1:1:1:1	0% (0)	100% (11)	11
305	3:2:2	27% (3)	73% (8)	11
309	3:2:1:1	45% (4)	55% (5)	9
312	3:1:1	100% (3)	0% (0)	3
401	4:1:1:1	60% (3)	40% (2)	5
405	3:2:2	67% (6)	33% (3)	9
607	2:2:1	0% (0)	100% (2)	2
	Total	36% (19)	64% (34)	53
	Without Council 304	45% (19)	55% (23)	42

Appendix D

Construction of Pivotal Swinger Index

For the purpose of constructing the Pivotal Swinger Index, a pivotal vote is defined as that vote or those votes necessary to form a simple majority in factional structures with one or more swingers. The pivotal vote may be controlled, then, by one or several swingers. The pivotal vote has a unit value of 1.0. If it is shared by two swingers, the share of each is .5; if it is shared by three swingers, the share of each is .33. If two pivotal votes are needed to form a simple majority, a single swinger is helpless and his vote has a value of zero; if there are two swingers casting their votes in the same way, the value of the vote of each is 1.0. But if there are three swingers acting jointly and only two pivotal votes are needed to form a simple majority, they share the two pivotal votes and the value of each share is 2/3 or .67. And so on. We shall indicate how the Index works by some simple illustrations.

1. *Five-member group with 3:2 factional split and one swinger in the majority faction.* If the swinger shifts, his vote decides the vote outcome. He is the pivotal swinger. He controls the unit value of the pivotal vote because only one vote is needed. The value of his vote is 1.0. (The same is the case in all other decisional structures where a single vote is controlling, as in 4:3, 5:4, etc. structures.)

2. *Five-member group with 3:2 factional split and two swingers in the majority.* As in the previous case, only one vote is needed for a simple majority. But if both swingers shift, the vote outcome is a 1:4 vote. In this case, then, the two swingers share the unit value of the single pivotal vote, and the share of each is .5. Both are in the pivotal group.

3. *Five-member group with 3:2 factional split, one swinger in the majority faction and one swinger in the minority faction; both shift simultaneously in*

Table XVII

*Swinger Patterns, Vote Outcome, and Swinger Vote Values in 3:2 Decisional Structures**

Number of Pivotal Votes Required for Simple Majority	Majority			Minority		Vote Outcome
	A	B	C	D	E	
0	−	−	−	+	+	5:0
				0.0	0.0	
0	−	−	−	+	−	4:1
				0.0		
1	+	−	−	−	−	2:3
	1.0					
1	+	+	−	−	−	1:4
	.5	.5				
1	+	+	+	−	−	0:5
	.33	.33	.33			
1	+	−	−	+	−	3:2
	0.0			1.0		
1	+	−	−	+	+	4:1
	0.0			.5	.5	
2	+	+	−	+	−	2:3
	1.0	1.0		0.0		
2	+	+	−	+	+	3:2
	0.0	0.0		1.0	1.0	
2	+	+	+	+	−	1:4
	.67	.67	.67	0.0		

* The symbol + denotes that the voter is a swinger, the symbol − that he is not a swinger. The value of each swinger vote is indicated beneath each swinger's behavior symbol.

opposite directions. The minority swinger is now allied with the two majority non-swingers and these three now form the simple majority that is needed. The majority swinger has joined the other minority member. In this case, then, the unit value of the pivotal vote is 1.0. But only the minority swinger is the pivotal swinger, for his vote has made the new simple majority possible. The value of his vote is 1.0. The majority swinger, now on the minority side, has lost influence over the vote outcome. The value of his vote is zero.

These illustrations should suffice. Under the assumption that each swinger will in fact shift away from his faction, it is possible to work out the value of his vote for every single contingency. Table xvii of this appendix presents the set of contingencies for the simple case of a 3:2 factional split. Similar tables can be developed for any other bipolar or multipolar structure. In this study, we have not made use of the values of each swinger's vote, but have only used the values to define the pivotal and non-pivotal swingers. In later analyses we expect to make use of the particular values.

Suggestions for Further Reading

Eulau, Heinz and Katherine Hinckley, "Legislative Institutions," in *Political Science Annual*, ed. James A. Robinson (Indianapolis: Bobbs-Merrill Company, 1966), Vol. I.

Fenno, Richard F., Jr., "The House Appropriations Committee as a Political System: The Problem of Integration," *American Political Science Review*, LVI (June 1962), 310-24.

Fiellin, Alan, "The Functions of Informal Groups in Legislative Institutions: A Case Study," *Journal of Politics*, XIV (February 1962), 72-91.

Francis, Wayne L., "Influence and Interaction in a State Legislative Body," *American Political Science Review*, LVI (December 1962), 953-60.

Huitt, Ralph K., "The Congressional Committee: A Case Study," *American Political Science Review*, XLVIII (June 1954), 340-65.

Jones, Charles O., "The Role of the Congressional Subcommittee," *Midwest Journal of Political Science*, VI (November 1962), 327-44.

Manley, John F., "The House Committee on Ways and Means: Conflict Management in a Congressional Committee," *American Political Science Review*, LIX (December 1965), 927-39.

McClosky, Herbert and Harold E. Dahlgren, "Primary Group Influence and Party Loyalty," *American Political Science Review*, LIII (September 1959), 757-76.

Patterson, Samuel, "Patterns of Interpersonal Relations in a State Legislative Group: The Wisconsin Assembly," *Public Opinion Quarterly*, XXIII (Spring 1959), 101-10.

Truman, David B., "The State Delegations and the Structure of Party Voting in the United States House of Representatives," *American Political Science Review*, L (December 1956), 1023-45.

Verba, Sidney, *Small Groups and Political Behavior—A Study of Leadership* (Princeton: Princeton University Press, 1961).